Modernity and Self-Identity

Modernity and Self-Identity

Self and Society in the Late Modern Age

Anthony Giddens

polity

First published in 1991 by Polity Press
in association with Blackwell Publishing Ltd.
Reprinted 1992, 1993, 1994, 1995, 1996, 1997, 1999, 2001, 2002, 2003

Editorial office:
Polity Press
65 Bridge Street
Cambridge CB2 1UR, UK

Marketing and production:
Blackwell Publishing Ltd
108 Cowley Road
Oxford OX4 1JF, UK

ISBN 0-7456-0889-2
ISBN 0-7456-0932-5 (pbk)

A CIP catalogue record for this book is available from the British Library.

Typeset in 11 on 12½ pt Times by Acorn Bookwork, Salisbury, Wiltshire.
Printed in Great Britain by T.J. International Ltd, Padstow, Cornwall
For further infomation on Polity, please visit our website: http:www.polity.co.uk

Contents

Acknowledgements

Many people have helped me, directly or indirectly, in the preparation of this book. I was fortunate enough to be able to discuss the ideas developed herein in extended seminar series in two particularly stimulating intellectual environments: the Faculty of Social and Political Sciences at Cambridge University, and the Department of Sociology at the University of California, Santa Barbara. I am grateful to the members of these seminars for numerous instructive comments and for their worthwhile advice. Several people have read the manuscript in a detailed and critical way. I am particularly indebted in this regard to Zygmunt Bauman, David Held, Lewis Coser and Dennis Wrong. I owe a very great deal indeed to Teresa Brennan, whose comments on the manuscript were marvellously helpful. Deirdre Boden's influence is apparent at many points in the book: I have gained enormously from the diverse materials and unpublished papers which she has sent me over a lengthy period, as well as from direct discussion with her. Ann Bone, who copy-edited the book, made many stylistic and substantive comments that helped transform the text. Others who have contributed much to the book, and whom I would like to thank are: Richard Appelbaum, Katy Giddens, Sam Hollick, Harvey Molotch, Helen Blunt, Avril Symonds and John Thompson.

Anthony Giddens

Introduction

The question of modernity, its past development and current institutional forms, has reappeared as a fundamental sociological problem at the turn of the twenty-first century. The connections between sociology and the emergence of modern institutions have long been recognised. Yet in the present day, we see not only that these connections are more complex and problematic than was previously realised, but that a rethinking of the nature of modernity must go hand in hand with a reworking of basic premises of sociological analysis.

Modern institutions differ from all preceding forms of social order in respect of their dynamism, the degree to which they undercut traditional habits and customs, and their global impact. However, these are not only extensional transformations: modernity radically alters the nature of day-to-day social life and affects the most personal aspects of our experience. Modernity must be understood on an institutional level; yet the transmutations introduced by modern institutions interlace in a direct way with individual life and therefore with the self. One of the distinctive features of modernity, in fact, is an increasing interconnection between the two 'extremes' of extensionality and intentionality: globalising influences on the one hand and personal dispositions on the other. The aim of this book is to analyse the nature of these interconnections and to provide a conceptual vocabulary for thinking about them. In this introductory discussion, I shall try to provide an overview and summary version of the themes of the study as a whole. I hope the reader will tolerate the slight elements of repetition which this strategy produces.

Although its main focus is on the self, this is not primarily a work of psychology. The overriding stress of the book is upon the emergence of new mechanisms of self-identity which are shaped by – yet also shape – the institutions of modernity. The self is not a passive entity, determined by external influences; in forging their self-identities, no matter how local their specific contexts of action, individuals contribute to and directly promote social influences that are global in their consequences and implications.

Sociology, and the social sciences more widely conceived, are inherent elements of the institutional reflexivity of modernity – a phenomenon fundamental to the discussion in this book. Not just academic studies, but all manner of manuals, guides, therapeutic works and self-help surveys contribute to modernity's reflexivity. On several occasions, therefore, I make fairly extensive reference to social research and practical 'guides to living', not as a means of documenting a definite subject-matter, but as symptomatic of social phenomena or trends of development I seek to identify. These are not just works 'about' social processes, but materials which in some part constitute them.

In general, the focus of this book is analytical rather than descriptive and at some key junctures relies on ideal-typical procedures in order to substantiate its points. I try to identify some structuring features at the core of modernity which interact with the reflexivity of the self: but I do not discuss in any detail how far some of the processes mentioned have proceeded in specific contexts, or what exceptions and countertrends to them exist.

The opening chapter sketches out a framework for the whole of the study. Taking as illustrative a specific piece of social research, it provides an appraisal of key aspects of modernity's development. Besides its institutional reflexivity, modern social life is characterised by profound processes of the reorganisation of time and space, coupled to the expansion of disembedding mechanisms – mechanisms which prise social relations free from the hold of specific locales, recombining them across wide time-space distances. The reorganisation of time and space, plus the disembedding mechanisms, radicalise and globalise pre-established institutional traits of modernity; and they act to transform the content and nature of day-to-day social life.

Modernity is a post-traditional order, but not one in which the sureties of tradition and habit have been replaced by the certitude of rational knowledge. Doubt, a pervasive feature of modern critical reason, permeates into everyday life as well as philosophical consciousness, and forms a general existential dimension of the contemporary social world. Modernity institutionalises the principle of radical doubt and insists that all knowledge takes the form of hypotheses: claims which may very well be true, but which are in principle always open to revision and may have at some point to be abandoned. Systems of accumulated expertise – which form important disembedding influences – represent multiple sources of authority, frequently internally contested and divergent in their implications. In the settings of what I call 'high' or 'late' modernity – our present-day world – the self, like the broader institutional contexts in which it exists, has to be reflexively made. Yet this task has to be accomplished amid a puzzling diversity of options and possibilities.

In circumstances of uncertainty and multiple choice, the notions of trust and risk have particular application. Trust, I argue, is a crucial generic phenomenon of personality development as well as having distinctive and specific relevance to a world of disembedding mechanisms and abstract systems. In its generic manifestations, trust is directly linked to achieving an early sense of ontological security. Trust established between an infant and its caretakers provides an 'inoculation' which screens off potential threats and dangers that even the most mundane activities of day-to-day life contain. Trust in this sense is basic to a 'protective cocoon' which stands guard over the self in its dealings with everyday reality. It 'brackets out' potential occurrences which, were the individual seriously to contemplate them, would produce a paralysis of the will, or feelings of engulfment. In its more specific guise, trust is a medium of interaction with the abstract systems which both empty day-to-day life of its traditional content and set up globalising influences. Trust here generates that 'leap into faith' which practical engagement demands.

Modernity is a risk culture. I do not mean by this that social life is inherently more risky than it used to be; for most people in the developed societies that is not the case. Rather, the concept of risk becomes fundamental to the way both lay actors and technical specialists organise the social world. Under conditions of modernity, the future is continually drawn into the present by means of the reflexive organisation of knowledge environments.

A territory, as it were, is carved out and colonised. Yet such colonisation by its very nature cannot be complete: thinking in terms of risk is vital to assessing how far projects are likely to diverge from their anticipated outcomes. Risk assessment invites precision, and even quantification, but by its nature is imperfect. Given the mobile character of modern institutions, coupled to the mutable and frequently controversial nature of abstract systems, most forms of risk assessment, in fact, contain numerous imponderables.

Modernity reduces the overall riskiness of certain areas and modes of life, yet at the same time introduces new risk parameters largely or completely unknown to previous eras. These parameters include high-consequence risks: risks deriving from the globalised character of the social systems of modernity. The late modern world – the world of what I term high modernity – is apocalyptic, not because it is inevitably heading towards calamity, but because it introduces risks which previous generations have not had to face. However much there is progress towards international negotiation and control of armaments, so long as nuclear weapons remain, or even the knowledge necessary to build them, and so long as science and technology continue to be involved with the creation of novel weaponry, the risk of massively destructive warfare will persist. Now that nature, as a phenomenon external to social life, has in a certain sense come to an 'end' – as a result of its domination by human beings – the risks of ecological catastrophe form an inevitable part of our horizon of day-to-day life. Other high-consequence risks, such as the collapse of global economic mechanisms, or the rise of totalitarian superstates, are an equally unavoidable part of our contemporary experience.

In high modernity, the influence of distant happenings on proximate events, and on intimacies of the self, becomes more and more commonplace. The media, printed and electronic, obviously play a central role in this respect. Mediated experience, since the first experience of writing, has long influenced both self-identity and the basic organisation of social relations. With the development of mass communication, particularly electronic communication, the interpenetration of self-development and social systems, up to and including global systems, becomes ever more pronounced. The 'world' in which we now live is in some profound respects thus quite distinct from that inhabited by human beings in previous periods of history. It is in many ways a single world, having a unitary framework of experience (for instance, in respect of basic axes of time and space), yet at the same time one which creates new forms of fragmentation and dispersal. A universe of social activity in which electronic media have a central and constitutive role, nevertheless, is not one of 'hyperreality', in Baudrillard's sense. Such an idea confuses the pervasive impact of mediated experience with the internal referentiality of the social systems of modernity – the fact that these systems become largely autonomous and determined by their own constitutive influences.

In the post-traditional order of modernity, and against the backdrop of new forms of mediated experience, self-identity becomes a reflexively organised endeavour. The reflexive project of the self, which consists in the sustaining of coherent, yet continuously revised, biographical narratives, takes place in the context of multiple choice as filtered through abstract systems. In modern social life, the notion of lifestyle takes on a particular significance. The more tradition loses its hold, and the more daily life is reconstituted in terms of the dialectical interplay of the local and the global, the more individuals are forced to negotiate lifestyle choices among a diversity of options. Of course, there are standardising influences too – most notably, in the form of commodification, since capitalistic production and distribution form core components of modernity's institutions. Yet because of the 'openness' of social life today, the pluralisation of contexts of action and the diversity of 'authorities', lifestyle choice is increasingly important in the constitution of self-identity and daily activity. Reflexively organised life-planning, which normally presumes consideration of risks as filtered through contact with expert knowledge, becomes a central feature of the structuring of self-identity.

A possible misunderstanding about lifestyle as it interconnects with life-planning should be cleared up right at the beginning. Partly because the term has been taken up in advertising and other sources promoting commodified consumption, one might imagine that 'lifestyle' refers only to the pursuits of the more affluent groups or classes. The poor are more or less completely excluded from the possibility of making lifestyle choices. In some substantial part this is true. Issues of class and inequality, within states and on a world-wide level, closely mesh with the arguments of this book, although I do not try to document those inequalities here. Indeed, class divisions and other fundamental lines of inequality, such as those connected with gender or ethnicity, can be partly *defined* in terms of differential access to forms of self-actualisation and empowerment discussed in what follows. Modernity, one should not forget, produces *difference*, *exclusion* and *marginalisation*. Holding out the possibility of emancipation, modern institutions at the same time create mechanisms of suppression, rather than actualisation, of self. Yet it would be a major error to suppose that the phenomena analysed in the book are confined in their impact to those in more privileged material circumstances. 'Lifestyle' refers also to decisions taken and courses of action followed under conditions of severe material constraint; such lifestyle patterns may sometimes also involve the more or less deliberate rejection of more widely diffused forms of behaviour and consumption.

At one pole of the interaction between the local and the global stands what I call the 'transformation of intimacy'. Intimacy has its own reflexivity and its own forms of internally referential order. Of key importance here is the emergence of the 'pure relationship' as prototypical of the new spheres of personal life. A pure relationship is one in which external criteria have become dissolved: the relationship exists solely for whatever rewards that relationship as such can deliver. In the context of the pure relationship, trust can be mobilised only by a process of mutual disclosure. Trust, in other words, can by definition no longer be anchored in criteria outside the relationship itself – such as criteria of kinship, social duty or traditional obligation. Like self-identity, with which it is closely intertwined, the pure relationship has to be reflexively controlled over the long term, against the backdrop of external transitions and transformations.

Pure relationships presuppose 'commitment', which is a particular species of trust. Commitment in turn has to be understood as a phenomenon of the internally referential system: it is a commitment to the relationship as such, as well as to the other person or persons involved. The demand for intimacy is integral to the pure relationship, as a result of the mechanisms of trust which it presumes. It is hence a mistake to see the contemporary 'search for intimacy', as many social commentators have done, only as a negative reaction to a wider, more impersonal social universe. Absorption within pure relationships certainly may often be a mode of defence against an enveloping outside world: but such relationships are thoroughly permeated by mediated influences coming from large-scale social systems, and usually actively organise those influences within the sphere of such relationships. In general, whether in personal life or in broader social milieux, processes of reappropriation and empowerment intertwine with expropriation and loss.

In such processes many different connections between individual experience and abstract systems can be found. 'Reskilling' – the reacquisition of knowledge and skills – whether in respect of intimacies of personal life or wider social involvements, is a pervasive reaction to the expropriating effects of abstract systems. It is situationally variable, and also tends to respond to specific requirements of context. Individuals are likely to reskill themselves in greater depth where consequential transitions in their lives are concerned or fateful decisions are to be made. Reskilling, however, is always partial and liable to be affected by the 'revisable' nature of expert knowledge and by internal dissensions between experts. Attitudes of trust, as well as more pragmatic acceptance, scepticism, rejection and withdrawal, uneasily coexist in the social space linking individual activities and expert systems. Lay attitudes towards science, technology and other esoteric forms of expertise, in the age of high modernity, tend to express the same mixed attitudes of reverence and reserve, approval and disquiet, enthusiasm and antipathy, which philosophers and social analysts (themselves experts of sorts) express in their writings.

The reflexivity of the self, in conjunction with the influence of abstract systems, pervasively affects the body as well as psychic processes. The body is less and less an extrinsic 'given', functioning outside the internally referential systems of modernity, but becomes itself reflexively mobilized. What might appear as a wholesale movement towards the narcissistic cultivation of bodily appearance is in fact an expression of a concern lying much deeper actively to 'construct' and control the body. Here there is an integral connection between bodily development and lifestyle – manifest, for example, in the pursuit of specific bodily regimes.

Yet much more wide-ranging factors are important, too, as a reflection of the socialising of biological mechanisms and processes. In the spheres of biological reproduction, genetic engineering and medical interventions of many sorts, the body is becoming a phenomenon of choices and options. These do not affect the individual alone: there are close connections between personal aspects of bodily development and global factors. Reproductive technologies and genetic engineering, for example, are parts of more general processes of the transmutation of nature into a field of human action.

Science, technology and expertise more generally play a fundamental role in which I call the sequestration of experience. The notion that modernity is associated with an instrumental relation to nature, and the idea that a scientific outlook excludes questions of ethics or morality, are familiar enough. However, I seek to reframe these issues in terms of an institutional account of the late modern order, developed in terms of internal referentiality. The overall thrust of modern institutions is to create settings of action ordered in terms of modernity's own dynamics and severed from 'external criteria' – factors external to the social systems of modernity. Although there are numerous exceptions and countertrends, day-to-day social life tends to become separated from 'original' nature and from a variety of experiences bearing on existential questions and dilemmas. The mad, the criminal and the seriously ill are physically sequestered from the normal population, while 'eroticism' is replaced by 'sexuality' – which then moves behind the scenes to become hidden away. The sequestration of experience means that, for many people, direct contact with events and situations which link the individual lifespan to broad issues of morality and finitude are rare and fleeting.

This situation has not come about, as Freud thought, because of the increasing psychological repression of guilt demanded by the complexities of modern social life. Rather, what occurs is an institutional repression, in which – I shall claim – mechanisms of shame rather than guilt come to the fore. Shame has close affiliations with narcissism, but it is a mistake, as noted earlier, to suppose that self-identity becomes increasingly narcissistic. Narcissism is one among other types of psychological mechanism – and, in some instances, pathology – which the connections between identity, shame and the reflexive project of the self bring into being.

Personal meaninglessness – the feeling that life has nothing worthwhile to offer – becomes a fundamental psychic problem in circumstances of late modernity. We should understand this phenomenon in terms of a repression of moral questions which day-to-day life poses, but which are denied answers. 'Existential isolation' is not so much a separation of individuals from others as a separation from the moral resources necessary to live a full and satisfying existence. The reflexive project of the self generates programmes of actualisation and mastery. But as long as these possibilities are understood largely as a matter of the extension of the control systems of modernity to the self, they lack moral meaning. 'Authenticity' becomes both a pre-eminent value and a framework for self-actualisation, but represents a morally stunted process.

Yet the repression of existential questions is by no means complete and in high modernity, where systems of instrumental control have become more nakedly exposed than ever before and their negative consequences more apparent, many forms of counter-reaction appear. It becomes more and more apparent that lifestyle choices, within the settings of local–global interrelations, raise moral issues which cannot simply be pushed to one side. Such issues call for forms of political engagement which the new social movements both presage and serve to help initiate. 'Life politics' – concerned with human self-actualisation, both on the level of the individual and collectively – emerges from the shadow which 'emancipatory politics' has cast.

Emancipation, the general imperative of progressivist Enlightenment, is in its various guises the condition for the emergence of a life-political programme. In a world still riven by divisions and marked by forms of oppression both old and new, emancipatory politics does not decline in importance. Yet these pre-existing political endeavours become joined by novel forms of life-political concern. In the concluding sections of the book I outline the main parameters of the life-political agenda. It is an agenda which demands an encounter with specific moral dilemmas, and forces us to raise existential issues which modernity has institutionally excluded.

1
The Contours of High Modernity

Let me open my discussion by describing some of the findings of a specific sociological study, plucked rather arbitrarily from a particular area of research. *Second Chances*, by Judith Wallerstein and Sandra Blakeslee, is an investigation of divorce and remarriage.[1] The book describes the impact of marriage break-up, over a period of some ten years, on sixty sets of parents and children. Divorce, the authors point out, is a crisis in individuals' personal lives, which presents dangers to their security and sense of well-being, yet also offers fresh opportunities for their self-development and future happiness. Separation and divorce, and their aftermath, can cause long-lasting anxieties and psychological disturbances; but at the same time the changes brought about by the dissolution of a marriage provide possibilities, as the authors put it, to 'grow emotionally', to 'establish new competence and pride' and to 'strengthen intimate relationships far beyond earlier capacities'.

The marital separation, Wallerstein and Blakeslee say, is a marker 'that freezes certain images which frame the courses of action that ensue. Anger is often rooted in and feeds on the way in which the marriage came apart: one partner suddenly finding the other having an affair with a mutual best friend; one partner leaving a note informing the other, without warning, that the marriage is dead; one parent departing suddenly, taking the children, providing no address . . .' A marriage that has come apart tends to be mourned, no matter how unhappy or desperate the partners may have been while they were together.

The longer two people have been with one another, the more protracted tends to be the period of mourning. Mourning derives from the loss of shared pleasures and experiences, plus the necessary abandoning of the hopes once invested in the relationship. Where no process of mourning occurs, the result is often the long-term persistence of hurt feelings, leading perhaps to despair and psychological breakdown. For the majority of people, in fact, the feelings engendered by divorce seem not to disappear completely with the passing of the years; they may be brought violently alive again by subsequent events, such as the remarriage of the previous partner, financial hardship, or quarrels over how the children should be brought up. Where a partner remains quite strongly involved emotionally with the other, even in a largely negative way, the results in such situations tends to be an upsurge of bitterness.

Going through a phase of mourning, according to Wallerstein and Blakeslee, is the key to 'reclaiming oneself' after divorce. Anyone who successfully 'decouples' from his or her previous spouse faces the task of establishing a 'new sense of self', a 'new sense of identity'. In a long-term marriage, each individual's sense of self-identity becomes tied to the other person, and indeed to the marriage itself. Following a broken marriage, each person must 'reach back into his or her early experience and find other images and roots for independence, for being able to live alone, and for undertaking the second chances provided by divorce'.

A separated or divorced person needs moral courage to try new relationships and find new interests. Many people in such circumstances lose confidence in their own judgements and capabilities, and may come to feel that planning for the future is valueless. 'They sense that life gives hard knocks and is essentially unpredictable; they conclude that the best-laid plans go awry and become discouraged about setting long-range or even short-range goals, much less working towards these goals'. Overcoming such feelings demands persistence in the face of setbacks and a willingness to alter established personal traits or habits. Similar qualities are needed by the children of divorced parents, who often suffer profoundly from the dissolution of the family household. 'The children of divorce', Wallerstein and Blakeslee say, 'face a more difficult task than the children of bereavement. Death cannot be undone, but divorce happens between living people who can change their minds. A reconciliation fantasy taps deep into children's psyches ... they may not overcome this fantasy of reconciliation until they themselves finally separate from their parents and leave home.'[2]

Personal problems, personal trials and crises, personal relationships: what can these tell us, and what do they express, about the social landscape of modernity? Not much, some would be inclined to argue, for surely personal feelings and concerns are much the same at all times and in all places. The coming of modernity, it might be accepted, brings about major changes in the external social environment of the individual, affecting marriage and the family as well as other institutions; yet people carry on their personal lives much as they always did, coping as best they can with the social transformations around them. Or do they? For social circumstances are not separate from personal life, nor are they just an external environment to them. In struggling with intimate problems, individuals help actively to reconstruct the universe of social activity around them.

The world of high modernity certainly stretches out well beyond the milieux of individual activities and personal engagements. It is one replete with risks and dangers, to which the term 'crisis', not merely as an interruption, but as a more or less continuous state of affairs, has particular application. Yet it also intrudes deeply into the heart of self-identity and personal feelings. The 'new sense of identity' which Wallerstein and Blakeslee mention as required following divorce is an acute version of a process of 'finding oneself' which the social conditions of modernity enforce on all of us. This process is one of active intervention and transformation.

Wallerstein and Blakeslee summarise the results of their research in a chapter called 'Danger and Opportunity'. Trite as it is, the phrase applies not only to marriage and its perturbations, but to the world of modernity as a whole. The sphere of what we have today come to term 'personal relationships' offers opportunities for intimacy and self-expression lacking in many more traditional contexts. At the same time, such relationships have become risky and dangerous, in certain senses of these terms. Modes of behaviour and feeling associated with sexual and marital life have become mobile, unsettled and 'open'. There is much to be gained; but there is unexplored territory to be charted, and new dangers to be courted.

Consider, as an example, a phenomenon discussed extensively by Wallerstein and Blakeslee: the changing nature of stepfamilies. Many people, adults and children, now live in stepfamilies – not usually, as in previous eras, as a consequence of the death of a spouse, but because of the re-forming of marriage ties after divorce. A child in a stepfamily may have two mothers and fathers, two sets of brothers and sisters, together with other complex kin connections resulting from the multiple marriages of parents. Even the terminology is difficult: should a stepmother be called 'mother' by the child, or called by her name? Negotiating such problems might be arduous and psychologically costly for all parties; yet opportunities for novel kinds of fulfilling social relations plainly also exist. One thing we can be sure of is that the changes involved here are not just external to the individual. These new forms of extended family ties have to be established by the very persons who find themselves most directly caught up in them.

Anxiety is the natural correlate of dangers of all types. It is caused by disturbing circumstances, or their threat, but also helps mobilise adaptive responses and novel initiatives. Terms such as pain, worry and mourning are repeatedly used by the authors of *Second Chances*. So are ones like courage and resolution. Life throws up personal problems in an apparently random way and, acknowledging this, some people take refuge in a sort of resigned numbness. Yet many are also able more positively to grasp the new opportunities which open up as pre-established modes of behaviour become foreclosed, and to change themselves. How new are these anxieties, dangers and opportunities? In what ways are they distinctively influenced by the institutions of modernity? These are the questions I shall try to answer in the pages that follow.

Second Chances is a work of sociology, but it will not only be read by sociologists. Therapists, family counsellors, social workers and other concerned professionals are likely to turn its pages. It is perfectly possible that members of the lay public, particularly if they have been recently divorced, will read the book and relate its ideas and conclusions to the circumstances of their own lives. The authors are clearly aware of this likelihood. Although the book is written mainly as a research study presenting a definite set of results, numerous passages scattered through the text suggest practical responses and courses of action which the newly separated or divorced might follow. No doubt few individual books influence overall social behaviour very much. *Second Chances* is one small contribution to a vast and more or less continuous outpouring of writings, technical and more popular, on the subject of marriage and intimate relationships. Such writings are part of the *reflexivity* of modernity: they serve routinely to organise, and alter, the aspects of social life they report on or analyse. Anyone who contemplates marriage today, or who faces a situation of the break-up of a marriage or a long-term intimate relationship, knows a great deal (not always on the level of discursive awareness) about 'what is going on' in the social arena of marriage and divorce. Such knowledge is not incidental to what is actually going on, but constitutive of it – as is true of all contexts of social life in conditions of modernity.

Not only this: everyone is in some sense aware of the reflexive constitution of modern social activity and the implications it has for her or his life. Self-identity for us forms a *trajectory* across the different institutional settings of modernity over the *durée* of what used to be called the 'life cycle', a term which applies much more accurately to non-modern contexts than to modern ones. Each of us not only 'has', but *lives* a biography reflexively organised in terms of flows of social and psychological information about possible ways of life. Modernity is a post-traditional order, in which the question, 'How shall I live?' has to be answered in day-to-day decisions about how to behave, what to wear and what to eat – and many other things – as well as interpreted within the temporal unfolding of self-identity.

Let us now move from the level of personal lives to a more institutional plane. To set the backdrop to this study as a whole, we have to provide a characterisation of this troubling and tumultuous phenomenon: modernity.

Modernity: some general considerations

In this book I use the term 'modernity' in a very general sense, to refer to the institutions and modes of behaviour established first of all in post-feudal Europe, but which in the twentieth century increasingly have become world-historical in their impact. 'Modernity' can be understood as roughly equivalent to 'the industrialised world', so long as it be recognised that industrialism is not its only institutional dimension.[3] I take industrialism to refer to the social relations implied in the widespread use of material power and machinery in production processes. As such, it is one institutional axis of modernity. A second dimension is captialism, where this term means a system of commodity production involving both competitive product markets and the commodification of labour power. Each of these can be distinguished analytically from the institutions of surveillance, the basis of the massive increase in organisational power associated with the emergence of modern social life. Surveillance refers to the supervisory control of subject populations, whether this control takes the form of 'visible' supervision in Foucault's sense, or the use of information to coordinate social activities. This dimension can in turn be separated from control of the means of violence in the context of the 'industrialisation of war'. Modernity ushers in an era of 'total war', in which the potential destructive power of weaponry, signalled above all by the existence of nuclear armaments, becomes immense.

Modernity produces certain distinct social forms, of which the most prominent is the nation-state. A banal observation, of course, until one remembers the established tendency of sociology to concentrate on 'society' as its designated subject-matter. The sociologist's 'society', applied to the period of modernity at any rate, is a nation-state, but this is usually a covert equation rather than an explicitly theorised one. As a sociopolitical entity the nation-state contrasts in a fundamental way with most types of traditional order. It develops only as part of a wider nation-state system (which today has become global in character), has very specific forms of territoriality and surveillance capabilities, and monopolises effective control over the means of violence.[4] In the literature of international relations, nation-states are often treated as 'actors' – as 'agents' rather than 'structures' – and there is a definite justification for this. For modern states are reflexively monitored systems which, even if they do not 'act' in the strict sense of the term, follow coordinated policies and plans on a geopolitical scale. As such, they are a prime example of a more general feature of modernity, the rise of the *organisation*. What distinguishes modern organisations is not so much their size, or their bureaucratic character, as the concentrated reflexive monitoring they both permit and entail. Who says modernity says not just organisations, but organisation – the regularised control of social relations across indefinite time-space distances.

Modern institutions are in various key respects *discontinuous* with the gamut of pre-modern cultures and ways of life. One of the most obvious characteristics separating the modern era from any other period preceding it is modernity's extreme dynamism. The modern world is a 'runaway world': not only is the *pace* of social change much faster than in any prior system, so also is its *scope*, and the *profoundness* with which it affects pre-existing social practices and modes of behaviour.[5]

What explains the peculiarly dynamic character of modern social life? Three main elements, or sets of elements, are involved – and each of them is basic to the arguments deployed in this book. The first is what I call the *separation of time and space*. All cultures, of course, have possessed modes of time-reckoning of one form or another, as well as ways of situating themselves spatially. There is no society in which individuals do not have a sense of future, present and past. Every culture has some form of standardised spatial markers which designate a special awareness of place. In pre-modern settings, however, time and space were connected *through* the situatedness of place.

Larger pre-modern cultures developed more formal methods for the calculation of time and the ordering of space – such as calendars and (by modern standards) crude maps. Indeed, these were the prerequisites for the 'distancing' across time and space which the emergence of more extensive forms of social system presupposed. But in pre-modern eras, for the bulk of the population, and for most of the ordinary activities of day-to-day life, time and space remained essentially linked through place. 'When' markers were connected not just to the 'where' of social conduct, but to the substance of that conduct itself.

The separation of time from space involved above all the development of an 'empty' dimension of time, the main lever which also pulled space away from place. The invention and diffusion of the mechanical clock is usually seen – rightly – as the prime expression of this process, but it is important not to interpret this phenomenon in too superficial a way. The widespread use of mechanical timing devices facilitated, but also presumed, deeply structured changes in the tissue of everyday life – changes which could not only be local, but were inevitably universalising. A world that has a universal dating system, and globally standardised time zones, as ours does today, is socially and experientially different from all pre-modern eras. The global map, in which there is no privileging of place (a universal projection), is the correlate symbol to the clock in the 'emptying' of space. It is not just a mode of portraying 'what has always been there' – the geography of the earth – but is constitutive of quite basic transformations in social relations.

The emptying out of time and space is in no sense a unilinear development, but proceeds dialectically. Many forms of 'lived time' are possible in social settings structured through the separation of time and space. Moreover, the severance of time from space does not mean that these henceforth become mutually alien aspects of human social organisation. On the contrary: it provides the very basis for their recombination in ways that coordinate social activities without necessary reference to the particularities of place. The organisations, and organisation, so characteristic of modernity are inconceivable without the reintegration of separated time and space. Modern social organisation presumes the precise coordination of the actions of many human beings physically absent from one another; the 'when' of these actions is directly connected to the 'where', but not, as in pre-modern epochs, via the mediation of place.

We can all sense how fundamental the separation of time from space is for the massive dynamism that modernity introduces into human social affairs. The phenomenon universalises that 'use of history to make history' so intrinsic to the processes which drive modern social life away from the hold of tradition. Such historicity becomes global in form with the creation of a standardised 'past' and a universally applicable 'future': a date such as the 'year 2000' becomes a recognisable marker for the whole of humanity.

The process of the emptying of time and space is crucial for the second major influence on modernity's dynamism, the *disembedding* of social institutions. I choose the metaphor of disembedding in deliberate opposition to the concept of 'differentiation' sometimes adopted by sociologists as a means of contrasting pre-modern with modern social systems. Differentiation carries the imagery of the progressive separation of functions, such that modes of activity organised in a diffuse fashion in pre-modern societies become more specialised and precise with the advent of modernity. No doubt this idea has some validity, but it fails to capture an essential element of the nature and impact of modern institutions – the 'lifting out' of social relations from local contexts and their rearticulation across indefinite tracts of time–space. This 'lifting out' is exactly what I mean by disembedding, which is the key to the tremendous acceleration in time-space distanciation which modernity introduces.

Disembedding mechanisms are of two types, which I term 'symbolic tokens' and 'expert systems'. Taken together, I refer to these as *abstract systems*. Symbolic tokens are media of exchange which have standard value, and thus are interchangeable across a plurality of contexts. The prime example, and the most pervasively important, is money. Although the larger forms of pre-modern social system have all developed monetary exchange of one form or another, money economy becomes vastly more sophisticated and abstract with the emergence and maturation of modernity. Money brackets time (because it is a means of credit) and space (since standardised value allows transactions between a multiplicity of individuals who never physically meet one another). Expert systems bracket time and space through deploying modes of technical knowledge which have validity independent of the practitioners and clients who make use of them. Such systems penetrate virtually all aspects of social life in conditions of modernity – in respect of the food we eat, the medicines we take, the buildings we inhabit, the forms of transport we use and a multiplicity of other phenomena. Expert systems are not confined to areas of technological expertise. They extend to social relations themselves and to the intimacies of the self. The doctor, counsellor and therapist are as central to the expert systems of modernity as the scientist, technician or engineer.

Both types of expert system depend in an essential way on *trust*, a notion which, as has been indicated, plays a primary role in this book. Trust is different from the form of confidence which Georg Simmel called the 'weak inductive knowledge' involved in formal transactions.[6] Some decisions in life are based on inductive inferences from past trends, or from past experience believed in some way to be dependable for the present. This kind of confidence may be an element in trust, but it is not sufficient in itself to define a trust relation. Trust presumes a leap to commitment, a quality of 'faith' which is irreducible. It is specifically related to absence in time and space, as well as to ignorance. We have no need to trust someone who is constantly in view and whose activities can be directly monitored. Thus, for example, jobs which are monotonous or unpleasant, and poorly paid, in which the motivation to perform the work conscientiously is weak, are usually 'low-trust' positions. 'High-trust' posts are those carried out largely outside the presence of management or supervisory staff.[7] Similarly, there is no requirement of trust when a technical system is more or less completely known to a particular individual. In respect of expert systems, trust brackets the limited technical knowledge which most people possess about coded information which routinely affects their lives.

Trust, of varying sorts and levels, underlies a host of day-to-day decisions that all of us take in the course of orienting our activities. But trusting is not by any means always the result of consciously taken decisions: more often, it is a generalised attitude of mind that underlies those decisions, something which has its roots in the connection between trust and personality development. We *can* make the decision to trust, a phenomenon which is common because of the third underlying element of modernity (already mentioned, but also further discussed below): its intrinsic reflexivity. But the faith which trust implies also tends to resist such calculative decision making.

Attitudes of trust, in relation to specific situations, persons or systems, and on a more generalised level, are directly connected to the psychological *security* of individuals and groups. Trust and security, risk and danger: these exist in various historically unique conjunctions in conditions of modernity. The disembedding mechanisms, for example, purchase wide arenas of relative security in daily social activity. People living in the industrialised countries, and to some extent elsewhere today, are generally protected from some of the hazards routinely faced in premodern times – such as those emanating from inclement nature. On the other hand, new risks and dangers are created through the disembedding mechanisms themselves, and these may be local or global. Foodstuffs purchased with artificial ingredients may have toxic characteristics absent from more traditional foods; environmental hazards might threaten the ecosystems of the earth as a whole.

Modernity is essentially a post-traditional order. The transformation of time and space, coupled with the disembedding mechanisms, propel social life away from the hold of pre-established precepts or practices. This is the context of the thoroughgoing *reflexivity* which is the third major influence on the dynamism of modern institutions. The reflexivity of modernity has to be distinguished from the reflexive monitoring of action intrinsic to all human activity. Modernity's reflexivity refers to the susceptibility of most aspects of social activity, and material relations with nature, to chronic revision in the light of new information or knowledge. Such information or knowledge is not incidental to modern institutions, but constitutive of them – a complicated phenomenon, because many possibilities of reflection about reflexivity exist in modern social conditions. As the discussion of *Second Chances* indicated, the social sciences play a basic role in the reflexivity of modernity: they do not simply 'accumulate knowledge' in the way in which the natural sciences may do.

Separation of time and space: the condition for the articulation of social relations across wide spans of time-space, up to and including global systems.

Disembedding mechanisms: consist of symbolic tokens and expert systems (these together = abstract systems). Disembedding mechanisms separate interaction from the particuliarities of locales.

Institutional reflexivity: the regularised use of knowledge about circumstances of social life as a constitutive element in its organisation and transformation.

Figure 1   *The dynamism of modernity*

In respect both of social and natural scientific knowledge, the reflexivity of modernity turns out to confound the expectations of Enlightenment thought – although it is the very product of that thought. The original progenitors of modern science and philosophy believed themselves to be preparing the way for securely founded knowledge of the social and natural worlds: the claims of reason were due to overcome the dogmas of tradition, offering a sense of certitude in place of the arbitrary character of habit and custom. But the reflexivity of modernity actually undermines the certainty of knowledge, even in the core domains of natural science. Science depends, not on the inductive accumulation of proofs, but on the methodological principle of doubt. No matter how cherished, and apparently well established, a given scientific tenet might be, it is open to revision – or might have to be discarded altogether – in the light of new ideas or findings. The integral relation between modernity and radical doubt is an issue which, once exposed to view, is not only disturbing to philosophers but is *existentially troubling* for ordinary individuals.

The local, the global and the transformation of day-to-day life

The globalising tendencies of modernity are inherent in the dynamic influences just sketched out. The reorganising of time and space, disembedding mechanisms and the reflexivity of modernity all presume universalising properties that explain the expansionist, coruscating nature of modern social life in its encounters with traditionally established practices. The globalisation of social activity which modernity has served to bring about is in some ways a process of the development of genuinely worldwide ties – such as those involved in the global nation-state system or the international division of labour. However, in a general way, the concept of globalisation is best understood as expressing fundamental aspects of time-space distanciation. Globalisation concerns the intersection of presence and absence, the interlacing of social events and social relations 'at distance' with local contextualities. We should grasp the global spread of modernity in terms of an ongoing relation between distanciation and the chronic mutability of local circumstances and local engagements. Like each of the other processes mentioned above, globalisation has to be understood as a dialectical phenomenon, in which events at one pole of a distanciated relation often produce divergent or even contrary occurrences at another. The *dialectic of the local and global* is a basic emphasis of the arguments employed in this book.

Globalisation means that, in respect of the consequences of at least some disembedding mechanisms, no one can 'opt out' of the transformations brought about by modernity: this is so, for example, in respect of the global risks of nuclear war or of ecological catastrophe. Many other aspects of modern institutions, including those operating on the small scale, affect people living in more traditional settings, outside the most strongly 'developed' portions of the world. In those developed sectors, however, the connecting of the local and global has been tied to a profound set of transmutations in the nature of day-to-day life.

We can understand these transmutations directly in terms of the impact of disembedding mechanisms, which act to deskill many aspects of daily activities. Such deskilling is *not* simply a process where everyday knowledge is appropriated by experts or technical specialists (since very often there are imponderable or hotly disputed features of their fields of expertise); and it is not only a one-way process, because specialist information, as part of the reflexivity of modernity, is in one form or another constantly reappropriated by lay actors. These observations apply to the writings of sociologists as much as to any other specialists: it has been seen that the findings of books such as *Second Chances* are likely to filter back into the milieux in which people take decisions about relationships, marriage and divorce. Trust in disembedding mechanisms is not confined to laypeople, because no one can be an expert about more than a tiny part of the diverse aspects of modern social life conditioned by abstract systems. Everyone living in conditions of modernity is affected by a multitude of abstract systems, and can at best process only superficial knowledge of their technicalities.

Awareness of the frailties and limits of abstract systems is not confined to technical specialists. Few individuals sustain an unswerving trust in the systems of technical knowledge that impinge on them, and everyone, whether consciously or not, selects among the competing possibilities of action that such systems (or disengagement from them) provide. Trust often merges with pragmatic acceptance: it is a sort of 'effort-bargain' that the individual makes with the institutions of modernity. Various attitudes of scepticism or antagonism towards abstract systems may coexist with a taken-for-granted confidence in others. For example, a person may go to great lengths to avoid eating foods that contain additives, but if that individual does not grow everything he or she eats, trust must necessarily be invested in the purveyors of 'natural foods' to provide superior products. Someone might turn towards holistic medicine after becoming disenchanted with the orthodox medical profession, but of course this is a transfer of faith. A sufferer from an illness might be so sceptical of the claims of all forms of expertise in healing that she avoids contact with medical practitioners altogether, no matter how the illness progresses. But even a person who effected a radical disengagement of this type would find it virtually impossible to escape altogether from the impact of systems of medicine and medical research, since these influence many aspects of the 'knowledge environment' as well as concrete elements of day-to-day life. For instance, they affect the regulations governing the production of foodstuffs – whether these be 'artificial' or 'natural' in character.

The mediation of experience

Virtually all human experience is mediated – through socialisation and in particular the acquisition of language. Language and memory are intrinsically connected, both on the level of individual recall and that of the institutionalisation of collective experience.[8] For human life, language is the prime and original means of time-space distanciation, elevating human activity beyond the immediacy of the experience of animals.[9] Language, as Lévi-Strauss says, is a time machine, which permits the re-enactment of social practices across the generations, while also making possible the differentiation of past, present and future.[10] The spoken word is a medium, a trace, whose evanescence in time and space is compatible with the preservation of meaning across time-space distances because of human mastery of language's structural charcteristics. Orality and tradition are inevitably related closely to one another. As Walter Ong puts it in his study of speaking and writing, oral cultures 'have a heavy investment in the past, which registers in their highly conservative institutions and in their verbal performances and poetic processes, which are formulaic, relatively invariable, calculated to preserve the hard-won knowledge garnered out of past experience which, since there is no writing to record it, would otherwise slip away'.[11]

Although Lévi-Strauss and others have skilfully explored the relation between writing and the emergence of 'hot', dynamic social systems, only Innis and, following him, McLuhan, have theorised the impact of media on social development in a sophisticated fashion, especially in relation to the emergence of modernity.[12] Both authors emphasise the connections between dominant kinds of media and time-space transformations. The degree to which a medium serves to alter time-space relations does not depend primarily on the content or the 'messages' it carries, but on its form and reproducibility. Innis points out, for example, that the introduction of papyrus as a medium for the inscribing of writing greatly extended the scope of administrative systems because it was so much easier to transport, store and reproduce than previously used materials.

Modernity is inseparable from its 'own' media: the printed text and, subsequently, the electronic signal. The development and expansion of modern institutions were directly bound up with the tremendous increase in the mediation of experience which these communication forms brought in their train. When books were produced by hand, readership was sequential: the book had to pass from one person to another. The books and texts of pre-modern civilisations remained substantially geared to the transmission of tradition, and were almost always essentially 'classical' in character. Printed materials cross space as easily as time because they can be distributed to many readers more or less simultaneously.[13] Only half a century after the appearance of Gutenberg's bible, hundreds of printing shops had sprung up in cities all over Europe. Today the printed word remains at the core of modernity and its global networks. Practically every known language of humankind has been set down in print, and even in those societies where levels of literacy are low, printed materials and the ability to produce and interpret them are indispensable means of administrative and social coordination. It has been calculated that, on a global level, the amount of printed materials produced has doubled every fifteen years since the days of Gutenberg.[14]

Printing was one of the main influences upon the rise of the early modern state, and other antecedent institutions of modernity, but when we look to the origins of high modernity it is the increasingly intertwined development of mass printed media and electronic communication that is important. The emergence of mass circulation printed materials is customarily thought of as belonging to an era prior to that of electronic messages – particularly by McLuhan, who radically set off one against the other. In terms of sheer temporal succession, it is true that the prime example of mass printed material – the newspaper – came into being about a century before the advent of television. Yet it is quite misleading to see one merely as a phase prior to the emergence of the other; from early on electronic communication has been vital to the development of mass printed media. Although the invention of the telegraph came some while after the first flourishing of dailies and periodicals, it was fundamental to what we now know as the newspaper and indeed to the very concept of 'news' itself. Telephone and radio communication further expanded this connection.

The early newspapers (and a whole diversity of other magazines and periodicals) played a major role in completing the separation of space from place, but this process only became a global phenomenon because of the integration of printed and electronic media. This is easily demonstrated by reference to the development of the modern newspaper. Thus Susan Brooker-Gross has examined changes in the time-space 'reach' of newspapers. She found that typical news items in an American paper from the mid-nineteenth century, before the diffusion of the telegraph, differed both from those of the early 1800s, and from those produced subsequently. The news items reported stories from cities some way distant in the US, but these did not have the immediacy the reader is used to with the newspapers of today.[15]

Prior to the coming of the telegraph, Brooker-Gross showed, news stories described events that were close at hand and recent; the further away a particular happening, the more it would appear at a very late date. News from afar came in the form of what she calls 'geographic bundling'. Materials from Europe, for example, literally came in packages from the ship, and would be presented in the form in which they were found: 'a ship arrived from London, and here is the news it brought.' In other words, channels of communication, and the pressures of time-space differences, directly shaped the presentation of the printed news-pages. Following the introduction of the telegraph, and then the telephone and other electronic media, it was the event that increasingly became the determining factor governing inclusion – rather than the place in which it occurred. Most news media preserve a sense of 'privileged place' in respect of their own position – giving a bias towards local news – but only against the backcloth of the pre-eminence of the event.[16]

The visual images which television, films and videos present no doubt create textures of mediated experience which are unavailable through the printed word. Yet, like newspapers, magazines, periodicals and printed materials of other sorts, these media are as much an expression of the disembedding, globalising tendencies of modernity as they are the instruments of such tendencies. As modalities of reorganising time and space, the similarities between printed and electronic media are more important than their differences in the constituting of modern institutions. This is so in respect of two basic features of mediated experience in conditions of modernity. One is the *collage effect*. Once the event has become more or less completely dominant over location, media presentation takes the form of the juxtaposition of stories and items which share nothing in common other than that they are 'timely' and consequential. The newspaper page and the television programme guide are equally significant examples of the collage effect. Does this effect mark the disappearance of narratives and even perhaps the severence of signs from their referents, as some have suggested?[17] Surely not. A collage is by definition not a narrative; but the coexistence of different items in mass media does not represent a chaotic jumble of signs. Rather, the separate 'stories' which are displayed alongside one another express orderings of consequentiality typical of a transformed time-space environment from which the hold of place has largely evaporated. They do not, of course, add up to a single narrative, but they depend on, and also in some ways express, unities of thought and consciousness.

Characteristic of mediated experience in modern times is a

second major feature: the *intrusion of distant events into everyday consciousness*, which is in some substantial part organised in terms of awareness of them. Many of the events reported on the news, for instance, might be experienced by the individual as external and remote; but many equally enter routinely into everyday activity. Familiarity generated by mediated experience might perhaps quite often produce feelings of 'reality inversion': the real object and event, when encountered, seem to have a less concrete existence than their media representation. Moreover many experiences that might be rare in day-to-day life (such as direct contact with death and the dying) are encountered routinely in media representations; confrontation with the real phenomena themselves is psychologically problematic. I shall expand on this phenomenon later in the book. In conditions of modernity, in sum, the media do not mirror realities but in some part form them; but this does not mean that we should draw the conclusion that the media have created an autonomous realm of 'hyperreality' where the sign or image is everything.

It has become commonplace to claim that modernity fragments, dissociates. Some have even presumed that such fragmentation marks the emergence of a novel phase of social development beyond modernity – a postmodern era. Yet the unifying features of modern institutions are just as central to modernity – especially in the phase of high modernity – as the disaggregating ones. The 'emptying' of time and space set in motion processes that established a single 'world' where none existed previously. In the majority of pre-modern cultures, including those of medieval Europe, time and space merged with domains of the gods and spirits as well as with the 'privileging of place'.[18] Taken overall, the many diverse modes of culture and consciousness characteristic of pre-modern 'world systems' formed a genuinely fragmented array of human social communities. By contrast, late modernity produces a situation in which humankind in some respects becomes a 'we', facing problems and opportunities where there are no 'others'.

High modernity and its existential parameters

High modernity is characterised by widespread scepticism about providential reason, coupled with the recognition that science and technology are double-edged, creating new parameters of risk and danger as well as offering beneficent possibilities for humankind. Such scepticism is not confined to the writings and ponderings of philosophers and intellectuals: we have seen that awareness of the existential parameters of reflexivity becomes part of reflexivity itself on a very broad level. To live in the 'world' produced by high modernity has the feeling of riding a juggernaut.[19] It is not just that more or less continuous and profound processes of change occur; rather, change does not consistently conform either to human expectation or to human control. The anticipation that the social and natural environments would increasingly be subject to rational ordering has not proved to be valid. The reflexivity of modernity is bound up in an immediate way with this phenomenon. The chronic entry of knowledge into the circumstances of action it analyses or describes creates a set of uncertainties to add to the circular and fallible character of post-traditional claims to knowledge.

Providential reason – the idea that increased secular understanding of the nature of things intrinsically leads to a safer and more rewarding existence for human beings – carries residues of conceptions of fate deriving from pre-modern eras. Notions of fate may of course have a sombre cast, but they always imply that a course of events is in some way preordained. In circumstances of modernity, traditional notions of fate may still exist, but for the most part these are inconsistent with an outlook in which risk becomes a fundamental element. To accept risk as risk, an orientation which is more or less forced on us by the abstract systems of modernity, is to acknowledge that no aspects of our activities follow a predestined course, and all are open to contingent happenings. In this sense it is quite accurate to characterise modernity, as Ulrich Beck does, as a 'risk society',[20] a phrase which refers to more than just the fact that modern social life introduces new forms of danger which humanity has to face. Living in the 'risk society' means living with a calculative attitude to the open possibilities of action, positive and negative, with which, as individuals and globally, we are confronted in a continuous way in our contemporary social existence.

Because of its reflexively mobilised – yet intrinsically erratic – dynamism, modern social activity has an essentially counterfactual character. In a post-traditional social universe, an indefinite range of potential courses of action (with their attendant risks) is at any given moment open to individuals and collectivities. Choosing among such alternatives is always an 'as if' matter, a question of selecting between 'possible worlds'. Living in circumstances of modernity is best understood as a matter of the routine contemplation of counterfactuals, rather than simply implying a switch from an 'orientation to the past', characteristic of traditional cultures, towards an 'orientation to the future'.

Given the extreme reflexivity of late modernity, the future does not just consist of the expectation of events yet to come. 'Futures' are organised reflexively in the present in terms of the chronic flow of knowledge into the environments about which such knowledge was developed – the very same process that, in an apparently paradoxical way, frequently confounds the expectations which that knowledge informs. The popularity of futurology in the system of high modernity is not an eccentric preoccupation, the contemporary equivalent of the fortune tellers of old. It signals a recognition that the consideration of counterfactual possibilities is intrinsic to reflexivity in the context of risk assessment and evaluation. In some respects, of course, such an outlook has long been built into modern institutions. Insurance, for example, has from fairly early on been linked not only to the risks involved in capitalist markets, but to the potential futures of a wide range of individual and collective attributes. Futures calculation on the part of insurance companies is itself a risky endeavour, but it is possible to limit some key aspects of risk in ways unavailable in most practical contexts of action. Risk calculation for insurance companies is actuarial and such companies typically attempt to exclude aspects or forms of risk which do not conform to the calculation of large-sample probabilities: that is, 'acts of God'.

Life has always been a risky business, fraught with dangers. Why should assessments of risk, and a proclivity for counterfactual thinking, be particularly significant in modern social life, as compared to pre-modern systems? We might add to this a question about expertise: is there anything distinctive about trust and abstract systems in modernity, since in pre-modern cultures also people consulted experts, such as magicians or healers, about their problems? In each of these respects, there are in fact major differences between the generality of pre-modern systems and the institutions of modernity. So far as the second question is concerned, the differences lie in the all-pervasive scope of abstract systems, together with the nature of the relation between technical and lay knowledge. There were experts in pre-modern societies but few technical systems, particularly in the smaller societies; hence it was often possible for the individual members of such societies to carry on their lives, if they so wished, almost solely in terms of their own local knowledge, or that of the immediate kinship group. No such disengagement is possible in modern times. This is true in some respects, as I have pointed out, for everyone on the face of the earth, but especially for those living in the core geographical areas of modernity.

The difference in the connections between technical and lay knowledge, when we compare pre-modern and modern systems, concerns the accessibility of expert skills and information to lay actors. Expert knowledge in pre-modern cultures tends to depend on procedures and symbolic forms that resist explicit codification; or, when such knowledge is codified, it is unavailable to lay individuals because literacy is the jealously guarded monopoly of the few. Preservation of the esoteric element of expert knowledge, particularly where this element is separated from 'skills and arts', is probably the main basis of whatever distinctive status experts achieve. The esoteric aspects of expertise in modern systems have little or nothing to do with its ineffability, but depend on a combination of lengthy training and specialisation – although, no doubt, experts (like sociologists) quite often put up a front of jargon and ritual to protect claims of technical distinctiveness. Specialisation is actually the key to the character of modern abstract systems. The knowledge incorporated in modern forms of expertise is in principle available to everyone, had they but the available resources, time and energy to acquire it. The fact that to be an expert in one or two small corners of modern knowledge systems is all that anyone can achieve means that abstract systems are opaque to the majority. Their opaque quality – the underlying element in the extension of trust in the context of disembedding mechanisms – comes from the very intensity of specialisation that abstract systems both demand and foster.

The specialised nature of modern expertise contributes directly to the erratic, runaway character of modernity. Modern expertise, in contrast to most pre-modern forms, is reflexively highly mobilised, and is generally oriented towards continual internal improvement or effectiveness. Expert problem-solving endeavours tend very often to be measured by their capacity to define issues with increasing clarity or precision (qualities that in turn have the effect of producing further specialisation). However, the more a given problem is placed precisely in focus, the more surrounding areas of knowledge become blurred for the individuals concerned, and the less likely they are to be able to foresee the consequences of their contributions beyond the particular sphere of their application. Although expertise is organised within wider abstract systems, expertise itself is increasingly more narrowly focused, and is liable to produce unintended and unforeseen outcomes which cannot be contained – save for the development of further expertise, thereby repeating the same phenomenon.[21]

This combination of specialised expertise and eccentric consequences forms one main reason why counterfactual thought, coupled to the centrality of the concept of risk, is so important in conditions of modernity. In pre-modern cultures, 'thinking ahead' usually means either the inductive use of stored experience, or consulting with soothsayers. Crops have to be sown, for example, in anticipation of future needs and with the changing of the seasons in mind. Traditionally established farming methods, perhaps accompanied by expert magical advice, would be employed to conjoin present need and future outcomes. In modern social life, individuals may be able to get along for periods of time by mixing established habits with consultation of specific experts for 'general repairs' and for unexpected contingencies. Experts themselves – who, to stress again, are not a clearly distinguishable stratum in the population – may proceed within their technical work by means of a resolute concentration on a narrow specialist area, paying little attention to broader consequences or implications. In such circumstances, risk assessment is fairly well 'buried' within more or less firmly established ways of doing things. But at any point these practices might become suddenly obsolete or subject to quite thoroughgoing transformation.

Expert knowledge does not create stable inductive arenas; new, intrinsically erratic situations and events are the inevitable outcome of the extension of abstract systems. There are still dangers constituted outside the reflexively infused spheres of action (for instance, from earthquakes or natural disasters), but most are filtered, and to some degree actively produced, by those spheres of action. We often think of risks in terms of parameters of probability that can be precisely assessed – rather in the manner in which insurance companies make their calculations. But in circumstances of late modernity, many forms of risk do not admit of clear assessment, because of the mutable knowledge environment which frames them; and even risk assessments within relatively closed settings are often only valid 'until further notice'.

Why modernity and personal identity?

Transformations in self-identity and globalisation, I want to propose, are the two poles of the dialectic of the local and the global in conditions of high modernity. Changes in intimate aspects of personal life, in other words, are directly tied to the establishment of social connections of very wide scope. I do not mean to deny the existence of many kinds of more intermediate connections – between, for example, localities and state organisations. But the level of time-space distanciation introduced by high modernity is so extensive that, for the first time in human history, 'self' and 'society' are interrelated in a global milieu.

Various factors, in circumstances of high modernity, directly influence the relation between self-identity and modern institutions. As has been stressed in the preceding pages, modernity introduces an elemental dynamism into human affairs, associated with changes in trust mechanisms and in risk environments. I do not think it is true that, as some have suggested, the modern age is specifically one of high anxiety, as contrasted to preceding eras. Anxieties and insecurities have plagued other ages besides ours, and there is probably little justification for the assumption sometimes made that life in smaller, more traditional cultures had a more even tenor than that of today. But the content and form of prevalent anxieties certainly have become altered.

The reflexivity of modernity extends into the core of the self. Put in another way, in the context of a post-traditional order, the self becomes a *reflexive project*. Transitions in individuals' lives have always demanded psychic reorganisation, something which was often ritualised in traditional cultures in the shape of *rites de passage*. But in such cultures, where things stayed more or less the same from generation to generation on the level of the collectivity, the changed identity was clearly staked out – as when an individual moved from adolescence into adulthood. In the settings of modernity, by contrast, the altered self has to be explored and constructed as part of a reflexive process of connecting personal and social change. This is a clear emphasis in Wallerstein and Blakeslee's study, and their work is not only a document about such a process, but also a constitutive contribution to it. The 'new sense of self' which, as they say, an individual has to cultivate after marital separation, is built as part of a process of pioneering innovative social forms, such as those involved in modern step-parenting (the very term 'parenting' is a relatively recent invention, helping to constitute what it now describes). The process of 'reaching back to one's early experiences' which Wallerstein and Blakeslee analyse is precisely part of a reflexive mobilising of self-identity; it is not confined to life's crises, but a general feature of modern social activity in relation to psychic organisation.

In such circumstances, abstract systems become centrally involved not only in the institutional order of modernity but also in the formation and continuity of the self. The early socialisation of children, for example, tends increasingly to depend on the advice and instruction of experts (paediatricians and educators), rather than on the direct initiation of one generation by another – and this advice and instruction is itself reflexively responsive to research in process. As academic disciplines, sociology and psychology are thus bound up in a direct way with the reflexivity of the self. Yet the most distinctive connection between abstract systems and the self is to be found in the rise of modes of therapy and counselling of all kinds. One way of interpreting the development of therapy is in purely negative fashion, as a response to the debilitating effects of modern institutions on self-experience and the emotions. Modernity, it might be said, breaks down the protective framework of the small community and of tradition, replacing these with much larger, impersonal organisations. The individual feels bereft and alone in a world in which she or he lacks the psychological supports and the sense of security provided by more traditional settings. Therapy offers someone to turn to, a secular version of the confessional.

I do not want to say that this standpoint should be dismissed altogether, since no doubt it contains elements of validity. But there is good reason to suppose that it is substantially inadequate. Self-identity becomes problematic in modernity in a way which contrasts with self–society relations in more traditional contexts; yet this is not only a situation of loss, and it does not imply either that anxiety levels necessarily increase. Therapy is not simply a means of coping with novel anxieties, but an expression of the reflexivity of the self – a phenomenon which, on the level of the individual, like the broader institutions of modernity, balances opportunity and potential catastrophe in equal measure.

This point will be amplified in the chapters that follow; but before expanding upon such issues, we have to take up some general problems to do with the self and self-identity. These considerations, together with the notions developed thus far, will form a general conceptual backdrop to the study as a whole.

2
The Self: Ontological Security and Existential Anxiety

An account of self-identity has to be developed in terms of an overall picture of the psychological make-up of the individual. In previous writings, I have suggested that such a picture should take the form of a 'stratification model'.[1] We begin from the premise that to be a human being is to know, virtually all of the time, in terms of some description or another, both what one is doing and why one is doing it. The logic of such a standpoint has been well explored within the perspectives of existential phenomenology and Wittgensteinian philosophy. The social conventions produced and reproduced in our day-to-day activities are reflexively monitored by the agent as part of 'going on' in the variegated settings of our lives. Reflexive awareness in this sense is characteristic of all human action, and is the specific condition of that massively developed institutional reflexivity spoken of in the preceding chapter as an intrinsic component of modernity. All human beings continuously monitor the circumstances of their activities as a feature of doing what they do, and such monitoring always has discursive features. In other words, agents are normally able, if asked, to provide discursive interpretations of the nature of, and the reasons for, the behaviour in which they engage.

The knowledgeability of human agents, however, is not confined to discursive consciousness of the conditions of their action. Many of the elements of being able to 'go on' are carried at the level of practical consciousness, incorporated within the continuity of everyday activities. Practical consciousness is integral to the reflexive monitoring of action, but it is 'non-conscious', rather than unconscious. Most forms of practical consciousness could not be 'held in mind' during the course of social activities, since their tacit or taken-for-granted qualities form the essential condition which allows actors to concentrate on tasks at hand. Yet there are no cognitive barriers separating discursive and practical consciousness, as there are divisions between the unconscious and consciousness taken generically. Unconscious modes of cognition and emotional governance, as a matter of definition, specifically resist being brought into consciousness, and appear there only in a distorted or transposed way.

Ontological security and trust

Practical consciousness is the cognitive and emotive anchor of the feelings of *ontological security* characteristic of large segments of human activity in all cultures. The notion of ontological security ties in closely to the tacit character of practical consciousness – or, in phenomenological terms, to the 'bracketings' presumed by the 'natural attitude' in everyday life. On the other side of what might appear to be quite trivial aspects of day-to-day action and discourse, chaos lurks. And this chaos is not just disorganisation, but the loss of a sense of the very reality of things and of other persons. Garfinkel's 'experiments' with ordinary language connect very closely here with philosophical reflection about the elemental characteristics of human existence.[2] To answer even the simplest everyday query, or respond to the most cursory remark, demands the bracketing of a potentially almost infinite range of possibilities open to the individual. What makes a given response 'appropriate' or 'acceptable' necessitates a shared – but unproven and unprovable – framework of reality. A sense of the shared reality of people and things is simultaneously sturdy and fragile. Its robustness is conveyed by the high level of reliability of the contexts of day-to-day social interaction, as these are produced and reproduced by lay agents. Garfinkel's experiments contravened conventions so firmly held that the reactions of those exposed to these breaches were dramatic and immediate.

Those reactions were ones of cognitive and emotional disorientation. The fragility of the natural attitude is evident to anyone who studies the protocols of Garfinkel's work. What happens is a flooding in of anxiety which the ordinary conventions of day-to-day life usually keep successfully at bay. The natural attitude brackets out questions about ourselves, others and the object-world which have to be taken for granted in order to keep on with everyday activity. Answers to these questions, if they were to be posed in a blunt way, are more radically uncertain than the sense in which knowledge as a whole 'lacks foundations'; or rather, the difficulties inherent in resolving them are a fundamental part of why more seemingly 'provable' forms of knowledge and claims cannot be given a completely secure base. To live our lives, we normally take for granted issues which, as centuries of philosophical enquiry have found, wither away under the sceptical gaze. Such issues include those quite properly called existential, whether posed on the level of philosophical analysis, or on a more practical level by individuals passing through a period of psychological crisis. They are questions of time, space, continuity and identity. In the natural attitude, actors take for granted existential parameters of their activity that are sustained, but in no way 'grounded' by the interactional conventions they observe. Existentially, these presume a tacit acceptance of the categories of duration and extension, together with the identity of objects, other persons and – particularly important for this study – the self.

To investigate such matters on the level of abstract philosophical discussion is, of course, quite different from actually 'living' them. The chaos that threatens on the other side of the ordinariness of everyday conventions can be seen psychologically as *dread* in Kierkegaard's sense: the prospect of being overwhelmed by anxieties that reach to the very roots of our coherent sense of 'being in the world'. Practical consciousness, together with the day-to-day routines reproduced by it, help bracket such anxieties not only, or even primarily, because of the social stability that they imply, but because of their constitutive role in organising an 'as if' environment in relation to existential issues. They provide modes of orientation which, on the level of practice, 'answer' the questions which could be raised about the frameworks of existence. It is of central importance to the analysis which follows to see that the anchoring aspects of such 'answers' are emotional rather than simply cognitive. How far different cultural settings allow a 'faith' in the coherence of everyday life to be achieved through providing symbolic interpretations of existential questions is, as we shall see below, very important. But cognitive frames of meaning will not generate that faith without a corresponding level of underlying emotional commitment – whose origins, I shall argue, are largely unconscious. Trust, hope and courage are all relevant to such commitment.

How is such faith achieved in terms of the psychological development of the human being? What creates a sense of ontological security that will carry the individual through transitions, crises and circumstances of high risk? Trust in the existential anchorings of reality in an emotional, and to some degree in a cognitive, sense rests on confidence in the reliability of persons, acquired in the early experiences of the infant. What Erik Erikson, echoing D. W. Winnicott, calls 'basic trust' forms the original nexus from which a combined emotive-cognitive orientation towards others, the object-world, and self-identity, emerges.[3] The experience of basic trust is the core of that specific 'hope' of which Ernst Bloch speaks, and is at origin of what Tillich calls 'the courage to be'. As developed through the loving attentions of early caretakers, basic trust links self-identity in a fateful way to the appraisals of others. The mutuality with early caretakers which basic trust presumes is a substantially unconscious sociality which precedes an 'I' and a 'me', and is a prior basis of any differentiation between the two.

Basic trust is connected in an essential way to the interpersonal organisation of time and space. An awareness of the separate identity of the parenting figures originates in the emotional acceptance of *absence*: the 'faith' that the caretaker will return, even though she or he is no longer in the presence of the infant. Basic trust is forged through what Winnicott calls the 'potential space' (actually, a phenomenon of time-space) which relates, yet distances, infant and prime caretaker. Potential space is created as the means whereby the infant makes the move from omnipotence to a grasp of the reality principle. 'Reality' here, however, should not be understood simply as a given object-world, but as a set of experiences organised constitutively through the mutuality of infant and caretakers.

From the early days of life, habit and routine play a fundamental role in the forging of relations in the potential space between infant and caretakers. Core connections are established between routine, the reproduction of coordinating conventions, and feelings of ontological security in the later activities of the individual. From these connections we can see why seemingly minor aspects of day-to-day routines come to be invested with the emotional significance which Garfinkels 'experiments' revealed. Yet at the same time, daily routines express deep-lying ambivalences which their early involvement with discipline implies. Routine activities, as Wittgenstein made clear, are never just carried out in an automatic way. In respect of control of the body and discourse, the actor must maintain constant vigilance in order to be able to 'go on' in social life. The maintaining of habits and routines is a crucial bulwark against threatening anxieties, yet by that very token it is a tensionful phenomenon in and of itself.

The infant, as Winnicott says, is 'all the time on the brink of unthinkable anxiety'. The very young child is not a 'being', but a 'going-on being', who has to be 'called into existence' by the nurturing environment which the caretaker provides.[4] The discipline of routine helps to constitute a 'formed framework' for existence by cultivating a sense of 'being', and its separation from 'non-being', which is elemental to ontological security. It includes orientations towards aspects of the object-world that carry symbolic residues into the later life of the individual. 'Transitional objects', in Winnicott's terminology, bridge the potential space between infant and caretakers. These first 'not-me' objects, like the routines with which they are virtually always connected, are both defences against anxiety and simultaneously links with an emerging experience of a stabilised world of objects and persons. Transitional objects predate 'reality testing' in Freud's sense, since they are part of the concrete means whereby the child passes from omnipotent control to control by means of manipulation.

The trust which the child, in normal circumstances, vests in its caretakers, I want to argue, can be seen as a sort of *emotional inoculation* against existential anxieties – a protection against future threats and dangers which allows the individual to sustain hope and courage in the face of whatever debilitating circumstances she or he might later confront. Basic trust is a screening-off device in relation to risks and dangers in the surrounding settings of action and interaction. It is the main emotional support of a defensive carapace or *protective cocoon* which all normal individuals carry around with them as the means whereby they are able to get on with the affairs of day-to-day life.

The sustaining of life, in a bodily sense as well as in the sense of psychological health, is inherently subject to risk. The fact that the behaviour of human beings is so strongly influenced by mediated experience, together with the calculative capacities which human agents possess, mean that every human individual could (in principle) be overwhelmed by anxieties about risks which are implied by the very business of living. That sense of 'invulnerability' which blocks off negative possibilities in favour of a generalised attitude of hope derives from basic trust. The protective cocoon is essentially a sense of 'unreality' rather than a firm conviction of security: it is a bracketing, on the level of practice, of possible events which could threaten the bodily or psychological integrity of the agent. The protective barrier it offers may be pierced, temporarily or more permanently, by happenings which demonstrate as real the negative contingencies built into all risk. Which car driver, passing by the scene of a serious traffic accident, has not had the experience of being so sobered as to drive more slowly – for a few miles – afterwards? Such an example is one which demonstrates – not in a counterfactual universe of abstract possibilities, but in a tangible and vivid way – the risks of driving, and thereby serves temporarily to pull apart the protective cocoon. But the feeling of relative invulnerability soon returns and the chances are that the driver then tends to speed up again.

Emphasising the interdependence of taken-for-granted routines and ontological security does not mean that a sense of 'the beneficence of things' derives from a dogged adherence to habit. On the contrary, a blind commitment to established routines, come what may, is a sign of neurotic compulsion. This is a compulsiveness which has its origins in the infant's failure – for whatever reason – to open out potential space in a way that generates basic trust. It is a compulsiveness born out of unmastered anxiety, which lacks that specific hope which creates social involvements over and above established patterns. If routine is a central element of the autonomy of the developing individual, it follows that the practical mastery of how to 'go on' in the contexts of social life is not inimical to creativity, but presumes it and is presumed by it. The paradigm case is the acquisition and use of language, but what applies in the discursive domain also applies to earlier forms of learning or experience.

Creativity, which means the capability to act or think innovatively in relation to pre-established modes of activity, is closely tied to basic trust. Trust itself, by its very nature, is in a certain sense creative, because it entails a commitment that is a 'leap into the unknown', a hostage to fortune which implies a preparedness to embrace novel experiences. However, to trust is also (unconsciously or otherwise) to face the possibility of loss: in the case of basic trust, the possible loss of the succour of the caretaking figure or figures. Fear of loss generates effort; the relations which sustain basic trust are 'worked at' emotionally by the child in conjunction with learning the cognitive work' that has to be put into even the most repetitive enactment of convention.

A creative involvement with others and with the object-world is almost certainly a fundamental component of psychological satisfaction and the discovery of 'moral meaning'. We do not need to resort to an arcane philosophical anthropology to see that the experience of creativity *as* a routine phenomenon is a basic prop to a sense of personal worth and therefore to psychological health. Where individuals cannot live creatively, either because of the compulsive enactment of routines, or because they have been unable to attribute full 'solidity' to persons and objects around them, chronic melancholic or schizophrenic tendencies are likely to result. Winnicott points out that an 'average expectable environment' in the early life of the child is the necessary condition of the development of such creative involvement. The infant has to go through a phase of 'madness' which, in Winnicott's words, 'enables the baby to be mad in one particular way that is conceded to babies', and which 'only becomes madness if it appears in later life'. The 'madness' of the infant is its creativity, at the stage at which early routines are being acquired and are opening out the potential space between the child and its caretakers. The infant 'creates an object but the object would not have been created as such if it had not already been there'.[5]

The establishing of basic trust is the condition of the elaboration of self-identity just as much as it is of the identity of other persons and of objects. The potential space between infant and caretakers provides the means of repudiating the other object as 'not-me'. From the phase of being merged with the main caretaking agent, the infant separates itself from that agent, at the same time as the caretaker reduces the degree of constant attention given to fulfilling the child's needs. The potential space which allows for an early (and unconscious) not-me to emerge through separation parallels the stage of separating attained at some point in adult psychotherapy. As in early infant attachments, a break which is not achieved through trust and reliability can produce traumatic consequences. In both infant and adult patient, trust is a mode of coping with the time-space absences implied in the opening out of potential space. Although in a more conscious and self-aware fashion, like an infant the patient lets go as part and parcel of a process of achieving autonomy, in which the separation is also tolerated by the analyst.

Anxiety and social organisation

I have argued in the preceding section that acquired routines, and forms of mastery associated with them, in the early life of the human being, are much more than just modes of adjusting to a pre-given world of persons and objects. They are constitutive of an emotional acceptance of the reality of the 'external world' without which a secure human existence is impossible. Such acceptance is at the same time the origin of self-identity through the learning of what is not-me. Although this position emphasises the emotional aspects of early encounters with reality, it is perfectly compatible with the view of the nature of external reality offered by Wittgenstein. Wittgensteinian philosophy has sometimes been pulled in a relativist direction by its interpreters, but it seems plain that Wittgenstein was not a relativist. There is a universally experienced world of external reality, but it is not directly reflected in the meaningful components of the conventions in terms of which actors organise their behaviour. Meaning is not built up through descriptions of external reality, nor does it consist in semiotic codes ordered independently of our encounters with that reality. Rather, 'what cannot be put into words' – interchanges with persons and objects on the level of daily practice – forms the necessary condition of what can be said and of the meanings involved in practical consciousness.

To know the meaning of words is thus to be able to use them as an integral part of the routine enactment of day-to-day life. We come to know reality not from perceiving it as it is, but as a result of the differences formed in daily practice. To come to know the meaning of the word 'table' is to get to know what a table is used for, which implies also knowing how the use of a table differs from other functional objects, like a chair or a bench. Meanings presuppose sets of differences, but these are differences accepted as part of reality as met with in daily experience, not only differences between signifiers in the structuralist sense.

Prior to the acquisition of language, the differences which are later elaborated into linguistic meanings are established in the potential space introduced between infant and caretakers. Reality is not just the here-and-now, the context of immediate sensory perception, but identity and change in what is *absent* – out of sight for the moment or, indeed, never directly encountered but simply accepted as 'there'. Learning about external reality hence is largely a matter of mediated experience. Although most of the richer textures of such experience depend on differentiated linguistic details, a grasp of the qualities of external reality begins much earlier. Learning the characteristics of absent persons and objects – accepting the real world as real – depends on the emotional security that basic trust provides. The feelings of unreality which may haunt the lives of individuals in whose early childhood basic trust was poorly developed may take many forms. They may feel that the object-world, or other people, have only a shadowy existence, or be unable to maintain a clear sense of continuity of self-identity.

Anxiety has to be understood in relation to the overall security system the individual develops, rather than only as a situationally specific phenomenon connected to particular risks or dangers. Anxiety, virtually all students of the subject agree, has to be distinguished from fear. Fear is a response to a specific threat and therefore has a definite object. As Freud says, anxiety, in contrast to fear, 'disregards the object': in other words, anxiety is a generalised state of the emotions of the individual. How far anxiety will be felt in any given situation, Freud goes on to point out, depends to a large degree on a person's 'knowledge and sense of power *vis-à-vis* the external world'.[6] A circumstance of 'anxious readiness' is different from anxiety as such, because it is a physiological, and functional, condition of preparedness of the organism to face a source of threat. Preparation for action, as it were, is what expedites an appropriate response to danger; anxiety itself is inexpedient, and tends to paralyse relevant actions rather than generate them.[7]

Because anxiety is diffuse, it is free-floating: lacking a specific object, it can come to be pinned to items, traits or situations which have an oblique (although unconsciously precise) reaction to whatever originally provoked it. Freud's writings contain many illustrations of people who exhibit fixations or obsessions of various kinds, but otherwise appear relatively free from anxious feelings. Anxiety is substitutive: the symptom replaces the anxiety, which is 'swallowed up' by the rigid pattern of behaviour that is adopted. The pattern is nonetheless a tensionful one, because an uprush of anxiety occurs when the person is unable to carry out, or is prevented from carrying out, the behaviour in question. Substitute formations have two advantages in respect of the management of anxiety: they avoid the direct experience of psychic conflict deriving from ambivalence, and they block off the further development of anxiety from its prime source. Anxiety, it seems reasonable to conclude, does not derive from unconscious repression; on the contrary, repression, and the behavioural symptoms associated with it, are created by anxiety. Anxiety is essentially fear which has lost its object through unconsciously formed emotive tensions that express 'internal dangers' rather than externalised threats. We should understand anxiety essentially as an unconsciously organised state of fear. Anxious feelings can to some degree be experienced consciously, but a person who says 'I feel anxious' is normally also aware of what he or she is anxious *about*. This situation is specifically different from the 'free-floating' character of anxiety on the level of the unconscious.

All individuals develop a framework of ontological security of some sort, based on routines of various forms. People handle dangers, and the fears associated with them, in terms of the emotional and behavioural 'formulae' which have come to be part of their everyday behaviour and thought. Anxiety also differs from fear in so far as it concerns (unconsciously) perceived threats to the integrity of the security system of the individual. The analysis of anxiety worked out by Harry Stack Sullivan, rather than that of Freud himself, is very useful here.[8] Sullivan emphasises that the need for a sense of security emerges very early on in the life of the child, and is 'much more important in the human being than the impulses resulting from a feeling of hunger, or thirst'.[9]

Like Winnicott and Erikson, Sullivan stresses that the infant's early sense of security comes from the nurturance of the caretaking agents – which he interprets in terms of the infant's sensitivity to parental approval or disapproval. Anxiety is felt through a – real or imagined – sensing of a caretaker's disapproval long before the development of consciously formed responses to the disapprobation of the other. Anxiety is felt as a 'cosmic' experience related to the reactions of others and to emerging self-esteem. It attacks the core of the self once a basic security system is set up, which is why it is so difficult for the individual to objectify it. Rising anxiety tends to threaten awareness of self-identity, since awareness of the self in relation to constituting features of the object-world becomes obscured. It is only in terms of the basic security system, the origin of the sense of ontological security, that the individual has the experience of self in relation to a world of persons and objects organised cognitively through basic trust.

The distinction between anxiety and fear, or apprehension that has an externally constituted object, has quite often been coupled to a further distinction between neurotic and normal anxiety.[10] However, this latter differentiation seems unnecessary if we recognise that anxiety depends fundamentally on unconscious operations. All anxiety is both normal and neurotic: normal because the mechanisms of the basic security system always involve anxiety-generating elements, and neurotic in the sense that anxiety 'has no object', in Freud's usage of that phrase. How far anxiety has a crippling effect on the personality, or expresses itself in, for instance, compulsive or phobic behaviour, varies according to the psychosocial development of the individual, but these characteristics are not a function of different types of anxiety. Rather, they concern the level of anxiety and the nature of the repressions to which it is linked.

Anxiety has its seeds in fear of separation from the prime

caretaking agent (usually the mother), a phenomenon which for the infant threatens the very core of the emerging self and of ontological security more generally. Fear of loss – the negative side of trust developed across the time-space absences of the parenting figures – is a permeating feature of the early security system. It is in turn associated with hostility, generated by feelings of abandonment: the antithesis of the sentiments of love which, combined with trust, generate hope and courage. The hostilities provoked by anxiety in the infant can most easily be understood as reactions to the pain of helplessness. Unless constrained and channelled, such hostilities can give rise to spiralling anxieties, especially where the expression of anger in the infant produces a reactive hostility on the part of parenting figures.[11]

Identification and projection form major means whereby potential spirals of anxiety and hostility are avoided. Identification is partial and contextual – the taking over of traits or patterns of behaviour of the other which are relevant to the resolution or diminishing of anxiety-creating patterns. It is always a tensionful affair, because it is partial, because mechanisms of projection are involved, and because it is fundamentally a defensive reaction to potential anxiety. Anxiety stimulated by the caretaker's absence, the time-space relation which is the arena for the development of basic trust, is the first impetus to identification, and also is the beginning of processes of cognitive learning whereby characteristics of the object-world are grasped. Becoming 'part of the other', that is to say, builds up a gradual understanding of absence and what 'the other' *is* as a separate person.

Since anxiety, trust and everyday routines of social interaction are so closely bound up with one another, we can readily understand the rituals of day-to-day life as coping mechanisms. This statement does not mean that such rituals should be interpreted in functional terms, as means of anxiety reduction (and therefore of social integration), but that they are bound up with how anxiety is socially managed. The observing of 'civil indifference' between strangers passing on the street, so brilliantly analysed by Goffman, serves to sustain attitudes of generalised trust on which interaction in public settings depends.[12] This is an elemental part of how modernity is 'done' in everyday interaction, as we can see by comparing the phenomenon to typical attitudes in pre-modern contexts.

Civil indifference represents an implicit contract of mutual acknowledgement and protection drawn up by participants in the public settings of modern social life. A person encountering another on the street shows by a controlled glance that the other is worthy of respect, and then by adjusting the gaze that he or she is not a threat to the other; and that other person does the same. In many traditional contexts where the boundaries between those who are 'familiars' and those who are 'strangers' is sharp, people do not possess rituals of civil indifference. They may either avoid the gaze of the other altogether, or stare in a way that would seem rude or threatening in a modern social environment.

Rituals of trust and tact in day-to-day life, as discussed by Goffman, are much more than merely ways of protecting one's own self-esteem and that of others (or, when used in particular ways, of attacking or undermining self-esteem). In so far as they concern the basic substance of everyday interaction – through control of bodily gesture, the face and the gaze, and the use of language – they touch on the most basic aspects of ontological security.

Existential questions

To be ontologically secure is to possess, on the level of the unconscious and practical consciousness, 'answers' to fundamental existential questions which all human life in some way addresses. Anxiety in a certain sense comes with human liberty, as Kierkegaard says; freedom is not a given characteristic of the human individual, but derives from the acquisition of an ontological understanding of external reality and personal identity. The autonomy which human beings acquire derives from their capacity to expand the range of mediated experience: to be familiar with properties of objects and events outside immediate settings of sensory involvement. With this in mind, we can reinterpret Kierkegaard's description of anxiety as 'the possibility of freedom'.[13] As a general phenomenon, anxiety derives from the capacity – and, indeed, necessity – for the individual to think ahead, to anticipate future possibilities counterfactually in relation to present action. But in a deeper way, anxiety (or its likelihood) comes from the very 'faith' in the independent existence of persons and objects that ontological security implies.

The prime existential question which the infant 'answers' in the course of early psychological development concerns *existence itself*: the discovery of an ontological framework of 'external reality'. When Kierkegaard analyses anxiety – or elemental dread – as 'the struggle of being against non-being', he points directly to this issue. To 'be', for the human individual, is to have ontological awareness.[14] This is not the same as awareness of self-identity, however closely the two may be related in the developing experience of the infant. The 'struggle of being against non-being' is the perpetual task of the individual, not just to 'accept' reality, but to create ontological reference points as an integral aspect of 'going on' in the contexts of day-to-day life. Existence is a mode of being-in-the-world in Kierkegaard's sense. In 'doing' everyday life, all human beings 'answer' the question of being; they do it by the nature of the activities they carry out. As with other existential questions to be mentioned below, such 'answers' are lodged fundamentally on the level of behaviour.

In pre-modern contexts, tradition has a key role in articulating action and ontological frameworks; tradition offers an organising medium of social life specifically geared to ontological precepts. In the first place, tradition orders time in a manner which restricts the openness of counterfactual futures. People in all cultures, including the most resolutely traditional, distinguish future, present and past, and weigh alternative courses of action in terms of likely future considerations. But as we saw in the previous chapter, where traditional modes of practice are dominant, the past inserts a wide band of 'authenticated practice' into the future. Time is not empty, and a consistent 'mode of being' relates future to past. In addition, tradition creates a sense of the firmness of things that typically mixes cognitive and moral elements. The world is as it is because it is as it should be. Of course, in many traditional cultures, and in virtually all rationalised religious systems, explicit ontological conceptions are found – although these may stand in considerable tension with the enactment of traditional practices themselves.

A second type of existential question concerns not so much the nature of being as the relations between the external world and *human life*. Here there is also a fundamental temporal aspect, in the guise of human finitude as compared to temporal infinity or the 'eternal'. All humans live in circumstances of what I have elsewhere called *existential contradiction*: we are of the inanimate world, yet set off against it, as self-conscious beings aware of our finite character. As Heidegger says, *Dasein* is a being who not only lives and dies, but is aware of the horizon of its own mortality. This is the 'existential awareness of non-being' of which Tillich speaks, 'the awareness that non-being is part of one's own being'.[15] When seen in a purely biological sense, death is relatively unproblematic – the cessation of the physiological functions of the organism. Kierkegaard points out that, in contrast to biological death, 'subjective death' is an 'absolute uncertainty' – something of which we can have no intrinsic understanding. The existential problem is how to approach subjective death: 'it is the case that the living individual is absolutely excluded from the possibility of approaching death in any sense whatever, since he cannot experimentally come near enough without comically sacrificing himself upon the altar of his own experiment, and since he cannot experimentally restrain the experiment, he learns nothing from it.'[16]

In psychoanalytic theory, the existential horizon of finitude does not have a prominent place in the origins of anxiety – or, rather, the unconscious cannot conceive of its own death, not for the reason given by Kierkegaard, but because the unconscious has no sense of time. Anxiety about death in Freud's theory comes primarily from fear of the loss of others, and is thus directly connected to the early mastery of absence. The discrepancy between these two interpretations, however, is more apparent than real. For if we cannot understand 'subjective death', then death is no more or less than the transition from being to non-being; and the fear of non-being becomes one of the primal anxieties of the developing infant. Threats to the being of the infant in the first instance are feelings or presentiments of loss – the realisation that the constancy of persons and objects is bound up with the stable relations provided by the caretaking agents. The possible loss of the caretakers provides the initiating framework from which fears of death and sickness emerge with regard to the self. It may be true that, on the level of the unconscious, the person cannot conceive of her death. As Freud says, unconsciously all of us think of surviving as spectators at our own deaths. But consciousness of finitude, which human beings develop with increasing cognitive mastery of temporal categories, is associated with anxieties of an utterly fundamental sort.

To accept the existential centrality of awareness of death for human actors does not necessitate endorsing the philosophy of 'authenticity' which Kierkegaard and Heidegger have built upon it. For Heidegger, death is the 'innermost possibility' of *Dasein*, a possibility which, in revealing itself as a necessity, renders 'authentic life' an option. Finitude is what allows us to discern moral meaning in otherwise transient events, something that would be denied to a being with no finite horizons. The 'call of conscience' which awareness of finitude brings stimulates human beings to realise their 'time essence as Beings-unto-death'. What Heidegger calls 'resolve' is the urgency which makes itself felt as the need to throw oneself into what life has to offer before time – for the individual – 'runs out'.[17] This view is not offered by Heidegger as a moral philosophy, but as an account of the actualities of human experience. Yet it is surely a position that is difficult to sustain on a transcendental basis. It is above all an outlook addressed to a civilisation afflicted by what Kierkegaard terms the 'sickness unto death' – by which he meant the inclination to accept that, for the individual, death is indeed the end.[18] While anxieties about finitude, deriving from the psychological development of the individual, are universal, cultural representations of death are not. Religious cosmologies may play on such anxieties in developing conceptions of the afterlife, or cycles of rebirth. Yet they do not by any means always cultivate moral meanings primarily by emphasising the impermanence of the individual's existence.

A third category of existential question concerns the existence of *other persons*. No issue was more thoroughly explored in the early literature of phenomenology, but we have to be careful to avoid the philosophical errors to which that literature fell prey. Husserl drew on Cartesian rationalism in his formulation of interpersonal knowledge. Given this position, although the individual can perceive the body of another person, he or she cannot perceive that individual as subject. 'I know my own soul better than my own body', Descartes wrote. But I can only know the body of the other, he continued, since I have no access to that person's consciousness.[19] According to Husserl, we are aware of another person's feelings and experiences only on the basis of empathic inferences from our own. As is well known, the inadequacy of this view proved to be one of the intractable difficulties of his philosophy. A transcendental philosophy of the ego terminates in an irremediable solipsism.

The difficulty is avoided in the position of the later Wittgenstein, as well as in the more sophistical versions of existentialist phenomenology. Self-consciousness has no primacy over the awareness of others, since language – which is intrinsically public – is the means of access to both. Intersubjectivity does not derive from subjectivity, but the other way around. How should we expand on this view in developmental terms, however, given that the early experiences of the child predate the acquisition of language? And in what sense is the existence of others an existential problem, if we break with Husserl's standpoint? The answers follow from the arguments already developed in the preceding pages. Learning the qualities of others is connected in an immediate way with the earliest explorations of the object-world and with the first stirrings of what later become established feelings of self-identity. The individual is not a being who at some sudden point encounters others; 'discovering the other', in an emotional-cognitive way, is of key importance in the initial development of self-awareness as such. The subsequent acquisition of language would not be possible were not those early developmental processes well in train by that time.

The 'problem of the other' is not a question of how the individual makes the shift from the certainty of her or his own inner experiences to the unknowable other person. Rather it concerns the inherent connections which exist between learning the characteristics of other persons and the other major axes of ontological security. Trust in others, in the early life of the infant and, in chronic fashion, in the activities of the adult, is at the origin of the experience of a stable external world and a coherent sense of self-identity. It is 'faith' in the reliability and integrity of others which is at stake here. Trust in others begins in the context of individual confidence – confidence in the caretaking figures. But it both precedes an awareness of those figures as 'persons' and later forms a generalised component of the intersubjective nature of social life. Trust, interpersonal relations and a conviction of the 'reality' of things go hand in hand in the social settings of adult life. The responses of the other are necessary to the sustaining of an 'observable/accountable' world, and yet there is no point at which they can be absolutely relied upon. Social reproduction unfolds with none of the causal determination characteristic of the physical world, but as an always contingent feature of the knowledgeable use of convention. The social world, moreover, should not be understood as a multiplicity of situations in which 'ego' faces 'alter', but one in which each person is equally implicated in the active process of organising predictable social interaction. The orderliness of day-to-day life is a miraculous occurrence, but it is not one that stems from any sort of outside intervention; it is brought about as a continuous achievement on the part of everyday actors in an entirely routine way. That orderliness is solid and constant; yet the slightest glance of one person towards another, inflexion of the voice, changing facial expression or gestures of the body may threaten it.

A fourth type of existential question concerns precisely: *self-identity*. But what exactly is self-identity? Since the self is a somewhat amorphous phenomenon, self-identity cannot refer merely to its persistence over time in the way philosophers might speak of the 'identity' of objects or things.[20] The 'identity' of the self, in contrast to the self as a generic phenomenon, presumes reflexive awareness. It is what the individual is conscious 'of' in the term 'self-consciousness'. Self-identity, in other words, is not something that is just given, as a result of the continuities of the individual's action-system, but something that has to be routinely created and sustained in the reflexive activities of the individual.

An anchoring discursive feature of self-identity is the linguistic differentiation of 'I/me/you' (or their equivalents). We cannot be satisfied, however, with G. H. Mead's formulation of the I/me couplet in relation to self-identity. In Mead's theory, the 'me' is the identity – a social identity – of which the 'I' becomes conscious in the course of the psychological development of the child. The 'I' is, as it were, the active, primitive will of the individual, which seizes on the 'me' as the reflection of social ties. We can agree with Mead that the infant begins to develop a self in response to the social context of its early experience. But the I/me (and I/me/you) relation is one internal to language, not one connecting the unsocialised part of the individual (the I) to the 'social self'. 'I' is a linguistic shifter, which gets its meaning from the networks of terms whereby a discursive system of subjectivity is acquired. The ability to use 'I', and other associated terms of subjectivity, is a condition for the emergence of self-awareness, but does not as such define it.

Self-identity is not a distinctive trait, or even a collection of traits, possessed by the individual. It is *the self as reflexively understood by the person in terms of her or his biography*. Identity here still presumes continuity across time and space: but self-identity is such continuity as interpreted reflexively by the agent. This includes the cognitive component of personhood. To be a 'person' is not just to be a reflexive actor, but to have a concept of a person (as applied both to the self and others). What a 'person' is understood to be certainly varies across cultures, although there are elements of such a notion that are common to all cultures. The capacity to use 'I' in shifting contexts, characteristic of every known culture, is the most elemental feature of reflexive conceptions of personhood.

The best way to analyse self-identity in the generality of instances is by contrast with individuals whose sense of self is fractured or disabled. Laing provides an important discussion of this issue.[21] The ontologically insecure individual, he points out, tends to display one or more of the following characteristics. In the first place she may lack a consistent feeling of biographical continuity. An individual may fail to achieve an enduring conception of her aliveness. Laing quotes a character from Kafka who says, 'There has never been a time in which I have been convinced from within myself that I am alive.'[22] Discontinuity in temporal experience is often a basic feature of such a sentiment. Time may be comprehended as a series of discrete moments, each of which severs prior experiences from subsequent ones in such a way that no continuous 'narrative' can be sustained. Anxiety about obliteration, of being engulfed, crushed or overwhelmed by externally impinging events, is frequently the correlate of such feelings. Secondly, in an external environment full of changes, the person is obsessively preoccupied with apprehension of possible risks to his or her existence, and paralysed in terms of practical action. The individual experiences what Laing calls an 'inner deadness' deriving from an inability to block off impinging dangers – an incapacity to sustain the protective cocoon of which

I spoke earlier. People engulfed by such anxieties may seek to 'blend with the environment' so as to escape being the target of the dangers which haunt them. Thirdly, the person fails to develop or sustain trust in his own self-integrity. The individual feels morally 'empty' because he lacks 'the warmth of a loving self-regard'.[23] Quite often, paradoxically, the actor subjects his behaviour and thoughts to constant scrutiny. Self-scrutiny in this guise is obsessional; its experiential outcome is much the same as in the other instances, a feeling that the living spontaneity of the self has become something dead and lifeless.

A normal sense of self-identity is the obverse of these characteristics. A person with a reasonably stable sense of self-identity has a feeling of biographical continuity which she is able to grasp reflexively and, to a greater or lesser degree, communicate to other people. That person also, through early trust relations, has established a protective cocoon which 'filters out', in the practical conduct of day-to-day life, many of the dangers which in principle threaten the integrity of the self. Finally, the individual is able to accept that integrity as worthwhile. There is sufficient self-regard to sustain a sense of the self as 'alive' – within the scope of reflexive control, rather than having the inert quality of things in the object-world.

The existential question of self-identity is bound up with the fragile nature of the biography which the individual 'supplies' about herself. A person's identity is not to be found in behaviour, nor – important though this is – in the reactions of others, but in the capacity *to keep a particular narrative going*. The individual's biography, if she is to maintain regular interaction with others in the day-to-day world, cannot be wholly fictive. It must continually integrate events which occur in the external world, and sort them into the ongoing 'story' about the self. As Charles Taylor puts it, 'In order to have a sense of who we are, we have to have a notion of how we have become, and of where we are going.'[24] There is surely an unconscious aspect to this chronic 'work', perhaps organised in a basic way through dreams. Dreaming may very well represent an unconscious selection and discarding of memories, which proceeds at the end of every day.[25]

A stable sense of self-identity presupposes the other elements of ontological security – an acceptance of the reality of things and of others – but it is not directly derivable from them. Like the

Existential questions concern basic parameters of human life, and are 'answered' by everyone who 'goes on' in the contexts of social activity. They presume the following ontological and epistemological elements:

Existence and being: the nature of existence, the identity of objects and events.

Finitude and human life: the existential contradiction by means of which human beings are of nature yet set apart from it as sentient and reflexive creatures.

The experience of others: how individuals interpret the traits and actions of other individuals.

The continuity of self-identity: the persistence of feelings of personhood in a continuous self and body.

Figure 2   *Existential questions*

other existential dimensions of ontological security, feelings of self-identity are both robust and fragile. Fragile, because the biography the individual reflexively holds in mind is only one 'story' among many other potential stories that could be told about her development as a self; robust, because a sense of self-identity is often securely enough held to weather major tensions or transitions in the social environments within which the person moves.

As with the other existential arenas, the 'content' of self-identity – the traits from which biographies are constructed – varies socially and culturally. In some respects this is obvious enough. A person's name, for example, is a primary element in his biography; practices of social naming, how far names express kin relations, whether or not names are changed at certain stages of life – all these things differ between cultures. But there are other more subtle, yet also more important, differences. Reflexive biographies vary in much the same ways as stories do – in terms, for instance, of form and style. As I will go on to argue, this issue is of fundamental importance in assessing mechanisms of self-identity under conditions of modernity.

Body and self

The self, of course, is embodied. Awareness of the contours and properties of the body is at the very origin of the original explorations of the world whereby the child learns the features of objects and others. A child does not learn that it 'has' a body, because self-consciousness emerges through bodily differentiation rather than the other way around. Wittgenstein again has a good deal to teach us about the relation of body and self. The child learns about its body primarily in terms of its practical engagements with the object-world and with other people. Reality is grasped through day-to-day *praxis*. The body is thus not simply an 'entity', but is experienced as a practical mode of coping with external situations and events (an emphasis also of Merleau-Ponty). Facial expressions and other gestures provide the fundamental content of that contextuality or indexicality which is the condition of everyday communication. To learn to become a competent agent – able to join with others on an equal basis in the production and reproduction of social relations – is to be able to exert a continuous, and successful, monitoring of face and body. Bodily control is a central aspect of what 'we cannot say in words' because it is the necessary framework for what we can say (or can say meaningfully).

The works of Goffman and Garfinkel in many ways represent an empirical exploration of the themes Wittgenstein raised on a philosophical level. They show how close, complete and unending is the control that the individual is expected to sustain over the body in all settings of social interaction. To be a competent agent, moreover, means not only maintaining such continuous control, but being seen by others to do so. A competent agent is one routinely seen to be so by other agents. He or she must avoid lapses of bodily control, or signal to others by gestures or exclamations that there is nothing 'wrong' if such events should occur.[26]

Routinised control of the body is crucial to the sustaining of the individual's protective cocoon in situations of day-to-day interaction. In ordinary situations, the person preserves a bodily orientation showing what Goffman calls 'easy control'.[27] Bodily experience and skills are influential features relevant to what an individual senses as pertinent dangers and therefore treats as alarming. As Goffman succinctly remarks, 'almost every activity that the individual easily performs now was at some time for him something that required serious mobilisation of effort. To walk, to cross a road, to utter a complete sentence, to wear long pants, to tie one's own shoes, to add a column of figures – all these routines that allow the individual unthinking, competent performance were attained through an acquisition process whose early stages were negotiated in a cold sweat.'[28] A person's ease in any given situation presumes long-term experience in confronting the threats and opportunities it presents. Actors acquire a 'survivably short reaction time': a brief interval needed to sense alarm and to respond appropriately. Bodily self-management, however, has to be so complete and constant that all individuals are vulnerable to moments of stress when competence breaks down – and the framework of ontological security is threatened.

The issue of the body in recent social theory is associated particularly with the name of Foucault. Foucault has analysed the body in relation to mechanisms of power, concentrating particularly on the emergence of 'disciplinary power' in circumstances of modernity. The body becomes the focus of power and this power, instead of trying to 'mark' it externally, as in pre-modern times, subjects it to the internal discipline of self-control. As portrayed by Foucault, disciplinary mechanisms produce 'docile bodies'.[29] Yet important though Foucault's interpretation of discipline may be, his view of the body is substantially wanting. He cannot analyse the relation between the body and agency since to all intents and purposes he equates the two. Essentially, the body plus power equals agency. But this idea will not do, and appears unsophisticated when placed alongside the standpoint developed prior to Foucault by Merleau-Ponty, and contemporaneously by Goffman. Bodily discipline is intrinsic to the competent social agent; it is transcultural rather than specifically connected with modernity; and it is a continuous feature of the flow of conduct in the *durée* of daily life. Most importantly, routine control of the body is integral to the very nature both of agency and of being accepted (trusted) by others as competent.

This double significance of the body in respect of agency may explain the apparently universal character of the I/me differentiation. Regularised control of the body is a fundamental means whereby a biography of self-identity is maintained; yet at the same time the self is also more or less constantly 'on display' to others in terms of its embodiment. The need to handle both of these aspects of the body simultaneously, which originates in the early experiences of the infant, is the main reason why a feeling of bodily integrity – of the self being safely 'in' the body – is so closely tied to the regular appraisals of others. What Goffman calls 'normal appearances' are part and parcel of routine contexts of interaction. Normal appearances are the (closely monitored) bodily mannerisms by means of which the individual actively reproduces the protective cocoon in situations of 'normalcy'. 'Normal appearances mean that it is safe and sound to continue on with the activity at hand with only peripheral attention given to checking up on the stability of the environment.'[30] They are the bodily manifestation of that 'bracketing out' process descri- bed earlier. Like all aspects of interaction in day-to-day life, normal appearances have to be managed with immense care, even though the seeming absence of such care is precisely a key feature of them.

How far normal appearances can be carried on in ways consis- tent with the individual's biographical narrative is of vital import- ance for feelings of ontological security. All human beings, in all cultures, preserve a division between their self-identities and the 'performances' they put on in specific social contexts. But in some circumstances the individual might come to feel that the whole flow of his activities is put on or false. An established routine, for one reason or another, becomes invalid. For instance, a husband may conceal from his wife the fact that he is having an affair and plans to divorce her. Ordinary routines then become false per- formances, staged routines from which the person feels a certain distance – the individual has to continue with ordinary appear- ances by acting as though nothing were up. What is habitually structured into practical consciousness becomes contrived, and probably unconsciously problematic. Playing the part of the dutiful husband in effect represents a false persona, but not one that seriously compromises the individual's own self-image.

Where the dissociation is more thoroughgoing, and less contex- tual, however, a more severe dislocation is likely to result. A person feels he is continually acting out most or all routines, rather than following them for valid reasons. If Laing is correct, such a situation characteristically leads to an 'unembodied' self. Most people are absorbed in their bodies, and feel themselves to be a unified body and self. Too radical a discrepancy between accepted routines and the individual's biographical narrative creates what Laing (following Winnicott) calls a false self – in which the body appears as an object or instrument manipulated by the self from behind the scenes. Disentanglement from the body – or perhaps a complete merging of self and body – in the form of spiritual ecstasy, is a common ideal of the world's religions, and appears there in a positive light. But when this dissociation happens as an unwanted feature of personality, it expresses existential anxieties impinging directly upon self-identity.

The disembodied person may feel unimplicated in bodily desire, and experiences dangers as though they were threats to another person. He or she may in fact be able to weather assaults on the physical well-being of the body more easily than an ordinary individual can; but the price of this capability is intense anxieties of other sorts. The narrative of self-identity in such instances is woven in a manner which allows the individual to witness the activities of her body with neutral detachment, cynicism, hatred or ironic amusement, as the case may be. Kierkegaard wrote of this phenomenon, speaking of the 'closure' of the self from the body; the individual's actions are as if under remote control.[31] Disembodiment has connections with reality inversion, mentioned in the preceding chapter. Prisoners in the Nazi concentration camps during the last war, subjected to horrendous physical and psychological pressures, experienced states of dissociation of body and self. For them, feeling 'out' of the body – a condition described as 'being like a dream', 'unreal' or 'like being a character in a play' – seems to have been a functional phenomenon, allowing distance from the physical deprivations which the body suffered.[32] Feelings of unreality on the part of schizoid individuals frequently have a similar form, and perhaps even involve parallel defence mechanisms. Disembodiment is an attempt to transcend dangers and be safe.

Disembodiment in more minor versions is a characteristic feature of disruptions in ontological security experienced by everyone in tensionful situations of daily life. The splitting is a temporary reaction to a danger which passes, not a chronic dissociation. It is not fanciful to discern a close connection between Winnicott, Laing and Lacan on this point. For if the hypothesis of the mirror stage is valid, perception of the body as separate – in the imaginary – is central to the formation of self-identity at a particular phase of child development. A narrative of self-identity cannot begin until this phase is transcended; or, more accurately, the emergence of such a narrative is the means of its transcendence. Against this backdrop, it is not surprising that, in circumstances of strain, feelings of separation from the body should be common. The individual enters a temporary schizoid state, and becomes detached from what the body is doing or what is being done to it.

Mirror image and self can effectively become reversed in more pronounced and semi-permanent schizoid personalities. The experience of agency is withdrawn from the body and attached to a fantasy world of narrative biography, separated from the intersecting of the imaginary and the reality principle upon which ordinary social activity depends. Self-identity is no longer inte-grated with the day-to-day routines in which the person is involved. The individual may in fact feel invisible to others, since the body in action ceases to be the 'vehicle of the self'. Freud notes that children often play at being invisible, and that the game may take place in front of a mirror. The child finds a method of making itself disappear – by ducking away from the mirror or moving out of sight of its own reflection. The game touches on deep anxieties. The fear of being invisible is con-nected to the early relations with parenting figures – and espe-cially the fear that the absent mother might never return. The child's exploration of its own disappearance is closely associated with the difficulty of grasping that the absent parent has not 'gone for good'.[33]

Feelings of invisibility are liable to become chronic if the threat of the parent's disappearance becomes linked to defences against being fully 'there' in the body. We see here again the central importance of the fact that, in 'normal' psychological develop-ment, the body is much more than a device for conveying minor feelings to others. The whole self is never to be seen on the surfaces of the body or in its gestures; but where it is not visible at all, ordinary feelings of embodiment – of being 'with' and 'in' the flow of day-to-day conduct – become dislocated or dissolved.

Laing identifies four characteristics of the pathology of such a false-self persona:

1 The false-self system becomes more and more enveloping and all-pervasive.
2 It becomes more autonomous from bodily routines.
3 It becomes 'harrassed' by compulsive behaviour fragments.
4 The actions of the body become more and more 'dead, unreal, false, mechanical'.[34]

The sense of more or less complete detachment from everyday routines is well conveyed in a case description Laing gives of a young schizophrenic man. This individual came to feel that the thoughts in his 'brain', as he expressed it, were not really his. He felt himself to be 'staging' all his reactions to the conventions of day-to-day social life, in respect of which he felt his body to be either machinelike and 'in neutral', or gripped by an unfathomable compulsion. For example, his wife would pour him a cup of tea, and in response he would smile and utter a word of thanks. Yet he would then immediately be overcome with revulsion: his wife had acted mechanically, and he had reacted in terms of the same 'social mechanics' (his phrase).

'Going on' in the contexts of daily social life involves constant and unremitting work on the part of all participants in social interaction. For ordinary individuals, much of this labour passes unnoticed, so deeply engrained is it in practical consciousness in terms of bodily control and facial expression. But for the schizoid or schizophrenic person, who cannot sustain such an unthinking acceptance of bodily integrity, the effort to keep up normal appearances may become a terrible burden – he or she may in the end be literally unable to 'go on' (in the double sense this phrase has) and retreat more or less wholly into an inner life of fantasy.

Of course, the body is not only a localised medium of action. It is a physical organism that has to be cared for by its possessor; it is sexed; and it is a source of pleasure and pain. A fundamental aspect of the human condition is that human beings cannot care for themselves during the first years of life. Routines of caring are elemental to the circumstances of trust in the life of the infant: the adult caretakers are also providers. Modes of providing food and other basic organic necessities are best regarded as *regimes* – the child learns early on that nourishment is not forthcoming on demand, but only periodically. Regimes are always partly a matter of individual influence and taste: even the neonate actively conditions the responses of the caretakers, sometimes in a very substantial way. But regimes are also always socially or culturally organised. How far food regimes, for the adult, are standardised and closely regulated, or left open to individual inclination, depends on the nature of a given culture. The same comments apply to sexual regimes, whether in respect of child or adult behaviour. Dress is another type of regime. In all cultures, dress is vastly more than simply a means of bodily protection: it is, manifestly, a means of symbolic display, a way of giving external form to narratives of self-identity.

Regimes differ from the ordinary routines of 'going on'. All social routines entail continuous control of the body, but regimes are learned practices that entail tight control over organic needs. With the partial exception of dress, regimes are enforced by the physiological character of the organism, no matter what symbolic elements they also acquire. Regimes centre on gratification/ deprivation, and hence are a focus of motivational energies – beginning, as Freud made clear, with the earliest unconscious adjustments to the reality principle. The types of regimes individuals build up as habits of behaviour, therefore, remain as unconscious conditioning elements of conduct, and are tied into enduring motivational patterns. Regimes are modes of self-discipline, but are not solely constituted by the orderings of convention in day-to-day life; they are personal habits, organised in some part according to social conventions, but also formed by personal inclinations and dispositions.

Regimes are of central importance to self-identity precisely because they connect habits with aspects of the visible appearance of the body. Habits of eating are ritual displays in themselves, but they also affect bodily form, perhaps indicating something about the background of the individual as well as a certain self-image which she or he has cultivated. Eating regimes also have their pathologies, and are connected with various persistent kinds of positive accentuations of bodily discipline. Asceticism, involving fasting and other forms of bodily deprivation, is commonly linked to the pursuit of religious values, as is the following of certain kinds of bodily regimes generally. On a more personal level, self-deprivation of physical resources is a frequent feature of psychologial disorders in all forms of society – as is indulgence. Much the same can be said about sexual regimes. Celibacy is a form of bodily denial prized in some religious orders, but can also be an expression of personality difficulties, as can sexual obsessions of different sorts. Regimes of self-adornment are similarly linked to key dynamics of personality. Dress is a means of self-display, but also relates directly to concealment/revelation in respect of personal biographies: it connects convention to basic aspects of identity.

How should we think of the body in relation to its sexual characteristics? Nothing is clearer than that gender is a matter of learning and continuous 'work', rather than a simple extension of biologically given sexual difference. In respect of this aspect of the body, we can return to the central themes of ethnomethodology as elaborated by Garfinkel. Ethnomethodology has become so closely identified with conversation analysis that it is easily forgotten that Garfinkel's work developed out of a direct concern with the managing of gender. The case of Agnes, the transsexual discussed in *Studies in Ethnomethodology*, shows that to be a 'man' or a 'woman' depends on a chronic monitoring of the body and bodily gestures. There is in fact no single bodily trait which separates all women from all men.[35] Only those few individuals who have something like a full experience of being a member of both sexes can completely appreciate how pervasive are the details of bodily display and management by means of which gender is 'done'.

Motivation

Reasons for action, as explained at the beginning of the chapter, are an intrinsic part of the reflexive monitoring of action carried on by all human agents. Reasons form an ongoing feature of action – rather than being linked as sequences or aggregates. All competent agents routinely 'keep in touch' with the grounds of their behaviour as an aspect of producing and reproducing that behaviour. Reasons are distinguishable from motives, which refer to the wellsprings of action. Motives do not impinge chronically on action in the manner in which reasons do. Many aspects of routine behaviour are not directly motivated – they are simply carried on as elements of day-to-day life. Motives do not exist as discrete psychological units, any more than reasons do. We should regard motivation as an underlying 'feeling state' of the individual, involving unconscious forms of affect as well as more consciously experienced pangs or promptings.

Infants do not have motives, but only needs or wants. A baby, of course, is not a passive organism, but one which actively and urgently prompts caretakers to respond to its wants by its reactions to whatever regimes they might seek to impose. Needs are not motives, however, because they do not imply a cognitive anticipation of a state of affairs to be realised – a defining characteristic of motivation. Motives are essentially born of anxiety, coupled with the learning processes whereby a sense of ontological security is engendered.

Motivation thus has to be analysed in terms of the characteristics of the basic security system, as portrayed earlier. More specifically, motives are bound up with the emotions linked to early relations of trust. Trust relations can be understood in terms of the formation of social *bonds* – emotively charged ties of dependence with other persons, beginning with the ties developed with caretakers.[36] Bonds established with early caretakers, which leave resonances affecting all close social relations formed in adult life, involve emotive gestures of various kinds. Although what 'an' emotion is has to be learned – and is substantively contextual, as the constructivist interpretation of emotion has demonstrated[37] – emotive reactions are intrinsic to the life of the very young infant. Emotional gestures, involving crying and facial expressions of contentment on the part of the child, and bodily expressions of care on the part of caretakers, are integral elements of developing social bonds.

Handling the emotional involvements of early life necessarily entangles the child in tensions affecting its bonds with caretakers. *Guilt* is one manifestation which the anxieties thus stimulated provoke. Guilt is anxiety produced by the fear of transgression: where the thoughts or activities of the individual do not match up to expectations of a normative sort. As Klein has persuasively demonstrated, the experience of guilt occurs much earlier in the life of the child than Freud implied. The mechanics of guilt have been very widely explored in the literature of psychoanalytic theory, but in respect of problems of self-identity, *shame*, which has been less extensively discussed, is more important. The obverse of guilt is reparation; guilt concerns things done or not done. Guilt experienced as a pervasive feature of the unconscious may affect more aspects of self-identity than shame, but its prime emphasis tends to be on discrete elements of behaviour and the modes of retribution that they suggest or entail.

Shame bears directly on self-identity because it is essentially anxiety about the adequacy of the narrative by means of which the individual sustains a coherent biography. It originates as early as guilt, since it is stimulated by experiences in which feelings of inadequacy or humiliation are provoked – feelings that long antedate the mastery of differentiated language. Some have argued that while guilt is a private anxiety-state, shame is a public one. Yet this is not the most appropriate way to distinguish the two since both, in their most pronounced forms, concern intro-jected figures – particularly on the level of the unconscious. Thus Sartre treats shame as essentially a visible phenomenon, giving as an example a man who makes a vulgar gesture when a particular event causes him some annoyance. He then realises that he is being observed: seeing himself suddenly through the eyes of the other, he feels shame.[38] But one might feel shame while entirely alone; indeed shame may be a persistent and very deep-lying form of affect, which signs that are visible to others do no more than trigger.[39] Shame depends on feelings of personal insuf-ficiency, and these can comprise a basic element of an individual's psychological make-up from an early age. Shame should be understood in relation to the integrity of the self, while guilt derives from feelings of wrongdoing.

Helen Lewis has distinguished two general states of shame, one of which she terms 'overt, undifferentiated', the other of which she calls 'bypassed' shame.[40] Overt shame refers to feelings experienced by a child when it is in some way humiliated by another person. Bypassed shame is the correlate of unacknow-ledged guilt: it is shame that comes from unconsciously experi-enced anxieties about inadequacies of self. As described by Lewis, bypassed shame links directly to feelings of ontological insecurity: it consists of repressed fears that the narrative of self-identity cannot withstand engulfing pressures on its coherence or social acceptability. Shame eats at the roots of trust more corro-sively than guilt, because shame is involved in a fundamental way with the fear of abandonment in infancy. Trust in others is the key to the development of a sense of ontological security in the young child; yet its inevitable accompaniment is the worry that absence induces.

Shame and trust are very closely bound up with one another, since an experience of shame may threaten or destroy trust. Where, for example, a person interprets – correctly or not – a response from another as indicating that her assumptions about others' views of her are false, the result might be to compromise a whole set of trust relations which has been built up. Basic trust is established in the child as part of the experiencing of a world that has coherence, continuity and dependability. Where such expectations are violated, the result can be that trust is lost, not only in other persons but in the coherence of the object-world. As Helen Lynd puts it, once this happens, 'we have become strangers in a world where we thought we were at home. We experience anxiety in becoming aware that we cannot trust our answers to the questions, "Who am I?" "Where do I belong?" . . . with every recurrent violation of trust we become again children unsure of ourselves in an alien world.'[41]

Shame is a negative side of the motivational system of the agent. The other side of shame is *pride*, or self-esteem: confidence in the integrity and value of the narrative of self-identity. A person who successfully fosters a sense of pride in the self is one who is able psychologically to feel that his biography is justified and unitary. Sustaining feelings of pride has effects which go further than simply protecting or enhancing self-identity, because of the intrinsic relations between the coherence of the self, its relations to others, and the sense of ontological security more generally. Where central elements of self-identity are threatened, for reasons analysed earlier, other aspects of the 'reality' of the world may be endangered.

Founded in the social bond, pride is continually vulnerable to the reactions of others, and the experience of shame often focuses on that 'visible' aspect of self, the body. Freud in fact specifically linked shame to fears of bodily exposure and nakedness: shame originates in being naked in front of the gaze of the onlooker. Fear of being caught naked, however, is primarily a symbolic phenomenon, expressive of the tension between pride and shame in social interaction. The difference between guilt and shame, in terms of their salience for self-identity, is indicated by the fact that guilt has no positive correlate corresponding to pride or self-esteem.

Before continuing the discussion, it may be useful here to adapt the work of Erikson and Lynd and contrast the 'guilt axis' with the 'shame axis' of the personality in a categorical way – while recognising that each enters into the attitudes and behaviour of the individual, often in the same situation.

Shame tends to have been relegated to a minor place in the psychoanalytical literature, partly because Freud wrote only sparingly about it, but more importantly because it bears on concepts – precisely those of self and self-identity – which are not easily integrated into mainstream psychoanalytic theory.[42] Piers and Singer link guilt and shame to the super-ego and ego-ideal

Guilt axis	*Shame axis*
Concerned with discrete acts related to the violation of codes or taboos	Concerned with the overall tissue of self-identity
Involves cumulative processes, in which autonomy is developed by surmounting repressions	Involves insight into the nature of the narrative of self-identity, which does not necessarily progress in a cumulative way
Exposure of misdemeanours or transgressions	Exposure of hidden traits which compromise the narrative of self-identity
Concern about violation of codes of 'proper behaviour' in respect of the body	Concern about the body in relation to the mechanisms of self-identity
Feeling of wrongdoing towards a respected or loved other	Feeling that one is inadequate for a respected or loved other
Trust based on absence of betrayal or disloyalty	Trust based on being 'known to the other', where self-revelation does not incur anxieties over exposure
Surmounting of guilt leads to sentiments of moral uprightness	Transcending of shame leads to secure self-identity

respectively.[43] Guilt is anxiety brought about whenever the constraints of the super-ego are transgressed, while shame derives from a failure to live up to expectations built into the ego-ideal. According to Piers and Singer, guilt is generated 'whenever a boundary is touched or transgressed', while shame 'occurs when a goal . . . is not being reached' and 'indicates a "short coming" '.[44] Rather than using the notion of ego-ideal, however we can draw on the work of Kohut to relate shame to the ideal self, a more encompassing and valuable concept. The ideal self is the 'self as I want to be'.

Shame has its roots in the 'archaic environment' in which the individual originally develops a sense of self-identity separate from those of the caretaking figures. The 'ideal self' is a key part of self-identity, because it forms a channel of positive aspirations in terms of which the narrative of self-identity is worked out. In many instances, early omnipotence becomes moulded into a reliable sense of self-esteem, through acceptance of the imperfections and limitations of the self. A 'gradual diminution of the domain and power of the grandiose fantasy', as Kohut puts it, 'is in general a precondition for mental health in the narcissistic sector of the personality.'[45] The experience of shame plays a basic role in this process. However, in some circumstances, specifically in the case of narcissistic personality disorders, the sense of pride in oneself and one's accomplishments becomes overdeveloped (although hiding feelings of inferiority) or fractured. This situation Kohut describes as

> the struggle of the patient who suffers from a narcissistic personality disorder to reassemble himself, the despair – the *guiltless despair*, I stress, of those who [for example] in late middle age discover the basic patterns of their self as laid down in their nuclear ambitions and ideals have not been realised . . . This is the time of utmost hopelessness for some, of utter lethargy, of that depression without guilt and self-directed aggression, which overtakes those who feel they have failed . . .[46]

Shame is directly related to narcissism, but should not be seen as necessarily accompanied by an ideal self that is overbearing in terms of its ambitions. Shame connects to difficulties individuals have in separating out their self-identity from their original 'oneness' with the caretaking agents, and with poorly constrained omnipotence. Lack of coherence in ideals, or the difficulty of finding worthwhile ideals to pursue, may be as important in relation to shame anxiety as circumstances in which goals are too demanding to be attained.

Erikson has observed that 'the patient of today suffers most under the problem of what he should believe in and who he should – or, indeed, might – be or become; while the patient of early psychoanalysis suffered most under inhibitions which prevented him from being what and who he thought he knew he was.'[47] In the following chapters of this study, I shall try to illuminate why such should be the case, and also indicate why, in conditions of modernity, shame rather than guilt tends to come to the fore as a feature of psychic organisation.

3
The Trajectory of the Self

In this chapter, elaborating upon the theme of the self, I shall follow the same course as in chapter 1, making use of analysis and advice which not only portray a 'subject-matter', but help constitute the fields of action they concern.

Self-Therapy, a work by Janette Rainwater, is a book directly oriented to practice. Like the study by Wallerstein and Blakeslee, it is only one among an indefinite variety of books on its subject, and it figures in this analysis for symptomatic reasons rather than on its own account. Subtitled *A Guide to Becoming Your Own Therapist*, it is intended as a programme of self-realisation that anyone can use:

> Possibly you're feeling restless. Or you may feel overwhelmed by the demands of wife, husband, children, or job. You may feel unappreciated by those people closest to you. Perhaps you feel angry that life is passing you by and you haven't accomplished all those great things you had hoped to do. Something feels missing from your life. You were attracted by the title of this book and wish that you really were in charge. What to do?[1]

What to do? How to act? Who to be? These are focal questions for everyone living in circumstances of late modernity – and ones which, on some level or another, all of us answer, either discursively or through day-to-day social behaviour. They are existential questions, although, as we shall see later, their relation to the existential issues discussed in the preceding chapter is problematic.

A key idea of Rainwater's perspective is set out very early in her book. Therapy with another person – psychiatrist or counsellor – she accepts, is an important, indeed frequently a crucial, part of a process of self-realisation. But, says Rainwater, therapy can only be successful when it involves the individual's own reflexivity: 'when the clients also start learning to do self-therapy.'[2] For therapy is not something which is 'done' to a person, or 'happens' to them; it is an experience which involves the individual in systematic reflection about the course of her or his life's development. The therapist is at most a catalyst who can accelerate what has to be a process of self-therapy. This proposition applies also, Rainwater notes, to her book, which can inform someone about possible modes and directions of self-change, but which must be interpretatively organised by the person concerned in relation to his or her life's problems.

Self-therapy is grounded first and foremost in continuous self-observation. Each moment of life, Rainwater emphasises, is a 'new moment', at which the individual can ask, 'what do I want for myself?' Living every moment reflectively is a matter of heightened awareness of thoughts, feelings and bodily sensations. Awareness creates potential change, and may actually induce change in and through itself. For instance, the question, 'Are you aware of your breathing right now?', at least when it is first posed, usually produces an instantaneous change. The raising of such an issue may make the person 'aware that she is inhibiting a normal full breathing cycle and allows her body to say "Whew!" in relief, take a deep breath, and then exhale it.' 'And', Rainwater adds parenthetically to the reader, 'how is your breathing right now, after having read this paragraph?'[3] – a question that I could echo to whosoever might be reading this particular text . . .

Present-awareness, or what Rainwater calls the 'routine art of self-observation', does not lead to a chronic immersion in current experience. On the contrary, it is the very condition of effectively planning ahead. Self-therapy means seeking to live each moment to the full, but it emphatically does not mean succumbing to the allure of the present. The question 'What do I want for myself right now?' is not the same as taking one day at a time. The 'art of being in the now' generates the self-understanding necessary to plan ahead and to construct a life trajectory which accords with the individual's inner wishes. Therapy is a process of growth, and one which has to encompass the major transitions through which a person's life is likely to pass. Keeping a journal, and developing a notional or actual autobiography, are recommended as means of thinking ahead. The journal, Rainwater suggests, should be written completely for oneself, never with the thought of showing it to anyone else. It is a place where the individual can be completely honest and where, by learning from previously noted experiences and mistakes, she can chart a continuing process of growth. Whether or not the journal itself has the explicit form of an autobiography, 'autobiographical thinking' is a central element of self-therapy. For developing a coherent sense of one's life history is a prime means of escaping the thrall of the past and opening oneself out to the future. The author of the autobiography is enjoined both to go back as far as possible into early childhood and to set up lines of potential development to encompass the future.

The autobiography is a corrective intervention into the past, not merely a chronicle of elapsed events. One of its aspects, for example, is 'nourishing the child-that-you-were'. Thinking back to a difficult or traumatic phase of childhood, the individual talks to the child-that-was, comforting and supporting it and offering advice. In this way, Rainwater argues, feelings of 'if only' can be got over and done with. 'The basic purpose of writing autobiographical material is to help you be done with the past . . .'[4] Another aspect is the 'corrective emotional experience exercise'. The person writes down an event from the past in the form of a short story written in the present, recalling what happened and the feelings involved as accurately as he or she can. Then the story is rewritten in the way the individual would have liked it to happen, with new dialogue, feelings and resolution of the episode.

Reconstruction of the past goes along with anticipation of the likely life trajectory of the future. Self-therapy presumes what Rainwater calls a 'dialogue with time' – a process of self-questioning about how the individual handles the time of her lifespan. Thinking about time in a positive way – as allowing for life to be lived, rather than consisting of a finite quantity that is running out – allows one to avoid a 'helpless-hopeless' attitude. Time which 'carries us along' implies a conception of fate like that found in many traditional cultures, where people are the prisoners of events and preconstructed settings rather than able to subject their lives to the sway of their own self-understanding. Holding a dialogue with time means identifying stressful events (actual events in the past and possible ones to be faced in the future) and coming to terms with their implications. Rainwater offers a 'rating scale' of stressful happenings, based on research literature in the area (pointing out also that such happenings can be causally linked to the onset of physical disease). Examples include death of a spouse, divorce or marital separation, losing one's job, being in financial difficulties, plus many other events or situations.

'Taking charge of one's life' involves risk, because it means confronting a diversity of open possibilities. The individual must be prepared to make a more or less complete break with the past, if necessary, and to contemplate novel courses of action that cannot simply be guided by established habits. Security attained through sticking with established patterns is brittle, and at some point will crack. It betokens a fear of the future rather than providing the means of mastering it:

> People who fear the future attempt to 'secure' themselves – with money, property, health insurance, personal relationships, marriage contracts. Parents attempt to bind their children to them. Some fearful childen are reluctant to leave the home nest. Husbands and wives try to guarantee the continuance of the other's life and services. The harsh psychological truth is that there is no permanence in human relationships, any more than there is in the stock market, the weather, 'national security', and so on . . . this clutching at security can be very discouraging to interpersonal relationships, and will impede your own self-growth. The more each of us can learn to be truly in the present with our others, making no rules and erecting no fences for the future, the stronger we will be in ourselves and the closer and happier in our relationships.

Finally . . . death: 'and the possibility that you're in charge here, too!'[5] Asking people to think about death, Rainwater says, typically provokes one of two attitudes. Either death is associated with fear, as in the case where individuals spend much of their present time worrying about their own death or that of loved ones; or death is regarded as unknowable, and therefore a subject to be avoided as far as possible. Both attitudes – fear of death and denial of death – can be countered by a programme of self-help that draws on the same techniques described elsewhere in Rainwater's book. Thinking back to the past, to the first experience of the death of another person, allows one to begin to ferret out hidden feelings about death. Looking ahead in this case involves contemplating the years of life which the person believes remain, and imagining the setting of one's own future death. An imaginary confrontation with death allows the question to be posed all over again: 'What to do?'

> Imagine that you have been told that you have just three years left to live. You will be in good health for these years. . . . What was your immediate response? . . . To start planning how you would spend your time? Or to be angry at how short the time is? Rather than 'raging against the dying of the light' or getting bogged down in the mechanics of how you die in this fantasy, decide how you want to spend your time, *how you want to live these last three years*.
>
> Where do you want to live?
> With whom do you want to live?
> Do you want to work?
> To study?
> Are there any ingredients from your fantasy life that you would like to incorporate into your current life?[6]

Self-identity, history, modernity

How distinctive in historical terms are the concerns and orientations expressed in Rainwater's 'self-help manual'? We might, of course, simply say that the search for self-identity is a modern problem, perhaps having its origins in Western individualism. Baumeister claims that in pre-modern times our current emphasis on individuality was absent.[7] The idea that each person has a unique character and special potentialities that may or may not be fulfilled is alien to pre-modern culture. In medieval Europe, lineage, gender, social status and other attributes relevant to identity were all relatively fixed. Transitions had to be made through the various stages of life, but these were governed by institutionalised processes and the individual's role in them was relatively passive. Baumeister's analysis recalls that of Durkheim: the 'individual', in a certain sense, did not exist in traditional cultures, and individuality was not prized. Only with the emergence of modern societies and, more particularly, with the differentiation of the division of labour, did the separate individual become a focus of attention.[8]

No doubt there is something in these views. But I do not think it is the existence of the 'individual' that is at stake, as a distinctive feature of modernity, and even less so the self. 'Individuality' has surely been valued – within varying limits – in all cultures and so, in one sense or another, has been the cultivation of individual potentialities. Rather than talking in general terms of 'individual', 'self' or even 'self-identity' as distinctive of modernity, we should try to break things down into finer detail. We can begin to do so by charting some of the specific points in, or implications of, Rainwater's portrayal of what therapy is and what it does. The following elements can be drawn out of her text:

1   The self is seen as a reflexive project, for which the individual is responsible (this theme figured in chapter 1 above). We are, not what we are, but what we make of ourselves. It would not be true to say that the self is regarded as entirely empty of content, for there are psychological processes of self-formation, and psychological needs, which provide the parameters for the reorganisation of the self. Otherwise, however, what the individual becomes is dependent on the reconstructive endeavours in which she or he engages. These are far more than just 'getting to know oneself' better: self-understanding is subordinated to the more inclusive and fundamental aim of building/rebuilding a coherent and rewarding sense of identity. The involvement of such reflexivity with social and psychological research is striking, and a pervasive feature of the therapeutic outlook advocated.

2   The self forms a trajectory of development from the past to the anticipated future. The individual appropriates his past by sifting through it in the light of what is anticipated for an (organised) future. The trajectory of the self has a coherence that derives from a cognitive awareness of the various phases of the lifespan. The lifespan, rather than events in the outside world,

becomes the dominant 'foreground figure' in the *Gestalt* sense. It is not quite the case that all outside events or institutions are a 'blur', against which only the lifespan has form and is picked out in clear relief; yet such events only intrude in so far as they provide supports for self-development, throw up barriers to be overcome or are a source of uncertainties to be faced.

3   The reflexivity of the self is continuous, as well as all-pervasive. At each moment, or at least at regular intervals, the individual is asked to conduct a self-interrogation in terms of what is happening. Beginning as a series of consciously asked questions, the individual becomes accustomed to asking, 'how can I use this moment to change?' Reflexivity in this sense belongs to the reflexive historicity of modernity, as distinct from the more generic reflexive monitoring of action. As Rainwater stresses, it is a practised art of self-observation:

> What is happening right now?
> What am I thinking?
> What am I doing?
> What am I feeling?
> How am I breathing?[9]

4   It is made clear that self-identity, as a coherent phenomenon, presumes a narrative: the narrative of the self is made explicit. Keeping a journal, and working through an autobiography, are central recommendations for sustaining an integrated sense of self. It is generally accepted among historians that the writing of autobiographies (as well as biographies) only developed during the modern period.[10] Most published autobiographies, of course, are celebrations of the lives or achievements of distinguished individuals: they are a way of singling out the special experiences of such persons from those of the mass of the population. Seen in this way, autobiography seems a rather peripheral feature of individual distinctiveness as a whole. Yet autobiography – particularly in the broad sense of an interpretative self-history produced by the individual concerned, whether written down or not – is actually at the core of self-identity in modern social life. Like any other formalised narrative, it is something that has to be worked at, and calls for creative input as a matter of course.

5   Self-actualisation implies the control of time – essentially, the establishing of zones of personal time which have only remote connections with external temporal orders (the routinised world of time-space governed by the clock and by universalised standards of measurement). The insistence on the primacy of personal time (the *durée* of day-to-day social life) is everywhere in Rainwater's book – although, as we have seen, it is not offered as a philosophy of the 'absolute present', but as a mode of controlling the available time of the lifespan. 'Holding a dialogue with time' is the very basis of self-realisation, because it is the essential condition of achieving satisfaction at any given moment – of living life to the full. The future is thought of as resonant with possibilities, yet not left open to the full play of contingency. So far as possible, the future is to be ordered by exactly those active processes of temporal control and active interaction on which the integration of the self's narrative depends.

6   The reflexivity of the self *extends to the body*, where the body (as suggested in the previous chapter) is part of an action system rather than merely a passive object. Observation of bodily processes – 'How am I breathing?' – is intrinsic to the continuous reflexive attention which the agent is called on to pay to her behaviour. Awareness of the body is basic to 'grasping the fullness of the moment', and entails the conscious monitoring of sensory input from the environment, as well as the major bodily organs and body dispositions as a whole. Body awareness also includes awareness of requirements of exercise and diet. Rainwater points out that people speak of 'going on a diet' – but we are all on a diet! Our diet is what we eat; at many junctures of the day we take decisions about whether or not to eat and drink, and exactly what to eat and drink. 'If you don't like the diet you are on, there is a new minute and a new choice-point coming up, and you can change your diet. You're in charge!'[11]
    Body awareness sounds similar to the regimes practised in some traditional religions, particularly religions of the East. And indeed Rainwater, like many others writing about self-actualisation or therapy today, draws on some such regimes in the programme she offers. Yet the differences are pronounced. For body awareness is presented by her as a means of constructing a differentiated self, not as one of the dissolution of the ego.

Experiencing the body is a way of cohering the self as an integrated whole, whereby the individual says 'this is where I live.'

7   Self-actualisation is understood in terms of a *balance between opportunity and risk*. Letting go of the past, through the various techniques of becoming free from oppressive emotional habits, generates a multiplicity of opportunities for self-development. The world becomes full of potential ways of being and acting, in terms of experimental involvements which the individual is now able to initiate. It would not be true to say that the psychologically liberated person faces risks while the more traditional self does not; rather, what is at stake is the *secular consciousness of risk*, as inherent in calculative strategies to be adopted in relation to the future.

The individual has to confront novel hazards as a necessary part of breaking away from established patterns of behaviour – including the risk that things could possibly get worse than they were before. Another book on self-therapy describes things in the following way:

> If your life is ever going to change for the better, you'll have to take chances. You'll have to get out of your rut, meet new people, explore new ideas and move along unfamiliar pathways. In a way the risks of self-growth involve going into the unknown, into an unfamiliar land where the language is different and customs are different and you have to learn your way around . . . the paradox is that until we give up all that feels secure, we can never really trust the friend, mate, or job that offers us something. True personal security does not come from without, it comes from within. When we are really secure, we must place our total trust in ourself.
>
> If we reject deliberate risk-taking for self growth, we will inevitably remain trapped in our situation. Or we end up taking a risk unprepared. Either way, we have placed limits on our personal growth, have cut ourselves off from action in the service of high self-worth.[12]

8   The moral thread of self-actualisation is one of *authenticity* (although not in Heidegger's sense), based on 'being true to oneself'. Personal growth depends on conquering emotional blocks and tensions that prevent us from understanding ourselves

as we really are. To be able to act authentically is more than just acting in terms of a self-knowledge that is as valid and full as possible; it means also disentangling – in Laing's terms – the true from the false self. As individuals we are not able to 'make history' but if we ignore our inner experience, we are condemned to repeat it, prisoners of traits which are inauthentic because they emanate from feelings and past situations imposed on us by others (especially in early childhood). The watchword in self-therapy is 'recover or repeat.'

The morality of authenticity skirts any universal moral criteria, and includes references to other people only within the sphere of intimate relationships – although this sphere is accepted as highly important to the self. To be true to oneself means finding oneself, but since this is an active process of self-construction it has to be informed by overall goals – those of becoming free from dependencies and achieving fulfilment. Fulfilment is in some part a moral phenomenon, because it means fostering a sense that one is 'good', a 'worthy person': 'I know that as I raise my own self-worth, I will feel more integrity, honesty, compassion, energy and love'.[13]

9   The life course is seen as a series of 'passages'. The individual is likely, or has to go through them, but they are not institutionalised, or accompanied by formalised rites. All such transitions involve loss (as well as, usually, potential gain) and such losses – as in the case of marital separation – have to be mourned if self-actualisation is to proceed on course. Life passages give particular cogency to the interaction of risk and opportunity spoken of earlier – especially, although by no means exclusively, when they are in substantial degree initiated by the individual whom they affect. Negotiating a significant transition in life, leaving home, getting a new job, facing up to unemployment, forming a new relationship, moving between different areas or routines, confronting illness, beginning therapy – all mean running consciously entertained risks in order to grasp the new opportunities which personal crises open up. It is not only in terms of the absence of rites that life passages differ from comparable processes in traditional contexts. More important is that such transitions are drawn into, and surmounted by means of, the reflexively mobilised trajectory of self-actualisation.

10   The line of development of the self is *internally referential*: the only significant connecting thread is the life trajectory as such. Personal integrity, as the achievement of an authentic self, comes from integrating life experiences within the narrative of self-development: the creation of a personal belief system by means of which the individual acknowledges that 'his first loyalty is to himself.' The key reference points are set 'from the inside', in terms of how the individual constructs/reconstructs his life history.

Of all this, of course, there are questions one could ask. How valid are these conceptions? Are they in some sense ideological? Are they more to do with therapy than with any changes which might have affected the self in modern social conditions? For the moment I want to bracket these issues. It seems to me justified to assert that, partial, inadequate and idiosyncratic as the ideas just outlined may be, they signal something real about self and self-identity in the contemporary world – the world of late modernity. How that may be we can begin to see by connecting them up to the institutional transformations characteristic of that world.

Lifestyles and life plans

The backdrop here is the existential terrain of late modern life. In a post-traditional social universe, reflexively organised, permeated by abstract systems, and in which the reordering of time and space realigns the local with the global, the self undergoes massive change. Therapy, including self-therapy, both expresses that change and provides programmes of realising it in the form of self-actualisation. On the level of the self, a fundamental component of day-to-day activity is simply that of *choice*. Obviously, no culture eliminates choice altogether in day-to-day affairs, and all traditions are effectively choices among an indefinite range of possible behaviour patterns. Yet, by definition, tradition or established habit orders life within relatively set channels. Modernity confronts the individual with a complex diversity of choices and, because it is non-foundational, at the same time offers little help as to which options should be selected. Various consequences tend to follow.

One concerns the primacy of *lifestyle* – and its inevitability for the individual agent. The notion of lifestyle sounds somewhat trivial because it is so often thought of solely in terms of a superficial consumerism: lifestyles as suggested by glossy magazines and advertising images.* But there is something much more fundamental going on than such a conception suggests: in conditions of high modernity, we all not only follow lifestyles, but in an important sense are forced to do so – we have no choice but to choose. A lifestyle can be defined as a more or less integrated set of practices which an individual embraces, not only because such practices fulfil utilitarian needs, but because they give material form to a particular narrative of self-identity.

Lifestyle is not a term which has much applicability to traditional cultures, because it implies choice within a plurality of possible options, and is 'adopted' rather than 'handed down'. Lifestyles are routinised practices, the routines incorporated into habits of dress, eating, modes of acting and favoured milieux for encountering others; but the routines followed are reflexively open to change in the light of the mobile nature of self-identity. Each of the small decisions a person makes every day – what to wear, what to eat, how to conduct himself at work, whom to meet with later in the evening – contributes to such routines. All such choices (as well as larger and more consequential ones) are decisions not only about how to act but who to be. The more post-traditional the settings in which an individual moves, the more lifestyle concerns the very core of self-identity, its making and remaking.

The notion of lifestyle is often thought to apply specifically to the area of consumption. It is true that the sphere of work is dominated by economic compulsion and that styles of behaviour in the workplace are less subject to the control of the individual than in non-work contexts. But although these contrasts clearly exist, it would be wrong to suppose that lifestyle only relates to

---

* The term 'lifestyle' is an interesting example of reflexivity. The *New York Times* columnist, William Safire, suggested that it derives from the writings of Alfred Adler, and from thence was taken up by radicals in the 1960s and, at about the same time, by advertising copywriters. According to Dennis Wrong, however, the main influence was actually Max Weber: 'style of life', as associated with *Stände* in Weberian usage, eventually became 'lifestyle' in everyday language.[14]

activities outside of work. Work strongly conditions *life chances*, in Weber's sense, and life chances in turn is a concept which has to be understood in terms of the availability of potential lifestyles. But work is by no means completely separate from the arena of plural choices, and choice of work and work milieu forms a basic element of lifestyle orientations in the extremely complex modern division of labour.

To speak of a multiplicity of choices is not to suppose that all choices are open to everyone, or that people take all decisions about options in full realisation of the range of feasible alternatives. In work, as in the area of consumption, for all groups which have become freed from the hold of traditional contexts of activity, a plurality of lifestyle choices exist. Naturally, as Bourdieu has emphasised, lifestyle variations between groups are also elementary structuring features of stratification, not just the 'results' of class differences in the realm of production.[15]

Overall lifestyle patterns, of course, are less diverse than the plurality of choices available in day-to-day and even in longer-term strategic decisions. A lifestyle involves a cluster of habits and orientations, and hence has a certain unity – important to a continuing sense of ontological security – that connects options in a more or less ordered pattern. Someone who is committed to a given lifestyle would necessarily see various options as 'out of character' with it, as would others with whom she was in interaction. Moreover, the selection or creation of lifestyles is influenced by group pressures and the visibility of role models, as well as by socioeconomic circumstances.

The plurality of choices which confronts individuals in situations of high modernity derives from several influences. First, there is the fact of living in a post-traditional order. To act in, to engage with, a world of plural choices is to opt for alternatives, given that the signposts established by tradition now are blank. Thus someone might decide, for example, to ignore the research findings which appear to show that a diet high in fruit and fibre, and low in sugar, fat and alcohol, is physically beneficial and reduces the risk of contracting some types of illnesses. She might resolutely stick to the same diet of dense, fatty and sugary foods that people in the previous generation consumed. Yet, given the available options in matters of diet and the fact that the individual has at least some awareness of them, such conduct still forms part of a distinctive lifestyle.

Second, there is what Berger calls the 'pluralisation of life-worlds'.[16] As he points out, throughout most of human history, people lived in social settings that were fairly closely connected with each other. Whether in situations of work, leisure or the family, an individual usually lived within a set of milieux of a comparable type – a phenomenon strongly reinforced by the dominance of the local community in most pre-modern cultures. The settings of modern social life are much more diverse and segmented. Segmentation includes particularly the differentiation between the public and private domains – but each of these is also subject internally to pluralisation. Lifestyles are characteristically attached to, and expressive of, specific milieux of action. Lifestyle options are thus often decisions to become immersed in those milieux, at the expense of the possible alternatives. Since individuals typically move between different milieux or locales in the course of their everyday life, they may feel uncomfortable in those settings that in some way place their own lifestyle in question.

Partly because of the existence of multiple milieux of action, lifestyle choices and activities very often tend to be segmental for the individual: modes of action followed in one context may be more or less substantially at variance with those adopted in others. I shall call these segments *lifestyle sectors*. A lifestyle sector concerns a time-space 'slice' of an individual's overall activities, within which a reasonably consistent and ordered set of practices is adopted and enacted. Lifestyle sectors are aspects of the regionalisation of activities.[17] A lifestyle sector can include, for instance, what one does on certain evenings of the week, or at weekends, as contrasted to other parts of the week; a friendship, or a marriage, can also be a lifestyle sector in so far as it is made internally cohesive by distinctive forms of elected behaviour across time-space.

A third factor conditioning plurality of choice is the existential impact of the contextual nature of warranted beliefs under conditions of modernity. As noted in the opening chapter, the Enlightenment project of replacing arbitrary tradition and speculative claims to knowledge with the certainty of reason proved to be essentially flawed. The reflexivity of modernity operates, not in a situation of greater and greater certainty, but in one of methodological doubt. Even the most reliable authorities can be trusted only 'until further notice'; and the abstract systems that penetrate so much of day-to-day life normally offer multiple possibilities rather than fixed guidelines or recipes for action. Experts can always be turned to, but experts themselves frequently disagree over both theories and practical diagnoses. Consider therapy itself. Someone contemplating therapy faces a bewildering variety of schools of thought and types of programme, and must also reckon with the fact that some psychologists discount the effectiveness of most forms of therapy entirely. The same applies in the hardest areas of hard science, particularly since the overall claims of science may be subject to doubt. Thus a person with a particular kind of medical problem may be faced with deciding not just between alternative forms of high-tech treatment, but also between the rival claims of scientific and holistic medicine (of which there may also be an indefinite variety proferring their particular solutions).

Fourth, the prevalence of mediated experience undoubtedly also influences pluralism of choice, in obvious and also in more subtle ways. With the increasing globalisation of media, a multifarious number of milieux are, in principle, rendered visible to anyone who cares to glean the relevant information. The collage effect of television and newspapers gives specific form to the juxtaposition of settings and potential lifestyle choices. On the other hand, the influence of the mass media plainly is not all in the direction of diversification and fragmentation. The media offer access to settings with which the individual may never personally come into contact; but at the same time some boundaries between settings that were previously separate are overcome. As Meyrowitz points out, the media, especially the electronic media, alter the 'situational geography' of social life: 'More and more, media make us "direct" audiences to performances that happen in other places and give us access to audiences that are not "physically present"'.[18] As a result, the traditional connection between 'physical setting' and 'social situation' has become undermined; mediated social situations construct new communalities – and differences – between preconstituted forms of social experience. Although criticisms can be made against

Meyrowitz's particular interpretations, the overall thrust of this view is surely correct.

In a world of alternative lifestyle options, strategic *life-planning* becomes of special importance. Like lifestyle patterns, life plans of one kind or another are something of an inevitable concomitant of post-traditional social forms.[19] Life plans are the substantial content of the reflexively organised trajectory of the self. Life-planning is a means of preparing a course of future actions mobilised in terms of the self's biography. We may also speak here of the existence of personal calendars or *life-plan calendars*, in relation to which the personal time of the lifespan is handled. Personal calendars are timing devices for significant events within the life of the individual, inserting such events within a personalised chronology. Like life plans, personal calendars are typically revised and reconstructed in terms of alterations in an individual's circumstances or frame of mind. 'When I got married,' as a basic date within a life-plan calendar, as the discussion in *Second Chances* indicates, may be largely ousted by 'when the marriage broke up' as a more significant psychological marker. Personal calendars very often incorporate elements of mediated experience – as when, for instance, a couple will remember that they got married 'two weeks after President Kennedy was assassinated'.[20]

Life-planning presupposes a specific mode of organising time because the reflexive construction of self-identity depends as much on preparing for the future as on interpreting the past, although the 'reworking' of past events is certainly always important in this process. Life-planning, of course, does not necessarily involve preparing strategically for future life as a whole, although Rainwater's book makes clear that thinking as far ahead as the imagined end of one's life, and about each of the major phases likely to intervene in the interim, is fundamental to self-actualisation.[21]

Lifestyle choices and life planning are not just 'in', or constituent of, the day-to-day life of social agents, but form institutional settings which help to shape their actions. This is one reason why, in circumstances of high modernity, their influence is more or less universal, no matter how objectively limiting the social situations of particular individuals or groups may be. Consider the position of a black woman, the head of a single-parent family of several children, living in conditions of poverty in the inner city. It might be assumed that such a person could only look on with bitter envy at the options available to the more privileged. For her there is only the drudgery of a daily round of activities carried on within strictly defined limits: she has no opportunities to follow a different lifestyle, and she could hardly plan her life, since it is dominated by external constraints.

Of course, for all individuals and groups, life chances condition lifestyle choices (and we should remember the point that lifestyle choices are often actively used to reinforce the distribution of life chances). Emancipation from situations of oppression is the necessary means of expanding the scope of some sorts of lifestyle option (see chapter 7 below on 'The Emergence of Life Politics'). Yet even the most underprivileged today live in situations permeated by institutional components of modernity. Possibilities denied by economic deprivation are different, and experienced differently – that is, as possibilities – from those excluded by the frameworks of tradition. Moreover, in some circumstances of poverty, the hold of tradition has perhaps become even more thoroughly disintegrated than elsewhere. Consequently, the creative construction of lifestyle may become a particularly characteristic feature of such situations. Lifestyle habits are constructed through the resistances of ghetto life as well as through the direct elaboration of distinctive cultural styles and modes of activity.

In such situations, the reflexive constitution of self-identity may be every bit as important as among more affluent strata, and as strongly affected by globalising influences. A black woman heading a single-parent household, however constricted and arduous her life, will nevertheless know about factors altering the position of women in general, and her own activities will almost certainly be modified by that knowledge. Given the inchoate nature of her social circumstances, she is virtually obliged to explore novel modes of activity, with regard to her children, sexual relations and friendships. Such an exploration, although it might not be discursively articulated as such, implies a reflexive shaping of self-identity. The deprivations to which she is subject, however, might make these tasks become an almost insupportable burden, a source of despair rather than self-enrichment.

Life planning is a specific example of a more general phenomenon that I shall discuss in some detail in a subsequent chapter as the 'colonisation of the future'. Rainwater's 'dialogue with time' is certainly carried on in very different ways in varying social contexts and within different social strata. The orientation towards the control of time which she describes (and advocates) generates refusals and temporal dislocations as well as the attempt reflexively to drag the future into the present. A teenager who 'drifts around', who refuses to think about a possible future career, and 'gives no thought to the future', rejects this orientation, but does so specifically in opposition to an increasingly dominant temporal outlook.

Finally, plurality of choice can also be connected directly to relations with others – to the transformation of intimacy.[22] I shall not offer a detailed discussion of whether personal relationships today are significantly different from close interpersonal ties in pre-modern contexts. We know that modern marriage differs quite dramatically from typical marriage institutions in pre-modern Europe, as well as from the generality of non-modern cultures. A parallel observation applies to friendship. The Greeks had no word for 'friend' in today's sense: *philos* was used to refer to 'anyone of one's "nearest and dearest", irrespective of whether they were kin, affines, or other people unrelated by blood'.[23] A person's *philos* network was largely given by that individual's social position; there was only a certain leeway for spontaneous choice. Such a situation is characteristic of many traditional cultures, in which, if a notion of 'friend' exists, it refers mainly to insiders, as contrasted to outsiders – strangers, and potential enemies.

It is characteristic of modern systems of sexual intimacy and friendship that partners are voluntarily chosen from a diversity of possibilities. Of course, proximity is ordinarily necessary for intimate relations to develop, and the extent of real choice varies according to many social and psychological differences. But the lonely hearts column, computer dating and other forms of introduction service demonstrate well enough that plural choice is easy to achieve if one is prepared to shed the last vestiges of traditional ways of doing things. Only when ties are more or less freely chosen can we speak at all of 'relationships' in the sense that term has recently acquired in lay discourse. Reasonably durable sexual ties, marriages and friendship relations all tend to approximate today to the *pure relationship*. In conditions of high modernity, again for reasons to be explored later, the pure relationship (which has nothing to do with sexual purity) comes to be of elementary importance for the reflexive project of the self. This much is evident from Rainwater's book, as it is of virtually all works of therapy, whether self-programmed or not.

The theory and practice of the pure relationship

The following passage appears under a heading 'Emotional Uncertainty in Relationships', in Shere Hite's study *Women and Love*. Hite's research is based on extensive comments obtained from American women about their experiences and feelings in relation to men. One woman responds as follows:

> I have a constant feeling of never being satisfied for some reason. Either he's not calling, or when he's calling, it's not romantic, and so on. . . . When I try to talk to him, really talk to him, I feel like I just can't get through. . . . It seems to revolve around a constant question of should I be asking myself "Is everything all right in terms of him (does he still love me)?" or "Is everything all right in terms of *me*? How am *I*?" If I am unhappy a lot, and he won't talk to me about the problems or resolve the issues, should I say, "Well, everything is really OK because he's OK and he's still there and still loves me"? Or should I say, "This relationship is terrible and I will leave it because he is not making me happy"? Loving him makes it difficult to leave him.
>
> Should I want to help him open up more, or should I worry about myself and break up with him? . . . The problem is that first he says he's vulnerable and in love – then later he denies it or doesn't act like it, acts cold. I ask myself, "Is the goal this man at any cost?" It's almost as if someone is egging me on to go into the deep end of the pool – and then when I get there (with my emotions) and really fall in love, trust him, he says "What? Why me?" I've been so scared all the way, thinking to myself, no matter what happened, giving him the benefit of the doubt, "Let me trust, let me trust", not letting myself believe the negative signals, thinking he was just insecure or reacting to something I had done in my *own* effort to seem invulnerable. I've always been so afraid, wondering, "Will somebody stay?"[24]

These reflections are those of a woman who is not living with the man concerned, and describe a relationship in its fairly early stages; yet, because of their 'exploratory' character, they give some insight into how relationships are constructed. Love is at the centre, and one might suppose that an exploration of intimacy, at least where a sexual component is involved, should concentrate on the nature of romantic attachment. The report recounts the experience of a woman, and although the point of view of the man involved is not given, we might conclude that gender relations should be the prime concern here. Without denying the significance of these features, I want to focus on other things. For there are core elements involved, as I shall try to show, which are also characteristic of other intimate and emotionally demanding relationships – between, for example, same-sex lovers or between very close friends. These are the elements of the pure relationship. They can be spelled out (in ideal-typical form) as follows.

1   In contrast to close personal ties in traditional contexts, the pure relationship is not anchored in external conditions of social or economic life – it is, as it were, free-floating. Consider, as an illustration, marriage as it once was. Marriage was a contract, often initiated by parents or relatives rather than by the marital partners themselves. The contract was usually strongly influenced by economic considerations, and formed part of wider economic networks and transactions. Even well into modern times, when the old frameworks of marriage had substantially disintegrated, the marital tie was anchored through an internal division of labour, the husband as breadwinner and wife preoccupied with children, hearth and home (although we should not forget that the labour force has always contained a considerable proportion of women). Some of these traditional characteristics of marriage persist, more pronounced among certain socioeconomic groups than others. In general, however, the tendency is towards the eradication of these pre-existing external involvements – a pheno-menon originally accompanied by the rise of romantic love as a basic motive for marriage. Marriage becomes more and more a relationship initiated for, and kept going for as long as, it delivers emotional satisfaction to be derived from close contact with another. Other traits – even such seemingly fundamental ones as having children – tend to become sources of 'inertial drag' on possible separation, rather than anchoring features of the rela-tionship.

Modern friendship exposes this characteristic even more clearly. A friend is defined specifically as someone with whom one has a relationship unprompted by anything other than the rewards that that relationship provides. One might become friendly with a colleague, and the proximity at work or shared interest generated by work might help instigate the friendship – but it *is* a friendship only in so far as the connection with the other person is valued for its own sake. This is why a sharp distinction is drawn between friends and kin. Even if they are now quite weak, there are obligations which relatives have towards one another, specified by the tie of kinship. Moreover, while these obligations may be general and vague, kin ties, where they are blood relations at any rate, cannot be broken off. Friendship attachments may have their own inertial elements, but in practice as well as in principle one normally stays a friend of another only in so far as sentiments of closeness are reciprocated for their own sake.

2   The pure relationship is sought only for what the relationship can bring to the partners involved. This point is the natural concomitant of (1), and it is precisely in this sense that the relationship is 'pure'. No doubt all personal relations of any duration are testing and tensionful as well as rewarding. But in relationships which only exist for their own sake, anything that goes wrong between the partners intrinsically threatens the relationship itself. Consequently, it is very difficult to 'coast along' in the way in which one can in a social relation dominated by external criteria. If one partner attempts to do so, the other is likely to be disaffected. The peculiar tensions this sets up are well evinced in other material contained in Hite's book, particularly that concerned with marriage:

> Women are deserting marriage in droves, either through divorce, or emotionally, leaving with a large part of their hearts. . . . Most, after an initial period of trying, have gone on to find other places to invest their emotional lives. Woman after woman, after the initial years of "trying to get through" gives up and begins to disengage quietly, gradually, perhaps even unnoticeably.[25]

Yet . . . the vast majority of women do not abandon the quest for love, or for a viable relationship:

As one woman says, love keeps returning to us, resurfacing perhaps as some kind of key: 'In some way which I cannot find the words for yet, romantic love contains the key to my identity – to discovering myself, my inner being.' Many women feel this way. Why? Perhaps women are right to come back, to try again to make love work or understand why it does not . . . most want not just 'love', but the kind of real love they are talking about. And so it is no surprise that women who are in relationships so often still talk about a 'deeper love' to come, have a hidden part of themselves that believes that there is more, more to life somehow. . . . And indeed, shouldn't there be?[26]

Again, one might think that it is love, or the demand for love, which is at issue here, rather than anything specifically to do with relationships as such. However love – ambiguous and difficult notion that it is – is really a codifying force organising the character of the sexual relationship, not in this context an independent value. Moreover, there is plenty of evidence that men are as concerned to find close emotive relationships as women are, and as attached to them.[27] They find such relationships harder to handle, and typically are less skilled at communicating their feelings and needs to the other, but these are different matters from the thread of discussion I am following. The difficulties of finding and continuing a satisfying relationship partly concern problems of love and gender asymmetries; but they also very substantially concern the intrinsic travails of the pure relationship. The feelings of 'never being satisfied' within the relationship, described by the respondent first quoted, reflect the difficulties inherent in creating or sustaining a relation in which there is balance and reciprocity, satisfactory to both partners, between what each brings and each derives from the tie.

3   The pure relationship is reflexively organised, in an open fashion, and on a continuous basis. This, too, is apparent enough in the quotation on p. 88, in which the question, 'Is everything all right?' figures as a leading motif. The more a relationship depends only upon itself, the more such a reflexive questioning comes to be its core – and contributes to the tensions noted in (2). The self-examination inherent in the pure relationship clearly connects very closely to the reflexive project of the self. 'How am I?' is an interrogation directly bound to the rewards the relation-

ship delivers as well as to the pain it can inflict. (The 'why me?' response of the partner is also a question relating to connections between self-identity and the demands of the pure relationship.)

The reflexive coordination of all close relationships today, no matter how distant they are from being 'fully pure', participates in the broader reflexivity of modernity. A host of magazine and newspaper articles, specialist texts and manuals, television and radio programmes convey research information and debates about close relationships, continuously reconstructing the pheno-menon they describe. Hite's own work stands in an interesting, but by no means untypical relation to such reflexivity. Her book, as with her previous studies,[28] is based on standard questionnaire procedures used in innumerable social research studies. Her work, however, has reached a large audience, whose attitudes will conform to the outlooks which the research charts, at the same time as their reading of the research results might modify those outlooks and related behavioural dispositions.

4   'Commitment' has a central role to play in pure relationships. Commitment would appear generic to many forms of human social activity, and one might readily suppose that it is found in all cultural contexts. For instance, the true believer in a religious order might be said to have a thoroughgoing commitment to the values and practices in question. Yet conviction is not the same as commitment, and when we speak of the second of these in respect of close relationships today we are probably concerned with something that is historically new. Commitment, within the pure relationship, is essentially what replaces the external anchors that close personal connections used to have in pre-modern situations. Love, in the sense of contemporary romantic love, is a form of commitment, but commitment is the wider category of the two. What is the 'committed person' in the context of a close relation-ship? She or he is someone who, recognising the tensions intrinsic to a relationship of the modern form, is nevertheless willing to take a chance on it, at least in the medium term – and who accepts that the only rewards will be those inherent in the relationship itself. A friend is *ipso facto* a committed person. Someone in a marriage is likely to be so to the degree that the relationship is not kept going only by external involvements or by inertial drag of

one kind or another. Commitment is recognised by participants to buy time: to provide emotional support which is guaranteed to persist through at least some of the perturbations which the relationship might undergo (although returns will almost certainly be demanded for this).

Commitment can to some extent be regularised by the force of love, but sentiments of love do not in and of themselves generate commitment, nor do they in any sense authorise it. A person only becomes committed to another when, for whatever reason, she or he decides to be so. The woman in the passage quoted from Hite's study feels she loves her partner, but her love does not supply the commitment she desires. Nor could it, because commitment must almost always be part of an effort-bargain; the pure relationship cannot exist without substantial elements of reciprocity. Rainwater's self-therapy programme recognises this, as do most forms of therapeutic endeavour. One of the reasons why the reflexivity of the self should produce more accurate and insightful self-knowledge is that it helps reduce dependency in close relationships. The well-functioning relationship, she says, is one in which each person is autonomous and sure of his or her self-worth. Where this is not the case, what I have called inertial drag sets in – as is found, for instance, in co-dependent relationships. 'Co-dependency' was first of all coined as a word to describe the position of individuals in relationships with others suffering from chemical addiction – to alcohol or other kinds of drugs. The co-dependent person is the partner who, no matter how much she or he detests the relationship or is unhappy within it, is psychologically unable to leave. For reasons which are opaque to the person concerned (although they may be uncovered by individual or family therapy), he or she has become dependent on a relationship which provides few psychic returns.[29]

Commitment is hard to build precisely because it presumes a mutual alignment within the pure relationship. It stands in uneasy connection with the reflexivity that is equally central to how the relationship is ordered. The committed person is prepared to accept the risks which the sacrificing of other potential options entails. In the initial phases of a relationship, each person is likely to be inspecting the activities of the other minutely, since too rapid an advance towards commitment on the part of one person may actively spark the withdrawal of the other from the nascent enterprise altogether. Hite's respondent demonstrates an astute sensitivity to just this aspect of her situation.

5   The pure relationship is focused on intimacy, which is a major condition of any long-term stability the partners might achieve. Intimacy has to be distinguished from the more negative phenomenon of lack of privacy, characteristic of most circumstances of life in pre-modern Europe and in many non-modern cultures generally. Physical proximity – and, in modern terms, the absence of privacy – were almost inevitable consequences of the architecture of day-to-day life in the small community, but were characteristic of the life of more affluent groups too.[30] Within households, but also in most other contexts of daily life, people were almost always in close range of one another. The development of 'personal' life during the early period of modernity has been well documented by historians, even if the nature of the causal connections involved is a matter of considerable dispute. Intimacy is the other face of privacy, or at least only becomes possible (or desired) given substantial privacy.[31]

Bensman and Lilienfeld have stressed the growing concern to achieve intimacy in modern societies: 'the demand for intimacy persists to the point where it is virtually compulsive.'[32] They explain this situation in terms of the alienating effects of the development of large, impersonal organisations in the modern world. Much of social life becomes run along impersonal lines, within contexts remote from the ordinary individual, and over which she or he has little or no control. A flight into intimacy is an attempt to secure a meaningful life in familiar environments that have not been incorporated in to these larger systems. I shall return to this thesis later, since other authors have also suggested something similar. I do not think it is entirely accurate. The search for intimacy has a positive valence. It is not just based on negative reactions to an enveloping world of large-scale systems and social processes. Privacy makes possible the psychic satisfactions that the achievement of intimacy has to offer.

The expectation of intimacy provides perhaps the closest links between the reflexive project of the self and the pure relationship. Intimacy, or the quest for it, is at the heart of modern forms of friendship and established sexual relationships. Most manuals of therapy, including that of Rainwater, make it clear that intimacy is usually obtained only through psychological 'work', and that it is only possible between individuals who are secure in their own self-identities. A therapeutic study referred to earlier sums the whole thing up well: an intimate friendship or partnership, the author says, is 'a *choice* between any two people who make a *commitment* to each other to share a meaningful *lifestyle*'.[33] She describes several types of relationship which are distinct from one within which a developed intimacy has been attained. Some relationships are full of conflict, and persistent rows or bickering become normalised: emotional pain becomes a familiar part of the relationship, and without it the relationship in fact might be broken up. Conflict-ridden relationships contrast with 'de-energised' ones. Here there is little direct antagonism between partners, but little in the way of a strong bond either: inertia sustains the relationship. The partners get along with one another in a reasonable enough way in day-to-day matters, but are often bored with and resentful of one another. A 'convenience' relationship is one in which the individuals concerned have overtly or tacitly agreed that they will 'settle for' what they have got in the light of external rewards, or because of the difficulties they might experience if the relationship were dissolved, or for the comfort of not being alone.

All of these 'get by' relationships contrast with intimate ties, which require a commitment to 'the quality of the relationship'; where the relationship threatens to lapse into one of the other types, 'a decision to recommit to each other and make whatever changes and choices necessary to grow close' has to be made. A commitment to 'one's own personal recovery' is also needed if one of the partners is unable to develop the integrity demanded for the pursuit of intimacy.[34] Intimacy, the author stresses, requires a defined measure of privacy on the part of each partner, because a balance between autonomy and the sharing of feelings and experiences has to be obtained if personal closeness is not to be replaced by dependence. According to such a conception, intimacy obviously is not to be confused with sexual ties. Developed intimacy is possible in non-sexual relationships or friendships; and a high level of sexual activity might be maintained in a conflict-ridden situation. On the other hand, sexual involvement is often part of achieving intimacy – and also part of the reflexivity of the body, which I shall discuss later.

6   The pure relationship depends on mutual trust between partners, which in turn is closely related to the achievement of intimacy. In the pure relationship, trust is not and cannot be taken as 'given': like other aspects of the relationship, it has to be worked at – the trust of the other has to be won. In most premodern situations, in which personal relations were stabilised by external criteria, in the sense noted above, trust tended to be geared to established positions. Kinspeople could by no means always be trusted in such settings, as the plots and counterplots between relatives scheming to obtain power in royal households demonstrate. Yet kinship obligations probably were accepted most of the time, and provided reasonably stable environments of trust within which day-to-day life was ordered. Stripped of such qualities, personal ties in the pure relationship require novel forms of trust – precisely that trust which is built through intimacy with the other. Such trust presumes the opening out of the individual to the other, because knowledge that the other is committed, and harbours no basic antagonisms towards oneself, is the only framework for trust when external supports are largely absent.[35]

To build up trust, an individual must be both trusting and trustworthy, at least within the confines of the relationship. Since it is so closely connected to intimacy, trust implies the same balance of autonomy and mutual disclosure necessary to sustain intimate exchanges. What matters in the building of trust in the pure relationship is that each person should know the other's personality, and be able to rely on regularly eliciting certain sorts of desired responses from the other. This is one reason (not the only one) why authenticity has such an important place in self-actualisation. What matters is that one can rely on what the other says and does. In so far as the capacity to achieve intimacy with others is a prominent part of the reflexive project of the self – and it is – self-mastery is a necessary condition of authenticity.

How is trust created in relationships? Again we can turn to the therapeutic manuals to provide a guide. Wegscheider-Cruse offers a range of practical proposals for building trust which derive from systematic research on relationships. One should 'take time to listen to each other daily,' since communication is so central to intimacy. Such talking and listening should not always be limited to trivial events of the day. Where there are substantive issues to be faced, they should be seriously discussed. Partners should 'stick with one issue until resolved, and then be done with it', for 'rehashing the same issues lessens trust and creates new problems.' Old disputes that fester unresolved are often more likely to destroy trust than new difficulties, which may be easier to face. One should 'get to the feelings behind issues,' because surface appearances may hide the true dynamics of a situation, and communication which is not 'in depth' cannot get at these. Other recommendations include nurturing an atmosphere of caring, aiming for a variety of recreational pleasures mutually engaged in, and learning to express anger in a constructive way.[36]

7   In a pure relationship, the individual does not simply 'recognise the other' and in the responses of that other find his self-identity affirmed. Rather, as follows from the preceding points, self-identity is negotiated through linked processes of self-exploration and the development of intimacy with the other. Such processes help create 'shared histories' of a kind potentially more tightly bound than those characteristic of individuals who share experiences by virtue of a common social position. Such shared histories may be quite divergent from the orderings of time and space that prevail in the wider social world. Yet it is important to emphasise – a point that will later be developed in some detail – that they are characteristically interpolated within that wider world rather than cut off from it. Shared histories are created and sustained, in fact, substantially in terms of how far they integrate participants' life-plan calendars.

The pure relationship is above all dyadic, but its implications and influence are not limited to two-person settings. A given individual is likely to be involved in several forms of social relation which tend towards the pure type; and pure relationships are typically interconnected, forming specific milieux of intimacy. These milieux, as will be discussed in the following chapter, express an institutionally affirmed division of private and public arenas.

Pure relationships come into existence primarily in the domains of sexuality, marriage and friendship. The degree to which intimate spheres are transformed in this way plainly varies according to context and differential socioeconomic position, in common with most of the traits of modernity discussed in this book. Relations between parents and children, and more extended kin relations, stay partly distinct from the purview of the pure relationship. Both remain substantially tied to external criteria: biological connections which form key conditions for the sustaining of the relation. But each also becomes permeated by some of the influences generating the pure relationship. In so far as kinship relations are stripped of their traditional duties and obligations, their continuance tends increasingly to depend on the qualities enumerated above. Either such relations become attenuated and nominal in character or they are reformed through the reflexive achievement of intimacy.

Parent–child relations are something of a special case, because of the radical imbalance of power involved, and because of their centrality for socialisation processes. The close bonds established between parents and children are formed in a context of infantile dependency, but they are also the psychological nexus within which the young child develops capacities to initiate intimate ties in later life. Yet in conditions of modernity, the more a child moves towards adulthood and autonomy, the more elements of the pure relationship tend to come into play. A person who has left home may keep in constant touch with his parents, as a matter of obligation; but reflexively ordered trust must be developed, involving mutually accepted commitment, if the relationship is to be deepened. Where a person becomes a step-parent of an older child, the connections established from the beginning take on the characteristics of the pure relationship.

What to do? How things are: these matters are linked through institutional reflexivity. What applies to the self, and to the domain of pure relationships, applies equally to the sphere of the body. The body, in other words, in late modernity becomes increasingly socialised and drawn into the reflexive organisation of social life.

The body and self-actualisation

'The body' sounds a simple notion, particularly as compared to concepts like 'self' or 'self-identity'. The body is an object in which we are all privileged, or doomed, to dwell, the source of feelings of well-being and pleasure, but also the site of illnesses and strains. However, as has been emphasised, the body is not just a physical entity which we 'possess', it is an action-system, a mode of praxis, and its practical immersion in the interactions of day-to-day life is an essential part of the sustaining of a coherent sense of self-identity.

Several aspects of the body having special relevance to self and self-identity can be distinguished. Bodily *appearance* concerns all those features of the surface of the body, including modes of dress and adornment, which are visible to the individual and to other agents, and which are ordinarily used as clues to interpret actions. *Demeanour* determines how appearance is used by the individual within generic settings of day-to-day activities: it is how the body is mobilised in relation to constitutive conventions of daily life. The *sensuality* of the body refers to the dispositional handling of pleasure and pain. Finally we have the *regimes* to which bodies are subject.

Certain types of bodily appearance and demeanour plainly become particularly important with the advent of modernity. In many settings of pre-modern cultures, appearance was largely standardised in terms of traditional criteria. Modes of facial adornment or dress, for example, have always been to some degree a means of individualisation; yet the extent to which this was either possible or desired was usually quite limited. Appearance primarily designated social identity rather than personal identity. Dress and social identity have certainly not become entirely dissociated today, and dress remains a signalling device of gender, class position and occupational status. Modes of dress are influenced by group pressures, advertising, socioeconomic resources and other factors that often promote standardisation rather than individual difference. But the fact that we have a special word, the 'uniform', to refer to styles of dress that are standardised in relation to given social positions indicates that in other settings choice of dress is relatively open. Appearance, to put the matter bluntly and in terms of the ideas discussed so far, becomes a central element of the reflexive project of the self.

Demeanour is strongly influenced by the pluralisation of milieux. Not only must an individual be prepared to interact with others in public places, where demeanour is expected to meet certain generalised criteria of everyday competence, but he or she must be able to maintain appropriate behaviour in a variety of settings or locales. Naturally, individuals adjust both appearance and demeanour somewhat according to the perceived demands of the particular setting. That this is so has led some authors to suppose that the self essentially becomes broken up – that individuals tend to develop multiple selves in which there is no inner core of self-identity. Yet surely, as an abundance of studies of self-identity show, this is plainly not the case. The maintaining of constants of demeanour across varying settings of interaction is one of the prime means whereby coherence of self-identity is ordinarily preserved. The potential for the unravelling of self-identity is kept in check because demeanour sustains a link between 'feeling at home in one's body' and the personalised narrative. Demeanour effectively has to be integrated into that narrative for a person both to be able to sustain 'normal appearances' and at the same time be convinced of personal continuity across time and space; in most circumstances this is accomplished without great difficulty (although at any point it may come under strain).

In the post-traditional environments of high modernity, neither appearance nor demeanour can be organised as given; the body participates in a very direct way in the principle that the self has to be constructed. Bodily regimes, which also bear directly on patterns of sensuality, are the prime means whereby the institutional reflexivity of modern social life is focused on the cultivation – almost, one might say, the creation – of the body.

Let us once again look to a particular guide as a means of investigating these matters. *Bodysense*, by Vernon Coleman, is one among a massive number of self-help works which aim to provide a way of steering between reliance on pre-established bodily habits and the barrage of new information developed within abstract systems (emanating from doctors – of which Coleman is one – holistic health practitioners, dieticians, and so forth).[37] Again, we look at it symptomatically.

The book offers a 'comprehensive screening programme', by means of which one can monitor many aspects of one's health and susceptibility to different ailments or disabilities. This is life-planning in a very concrete sense: a checklist is included, for example, which allows the calculation of a person's life expectancy. Each section of the book (referred to as a 'clinic') contains a health area questionnaire, a 'truth file' (which summarises the current state of medical fact about the subject or subjects concerned) and an 'action plan' (what the individual might do to improve his health in the relevant respects). The concept of risk is pivotal to the work as a whole. The questionnaires allow the individual to collect points designed to give an estimate of his risk of contracting particular diseases – in particular, cancer, heart and circulatory problems, respiratory disease, digestive problems and muscle or joint difficulties.

Two of the most prominent sections are to do with eating habits and health care. Each provides an object lesson in the difficulties even professionals have in sifting through the diversity of claims and counterclaims characteristic of expert systems. As Coleman puts it:

> If you believed everything you read about foodstuffs these days, you'd probably never eat again. Turn on the TV or the radio, open a magazine or newspaper and you'll see horrifying stories about the dreadful things your grocer is doing to you. That in itself would be bad enough. It's not much fun sitting down to a good-looking meal if you're worried that it might be your last. But the whole business has been made even more worrying by the fact that the information being offered now frequently conflicts with last week's data . . . so what is the truth about the food we eat? . . . What is good for you and what is bad for you? What should you avoid and what can you eat with impunity?[38]

Coleman tries to provide authoritative answers, although he has to recognise that many of the things he says might be disputed by other experts; and in many instances risks cannot be calculated because existing knowledge is too incomplete.

According to Coleman's programme, cholesterol intake is to be reduced; the eating of animal fats, salt and sugar, and the drinking of alcohol, is to be brought down to a minimum: these recommendations are made quite confidently. By contrast, coffee – which, for example, Rainwater recommends cutting out entirely on health grounds – is held not to have deserved its bad press, for 'there really is no solid evidence to support the theory that coffee is bad for you.'[39] Fibre, bran and roughage are advocated as important for a healthy digestive system, while additives are treated more ambivalently by the author. Pointing out that a massive range of additives is now regularly used in the manufacture of processed foods, and pesticides sprayed on crops, Coleman emphasises that many of these chemicals have been only inadequately tested in terms of their effects on health – indeed, that testing for their long-term effects is almost impossible. It is suggested that, while it would be very difficult to eradicate all artificial additives from the diet, as much as possible can be bought from local market gardeners, local farmers and shops selling fresh or organically grown food.

'Bodysense' entails 'body care', and that is something, Coleman says, which cannot be provided by experts. Although professionals should be consulted where appropriate, resisting illness has to be primarily a matter of developing the body's 'own skills'. Body care means constantly 'listening to the body', both in order to experience fully the benefits of good health and to pick up signs that something might be going wrong. Body care delivers 'bodypower', the increased capability to avoid serious illness and the capacity to deal with minor symptoms without drugs. Bodypower can help a person retain, and even improve on, her or his appearance: understanding how the body functions and closely monitoring this functioning in an alert fashion keeps a person's skin fresh and body slim.

What does it mean to say that the body has become part of the reflexivity of modernity? Body regimes and the organisation of sensuality in high modernity become open to continuous reflexive attention, against the backdrop of plurality of choice. Both life-planning and the adoption of lifestyle options become (in principle) integrated with bodily regimes. It would be quite short-sighted to see this phenomenon only in terms of changing ideals of bodily appearance (such as slimness or youthfulness), or as solely brought about by the commodifying influence of advertising. We become responsible for the design of our own bodies, and in a certain sense noted above are forced to do so the more post-traditional the social contexts in which we move.

The study of anorexia nervosa, apparently purely an obsession with bodily appearance and slimness, provides a means of placing this point in stark relief.

Anorexia nervosa and the reflexivity of the body

The following is a personal description of an episode of anorexic compulsion, written by a woman who eventually managed to fight free from its yoke:

> I started to wear odd clothes; from jumble sales and of my own making. And make-up – strange make-up – white or black lips; dark, violent-coloured eyelids. I plucked my eyebrows away and back-combed my hair. My mother was outraged and she shouted at me. She wouldn't let me out looking like that, so I removed it all and put it on again on the bus. And it was all a façade: underneath I was scared and lonely but I desperately wanted to be myself, to define who I was, to express my very nature. I couldn't find the words so I used my face. I looked at photographs in magazines: there the girls were beautiful and thin. They seemed to express something that I felt. Yet I wasn't thin and I wanted to be. I stopped eating, not dramatically, but little by little. I became a vegetarian and my mother fussed. I lost weight. My mother took me to the doctor who tried to persuade me to eat fish, at least, so I did. . . .

Later she was taken into hospital to have her appendix out:

> Two months after the operation I went to a party. There I met an old acquaintance. He remarked on my weight loss and said that it suited me; in fact, he said, I looked much more attractive. I reduced my intake of food, considerably, from that moment on. I stopped eating potatoes and bread; then butter and cheese. I started to 'eat up' all the information I could get about calories; I read diet books with consuming interest. My food was weighed; measured according to calorific value. . . . My diet was unvaried. Every day had to be the same. I panicked if the shop did not have exactly the brand of crispbread I wanted; I panicked if I could not eat, ritually, at the same time . . .

Eventually she found a sympathetic and knowledgeable doctor, who helped her to begin to eat more substantial foods again

> I trusted her. I needed her; this person who listened so carefully to what I said, who didn't judge me, who didn't tell me what to do, who let me be. I tried, with her help, to unravel the tangle of my confusing and conflicting emotions.
>
> But in the end it was up to me. It was so hard to accept. She would help me but she couldn't tell me how to live. It was my life, after all. It belonged to me. I could cultivate it; I could nourish it or I could starve it. I could choose. It was such a burden, that choice, that sometimes I thought I could not bear it on my own. . . . It is a risky business, being a woman. I have found different strategies to cope; ones that are under my control. The struggle to be myself, autonomous and free, goes on.[40]

Fasting, and the self-denial of various kinds of foodstuffs, have obviously long been part of religious practices, and are found in many different cultural frameworks. It was relatively common in medieval Europe for individuals seeking salvation to undergo prolonged fasts. Female holiness achieved through food deprivation was particularly important. A variety of chronicles from medieval times recount stories of female saints whose regular fastings helped them achieve spiritual grace – physicians of the seventeenth and eighteenth centuries labelled the practice anorexia mirabilis, miraculously inspired loss of appetite.[41] However, it is generally agreed that anorexia mirabilis is quite distinct from anorexia nervosa, which belongs to modern times, and is particularly characteristic of the contemporary period – the phase of late modernity. Anorexia mirabilis was not especially pronounced among teenage or young adult women, as is often the case today; and was not bound up with the cultivation of bodily appearance, but was rather concerned with overcoming sensual appetites in the pursuit of higher values. Anorexia nervosa begins with the phenomenon of 'fasting girls', noted in the late nineteenth century, although this is still largely a transitional syndrome, as it were, 'a provocative relic, in a secularising age, of an older female religious culture.'[42] The condition proper has only become widespread since the rise of 'dieting', in the restricted sense of that term, from about the 1920s through to the present day.

The fact that anorexia is so closely linked to a gender divide is undoubtedly to do with the association between dieting and changing values about bodily appearance. The pre-established connection between a corpulent figure and prosperity had virtually disappeared by the end of the first two or three decades of the twentieth century. Women began to become concerned about weight in ways that, for the most part, men did not. Yet it is important to recognise that the 1920s was also a period at which 'diet' in the broader sense for the first time became associated with the control of weight and the self-regulation of health; and this was also the period at which the manufacture of foods began to accelerate, leading to a much wider diversity of foodstuffs becoming available. 'Being on a diet' in the narrow meaning of the phrase is only a particular version of a much more general phenomenon – the cultivation of bodily regimes as a means of reflexively influencing the project of the self.

From this point of view, anorexia, and its apparent opposite, compulsive overeating, should be understood as casualties of the need – and responsibility – of the individual to create and maintain a distinctive self-identity.[43] They are extreme versions of the control of bodily regimes which has now become generic to the circumstances of day-to-day life.

Anorexia is a complex phenomenon, about which there is now a voluminous literature, and it would scarcely be possible in this context to offer a properly detailed analysis of it. I want to concentrate only on those features directly relevant to the overall theses of this book. Anorexia can be understood as a pathology of reflexive self-control, operating around an axis of self-identity and bodily appearance, in which shame anxiety plays a preponderant role. All of the important elements to do with anorexia appear in the experience of the individual described at some length above. Her concern to become thin emerged, not as a sudden antipathy towards food, but as a controlled and progressive phenomenon, which happened 'little by little'; she devoted a great deal of care and concern to her diet, a deliberate asceticism in bodily regime amid the plural choices of food available; there was a marked reflexive component, as signalled by her determination to 'eat up' all the information about calories she could obtain; awarenes of the need to forge a distinctive lifestyle, in relation to her self-identity, emerges very clearly; and a polarity of shame and pride comes out plainly in the 'façade' she sought to construct as contrasted to her eventual conviction that she could 'nourish' her self-esteem rather than 'starve' it.

Why should anorexia nervosa be primarily characteristic of women, especially relatively younger women? One reason is no doubt the greater premium placed on physical attractiveness for women as opposed to men (although this imbalance is changing), coupled to the fact that early adulthood is a crisis phase in identity formation. A common view of anorexia is that it represents a 'refusal to become an adult' – in effect, a denial of puberty, the wish to remain a girl rather than become a woman. But this interpretation is not convincing and, as one observer remarks, treats anorexia misleadingly as a specific pathology rather than as 'an extremely complicated response to a confusing self-identity'.[44] Anorexia should rather be understood in terms of the plurality of options which late modernity makes available – against the backdrop of the continuing exclusion of women from full participation in the universe of social activity which generates those options. Women today have the nominal opportunity to follow a whole variety of possibilities and chances: yet, in a masculinist culture, many of these avenues remain effectively foreclosed. Moreover, to embrace those which do exist, women have to abandon their older, 'fixed' identities in a more thorough-going way than do men. In other words, they experience the openness of late modernity in a fuller, yet more contradictory, way.

Anorexia, as Orbach puts it, is a form of protest: one character-ised not by withdrawal, but by a sustained engagement with the reflexivity of bodily development.[45] In previous times, when women's social positions were in general tightly defined, women expressed rebellion in the body in the form of hysterical symp-toms. Today, their protest is intertwined with the reflexive con-trol which a post-traditional order implies: 'The anorectic woman encompasses in her symptom a way of being entirely at odds with the phlegmatic response of her nineteenth-century hysterical sister. Not for her the fainting, falling, or flailing fists; her protest is marked by the achievement of a serious and successful transfor-mation of her body . . .'[46] When the options open to a woman were few and narrowly focused, her unconscious resistance through the body was diffuse; in a situation of an apparent multiplicity of possibilities, her reaction is confined and exhibits tight control. As Orbach points out, the anorectic individual is not the passive victim of the dietician: on the contrary, anorexia involves body regimes that are highly active and coordinated.

In anorectic lifestyles, then, we see a specific version of Rainwater's admonition: 'You're in charge,' save that the attempt at mastery becomes compulsive. The body regimes of anorectic individuals are often extreme. A person may, for example, run for several miles, take part in a punishing and lengthy exercise class and then go on to work out for a period on exercise machines. Such activities bring about a sense of achievement, rather than simply despair, and one can clearly see in them important aspects of empowerment. There is 'an urgency and strength' in the asceticism of anorexia, which is thus more to do with the self-denial *per se* rather than with a body image of slimness. 'Starving to death in a sea of objects,' as John Sours puts it, is a denial which paradoxically asserts with great force the reflexive making of self-identity and body.[47]

Compulsive mastery is quite different from authentic reflexive monitoring, however, and it is hardly surprising that the anorectic person frequently feels herself 'taken over' by the very regime to which she submits her body. In the terms of Winnicott and Laing, the body becomes part of a false-self system, detached from, yet rigorously governed by, the individual's inner aspirations. Feelings of destructiveness, deriving from unconscious shame, become focused on body regimes. The extraordinary intensity which anorectic asceticism can assume carries the hallmark of a ruthless inner dedication, of whose sources in the project of self-identity the individual is only partly aware. The 'alienness' of the body – in which the self cannot feel at home – helps explain why anorectic regimes may sometimes be pursued even to the level of an actual 'fasting unto death'. The individual only feels 'worthy' on the basis of a regime of self-regulation so complete that the slightest lapse is threatening.

Anorexia represents a striving for security in a world of plural, but ambiguous, options. The tightly controlled body is an emblem of a safe existence in an open social environment. As we read earlier in the personal account: 'It's a risky business, being a woman.' The making of a self-identity and body occurs in the framework of a risk culture, which it will be the business of the next chapter to look at more directly.

4
Fate, Risk and Security

Fate, fatalism, fateful moments

To live in the universe of high modernity is to live in an environment of chance and risk, the inevitable concomitants of a system
geared to the domination of nature and the reflexive making of
history. Fate and destiny have no formal part to play in such a
system, which operates (as a matter of principle) via what I shall
call open human control of the natural and social worlds. The
universe of future events is open to be shaped by human intervention – within limits which, as far as possible, are regulated by risk
assessment. Yet the notions of fate and destiny have by no means
disappeared in modern societies, and an investigation into their
nature is rich with implications for the analysis of modernity and
self-identity.

Sweeping though the assertion may be, it can be said with some
confidence that there is no non-modern culture which does not in
some sense incorporate, as a central part of its philosophy, the
notions of fate and destiny. The world is not seen as a direction-
less swirl of events, in which the only ordering agents are natural
laws and human beings, but as having intrinsic form which relates
individual life to cosmic happenings. A person's destiny – the
direction his or her life is due to take – is specified by that
person's fate, what the future holds in store. Although there is an
enormous variety of beliefs which could be grouped under these
two terms, in most of them the connecting point between destiny
and fate is death. In Greek thought, fate (*moira*) was the bringer
of doom and death, and was thought of as a great power – more
ancient than the oldest gods.[1]

Given the nature of modern social life and culture, we tend

now to counterpose fate and the openness of future events. Fate is taken to mean a form of preordained determinism, to which the modern outlook stands opposed. Yet while the concept of fate does have the connotation of a partly 'settled' future, it typically also involves a moral conception of destiny and an esoteric view of daily events – where 'esoteric' means that events are experienced not just in terms of their causal relation to one another, but in terms of their cosmic meaning. Fate in this sense has little connection with *fatalism*, as this term is ordinarily understood today. Fatalism is the refusal of modernity – a repudiation of a controlling orientation to the future in favour of an attitude which lets events come as they will.

A main connecting point between pre-existing ideas of fate and those of the post-medieval period was the concept of *fortuna*, which originally derived from the name of the Roman goddess of 'fortune', and came into uneasy tension with the dominant Christian beliefs. The idea of Divine Providence was clearly a version of fate but, as Max Weber pointed out, Christianity introduced a more dynamic role for human beings on this earth than was characteristic of the traditional religions of Greece and Rome.[2] The goddess was frowned on by the Church, since the idea of 'fortune' implied that one could achieve grace without having to work as God's instrument in the world. Yet the idea of *fortuna* remained important and often outweighed providential reward in the afterlife as a feature of local cultural belief. Machiavelli's use of *fortuna* marked a significant transition between the traditional use of the notion and the emergence of new modes of social activity from which fate is excluded. In *The Prince* he says:

Many have held, and still hold the opinion that the things of this world are, in a manner, controlled by *fortuna* and by God, that men in their wisdom cannot control them, and, on the contrary, that men can have no remedy whatsoever for them; and for this reason they might judge that they need not sweat much over such matters but let them be governed by fate. . . . I judge it to be true that *fortuna* is the arbiter of one half of our actions, but that she still leaves the control of the other half, or almost that, to us . . . I say that one sees a prince prosper today and come to ruin tomorrow without having seen him change his character or any of his traits . . . a prince who relies completely upon fortune will come to ruin as soon as she changes; I also believe that the man who adapts his course of action to the nature of the times will succeed and, likewise, that the man who sets his course of action out of tune with the times will come to grief.[3]

It is not surprising that the study of politics should provide the initial area within which notions of fate become transformed, for although the propaganda of nations may see them as driven by fate to a specific destiny, the practice of politics – in the modern context – presumes the art of conjecture. Thinking how things might turn out if a given course of action is followed, and balancing this against alternatives, is the essence of political judgement. Machiavelli is celebrated as the originator of modern political strategy, but his work gives voice to some rather more fundamental innovations. He foreshadows a world in which risk, and risk calculation, edge aside *fortuna* in virtually all domains of human activity. There seems to have been no generic word for risk in Machiavelli's time, however; the notion appears in European thought about a century later. (In English until the nineteenth century the word was usually spelled in its French version, as *risque*. For some while the French spelling continued to be used alongside the new Anglicised word, which was first of all employed with reference to insurance. The term *risqué*, meaning a joke that risks giving offence, still retains the old form.)[4]

The notion of risk becomes central in a society which is taking leave of the past, of traditional ways of doing things, and which is opening itself up to a problematic future. This statement applies just as much to institutionalised risk environments as to other areas. Insurance, as we saw in chapter 1, is one of the core elements of the economic order of the modern world – it is part of a more general phenomenon concerned with the control of time which I shall term the *colonisation of the future*. The 'openness' of things to come expresses the malleability of the social world and the capability of human beings to shape the physical settings of our existence. While the future is recognised to be intrinsically unknowable, and as it is increasingly severed from the past, that future becomes a new terrain – a territory of counterfactual possibility. Once thus established, that terrain lends itself to colonial invasion through counterfactual thought and risk calculation. The calculation of risk, as I have mentioned previously, can never be fully complete, since even in relatively confined risk environments there are always unintended and unforeseen outcomes. In milieux from which fate has disappeared, all action, even that which sticks to strongly established patterns, is in principle 'calculable' in terms of risk – some sort of overall assessment of likely risks can be made for virtually all habits and activities, in respect of specific outcomes. The intrusion of abstract systems into day-to-day life, coupled with the dynamic nature of knowledge, means that awareness of risk seeps into the actions of almost everyone.

A more extended discussion of risk, and its relation to self-identity, will be given shortly. First, however, it is necessary to introduce one or two other notions connected with that of fate. We have to say a little bit more about *fatalism*, a term which, as mentioned has more to do with modern social life than with more traditional cultures. Fatalism, as I understand it here, differs from stoicism, an attitude of strength in the face of life's trials and tribulations. A fatalistic outlook is one of resigned acceptance that events should be allowed to take their course. It is an outlook nourished by the main orientations of modernity, although it stands in opposition to them.

Fatalism should be separated from a sense of the *fatefulness* of events. Fateful happenings, or circumstances, are those which are particularly consequential for an individual or group.[5] They include the undesired outcomes faced in what I have termed high-consequence risks, risks affecting large numbers of people in a potentially life-threatening way, but they also figure at the level of the individual. *Fateful moments* are those when individuals are called on to take decisions that are particularly consequential for their ambitions, or more generally for their future lives. Fateful moments are highly consequential for a person's destiny.

Fateful moments can be understood in terms of the broader traits of consequential activities that an individual carries on in day-to-day life and over the course of the lifespan. Much of the daily life, so far as the individual is concerned, is inconsequential, and is not seen to be particularly fateful for overall goals. However, some avenues of activity are usually thought of by the person in question as more generally consequential than others – such as activity carried on in the sphere of work. Consider the phenomenon of 'dead' or 'killed' time, analysed with characteristic brilliance by Goffman.[6] Time that has to be killed is also, interestingly, quite often called 'free' time – it is time which is filled in, in between the more consequential sectors of life. If a person finds she has half an hour between one engagement and the next, she might decide to spend that time pottering around or reading the newspaper until her next appointment, rather than putting the time to 'good' use. Killed time is bounded off from the rest of an individual's life and (unless something unexpected happens) has no consequences for it.

By contrast, many more consequential activities of life are routinised. Most 'time on' activities – whether in the formal or more informal sectors of social life – are not problematic, or are so only in terms of the ordinary management of the tasks concerned. In other words, difficult decisions may often have to be taken, but they are handled by strategies evolved to cope with them as part of the ongoing activities in question. Sometimes, however, a particular situation or episode may be both highly consequential and problematic: it is these episodes that form fateful moments. Fateful moments are times when events come together in such a way that an individual stands, as it were, at a crossroads in his existence; or where a person learns of information with fateful consequences.[7] Fateful moments include the decision to get married, the wedding ceremony itself – and, later, perhaps the decision to separate and the actual parting. Other examples are: taking examinations, deciding to opt for a particular apprenticeship or course of study, going on strike, giving up one job in favour of another, hearing the result of a medical test, losing a large amount in a gamble, or winning a large sum in a lottery. It often happens that fateful moments occur because of events that impinge upon an individual's life willy-nilly; but such moments are also quite commonly engineered, as, for example, when a person decides to get together the whole of her savings and start a business. There are, of course, fateful moments in the history of collectivities as well as in the lives of individuals. They are phases at which things are wrenched out of joint, where a given state of affairs is suddenly altered by a few key events.

Fateful moments, or rather that category of possibilities which an individual defines as fateful, stand in a particular relation to risk. They are the moments at which the appeal of *fortuna* is strong, moments at which in more traditional settings oracles might have been consulted or divine forces propitiated. Experts are often brought in as a fateful moment approaches or a fateful decision has to be taken. Quite commonly, in fact, expertise is the vehicle whereby a particular circumstance is pronounced as fateful, as for instance in the case of a medical diagnosis. Yet there are relatively few situations where a decision as to what to do becomes clear-cut as a result of experts' advice. Information derived from abstract systems may help in risk assessment, but it is the individual concerned who has to run the risks in question. Fateful decisions are usually almost by definition difficult to take because of the mixture of the problematic and the consequential that characterises them.

Fateful moments are threatening for the protective cocoon which defends the individual's ontological security, because the 'business as usual' attitude that is so important to that cocoon is inevitably broken through. They are moments when the individual must launch out into something new, knowing that a decision made, or a specific course of action followed, has an irreversible quality, or at least that it will be difficult thereafter to revert to the old paths. Fateful moments do not necessarily mean facing a strong possibility that things will go awry, that is, circumstances with a high probability of losing out. What tends to make the risk environment difficult to confront is rather the scale of the consequential penalties for getting things wrong. Fateful moments disclose high-consequence risks for the individual comparable to those characteristic of collective activity.

The parameters of risk

Since risk, and attempts at risk assessment, are so fundamental to the colonising of the future, the study of risk can tell us much about core elements of modernity. Several factors are involved here: a reduction in life-threatening risks for the individual, consequent on large tracts of security in daily activity purchased by abstract systems; the construction of institutionally bordered risk environments; the monitoring of risk as a key aspect of modernity's reflexivity; the creation of high-consequence risks resulting from globalisation; and the operation of all this against the backdrop of an inherently unstable 'climate of risk'.

Preoccupation with risk in modern social life has nothing directly to do with the actual prevalence of life-threatening dangers. On the level of the individual lifespan, in terms of life expectation and degree of freedom from serious disease, people in the developed societies are in a much more secure position than most were in previous ages. In the late eighteenth century in Britain, at that time the most economically advanced society in the world, deadly epidemics which killed hundreds of thousands of people were still commonplace. A proliferation of endemic illnesses had to be endured, even when they were not necessarily fatal. Many had cause to observe:[8]

The weariness, the fever and the fret,
Here, where men sit and hear each other groan,
Where palsy shakes a few sad last grey hairs,
Where youth grows pale, and spectre-thin, and dies.

Only since the early twentieth century have sufficient statistics been available to chart out with any precision the changes which have affected life-threatening outcomes. A study which took the year 1907 as its point of departure showed that at that time newborn infants 'stepped into a minefield'[9] (although rates of infant mortality had been vastly reduced as compared to a century before). On a chart for 1907, about one in seven died in the first year of life, as contrasted to one in sixty-seven on a 1977 chart taken as a basis for comparison. The list given below records some of the most important risk-reducing advances relevant to health which occurred during the years 1907–77 – that is, the years spanning the life of a seventy-year-old in 1977:

Safe drinking water
Sanitary sewage disposal
Hygienic food preparation
Pasteurised milk
Refrigeration
Central heating
Scientific principles of nutrition widely applied
Scientific prinicples of personal hygiene widely applied
Eradication of major parasitic diseases, including malaria
Rodent and insect control
Continually improved prenatal and postnatal care

Continually improved care of babies and infants
Continually improved care of infectious diseases
Continually improved surgical treatment
Continually improved anaesthesia and intensive care
Scientific principles of immunisation widely applied
Blood transfusion made practical
Organisation of intensive care units in hospitals
Continually expanded and improved diagnostic procedures
Continually improved treatment of cancer
Continually improved treatment of occlusive arterial disease
Planned parenthood made feasible and practical
Improved and legalised methods for interrupting pregnancy
Safety in the workplace widely accepted
Safety belts in cars
Continually improved methods for preserving teeth, vision and
hearing
Smoking, obesity, high blood pressure and sedentary life recognised as damaging to health.[10]

We cannot tell in full how far each of the items on this list has affected the changes highlighted in the 1907–77 comparison, since the full impact of some, or even many, of them may only be felt by subsequent generations. Against such risk-reducing changes, moreover, we have to place a considerable number of negative influences. Two world wars, involving massive destruction of life, have occurred during the lifetime of the 1907 generation. Risk of death or serious injury from car crashes has increased steadily over most of this period. From the 1930s to the late 1960s, this generation consumed many drugs that, by current standards, were inadequately tested before being made available. The members of this generation drank a great deal of alcohol, and smoked millions of tobacco goods, before the toxic effects of these were fully realised; environmental pollution, believed by many medical specialists to increase susceptibility to major diseases of various sorts, has sharply increased; and for much of their lives they have eaten food containing many additives and treated by chemical fertilisers, with consequences for health that are at best unknown and at worst may help produce some of the leading killer diseases.

In terms of basic life security, nonetheless, the risk-reducing elements seem substantially to outweigh the new array of risks.

There are various ways in which this can be tentatively assessed. One is by calculating how the 1907 cohort actually fared with how it would have fared if the major known life-threatening risks pertaining in 1907 had continued to prevail through the lifetimes of those born in that year – a speculative calculation, but one that can be undertaken with a reasonable degree of statistical backing. Such a calculation indicates no differential, in terms of survival percentages, up to age twenty. After this age, the curve of actual survival begins to rise above the curve given by the newly constructed data in a progressive way, the more so in the later period.

Comparisons can also be made between the 1907 chart and that of 1977 by contrasting life expectancies of the 1907 group with those predicted for the 1977 generation. These show a substantial divergence, starting from the very first year of life and up to old age, in favour of the 1977 cohort (although, of course, we have no way of knowing fully what additional factors might influence life-threatening risks for that generation in years to come).

Risk concerns future happenings – as related to present practices – and the colonising of the future therefore opens up new settings of risk, some of which are institutionally organised. In relatively minor contexts such settings have always existed, for instance in the culturally widespread case of gambling. Occasionally there have been organised risk environments in non-modern cultures where no equivalent institutionalised forms are found in modern social life. Thus Firth describes an institutionalised type of attempted suicide in Tikopia.[11] It is accepted practice for a person with a grievance to put out to sea in a canoe. Since the waters are treacherous, there is a substantial chance that the individual will not survive the experience; chances of survival are also affected by how quickly others in the community notice and respond to the person's absence. While this risk-taking endeavour clearly bears some affinities with risk-taking in suicide attempts in modern settings, in the second of these the institutionalised element is lacking.[12]

For the most part, however, institutionally structured risk environments are much more prominent in modern than pre-modern societies. Such institutionalised systems of risk affect virtually everyone, regardless of whether or not they are 'players' within them – competitive markets in products, labour power, investments or money provide the most significant example. The difference between such institutionalised systems and other risk parameters is that they are constituted through risk, rather than certain risks being incidental to them. Institutionalised risk environments link individual and collective risks in many ways – individual life chances, for instance, are now directly tied to the global capitalistic economy. But in relation to the present discussion they are most important for what they reveal about how the future is colonised.

Take the stock exchange as an example. The stock exchange is a regulated market which provides a range of securities (an interesting term in itself) that borrowers issue and savers hold, creating a choice of ways of structuring the risks of both borrowers and savers in their objective of achieving financial gain. It also has the effect of valuing securities in relation to their expected returns, taking into account investors' risks.[13] Savers and borrowers have a variety of financial desiderata. Some savers want to accumulate money in the long term, while others are looking for more short-term gains and may be prepared to take considerable risks with their capital with this end in view. Borrowers normally want money for the long term, but a certain risk of loss on the part of lenders is unavoidable. In the stock market, investors can choose from a range of risks and modes of hedging against them, while borrowers can seek to adjust the terms of their received capital against the risks of the business endeavours for which they utilise it. The stock market is a theorised domain of sophisticated reflexivity – a phenomenon which directly influences the nature of the hazards of saving and borrowing. Thus studies indicate that price–earnings ratios seem to be poor predictors of subsequent earnings or dividend growth. Some theories applied in stock market investment take this as evidence that the stock market cannot identify which companies will utilise scarce financial resources most satisfactorily, and calculate risk strategies accordingly. Others hold that retention of earnings, plus other specifiable factors, account for this finding, and adopt correspondingly different strategies. A measure of the reflexive complexity of such a situation is provided by the fact that retention policies themselves are likely to be influenced by the type of theory adopted.[14]

Stock markets, like other institutionalised risk environments, use risk actively to create the 'future' that is then colonised. This is well understood by participants. One of the best illustrations of this is the specific existence of futures markets. All savings and borrowings create possible future worlds through the mobilising of risk. But futures markets mortgage the future in a direct fashion, securing a bridgehead in time that offers a peculiar security for certain types of borrowers.

The reflexive monitoring of risk is intrinsic to institutionalised risk systems. In respect of other risk parameters it is extrinsic, but no less fundamental for life chances and life-planning. A significant part of expert thinking and public discourse today is made up of *risk profiling* – analysing what, in the current state of knowledge and in current conditions, is the distribution of risks in given milieux of action. Since what is 'current' in each of these respects is constantly subject to change, such profiles have to be chronically revised and updated.

Consider 'what we die of' – representing the major risks associated with mortality.[15] Risk profiling of the main life-threatening illnesses shows major differences between the turn of the century and the present-day in the developed countries. By 1940 infectious diseases like tuberculosis, nephritis or diphtheria had dropped out of the top ten causes of death. Deaths attributed to heart disease and cancer moved into first and second place after 1940, where they have stayed. The main reason for this change is thought to be the greater proportion of people living to age fifty or more, but this view is challenged by some who hold dietary and environmental factors responsible. One should note that the concepts used to identify the major causes of death have changed substantially since 1900. What was first generally termed 'intracranial lesions of vascular origin' at the turn of the century became 'vascular lesions affecting the central nervous system' in the 1960s, and has since altered to 'cerebrovascular diseases'. Such changes are more than fads: they reflect alterations in medical outlook towards the pathologies in question.

Some two-thirds of the population over thirty-five years of age in countries with high rates of coronary heart disease, like Britain or the United States, are believed to have some degree of narrowing in their coronary arteries, although not enough to bring about distinct pathological symptoms or changes in an electrocardiogram. Each year, about one person in eighty over the age of thirty-five has a heart attack, although only a certain proportion of these are fatal. Heart disease is more common in men than women, although the gap is closing. In the United States and one or two other countries, after a steady increase for many years, the rate of deaths due to coronary heart disease has begun to drop. There is much debate as to why this is so; it may be due to changes in diet, improved emergency care, a decrease in smoking or greater adult participation in regular exercise. It is generally agreed that lifestyle factors of one kind or another strongly influence the risk of contracting heart disease. There is a good deal of comparative evidence on the issue. Thus Japan has the lowest rate of coronary heart disease of any of the industrialised societies. The children and grandchildren of Japanese immigrants to the United States, however, have rates of the disease comparable to that of the US, not Japan. Yet it is not at all clear what influence diet, as compared to other aspects of lifestyle, has in the aetiology of heart illnesses. France, for example, reports low rates of death from coronary heart disease, although the French diet is high in the substances thought to produce it.

Cancer is not a single disease entity, at least in respect of the risks of death associated with it. From the turn of the century, the different forms of the disease have followed divergent paths. For instance, there has been a steady increase in rates of death from lung cancer since about 1930, the continuation of that increase presumably being due to the delayed effects of the widespread popularity of smoking until about the late 1960s. On the other hand, there has been a steady drop in some other types of cancer. The experts disagree about why this is so. They also disagree about whether or not, or to what degree, diet and environmental factors play a part in the onset of the disease.

The regular and detailed monitoring of health risks, in relation to information such as that just described, provides an excellent example, not just of routine reflexivity in relation to extrinsic risk, but of the interaction between expert systems and lay behaviour in relation to risk. Medical specialists and other researchers produce the materials from which risk profiling is carried out. Yet risk profiles do not remain the special preserve of the experts. The general population is aware of them, even if it is often only in a rough and ready way, and indeed the medical profession and other agencies are concerned to make their findings widely available to laypeople. The lifestyles followed by the population at large are influenced by the reception of those findings, although there are normally class differences in the altering of behaviour patterns, with professional and more highly educated groups in the lead. Yet the consensus of expert opinion – if there is any such consensus – may switch even as the changes in lifestyle they called for previously become adopted. We might recall that smoking was once advocated by some sectors of the medical profession as a relaxant; while red meat, butter and cream were said to build healthy bodies.

Medical concepts and terminologies change as theories are revised or discarded. Moreover, at any one time, there is substantial, sometimes radical, disagreement within the medical profession about risk factors as well as about the aetiology of major health hazards. Even with illnesses as serious as coronary heart disease and cancer, there are many practitioners of alternative medicine – some of whom are now taken much more seriously by orthodox medical specialists than used to be the case – who dispute the more mainline positions. The assessment of health risks is very much bound up with 'who is right' in these disputes. For although a risk profile drawn up at any one point in time looks objective, the interpretation of risk for an individual or category of individuals depends on whether or not lifestyle changes are introduced, and how far these are in fact based on valid presumptions. Once set up, a lifestyle sector – say, the following of a particular diet – may be quite difficult to break, because it is likely to be integrated with other aspects of a person's behaviour. All these considerations influence the reflexive adoption by laypeople of risk parameters as filtered through abstract systems. In the face of such complexity, it is not surprising that some people withdraw trust from virtually all medical practitioners, perhaps consulting them only in times of desperation, and stick doggedly to whatever established habits they have formed for themselves.

In contrast to health dangers, high-consequence risks by definition are remote from the individual agent, although – again, by definition – they impinge directly on each individual's life chances. It would clearly be a mistake to suppose that people living in modern social conditions are the first to fear that terrible catastrophes might befall the world. Eschatological visions were quite common in the Middle Ages, and there have been other cultures in which the world has been seen as fraught with massive hazards. Yet both the experience and nature of such hazardous visions are in some respects quite distinct from the awareness of high-consequence risks today. Such risks are the result of burgeoning processes of globalisation, and even half a century ago humanity did not suffer from the same kind of threat.

Such risks are part of the dark side of modernity, and they, or comparable risk factors, will be there so long as modernity endures – so long as the rapidity of social and technological change continues, throwing off unanticipated consequences. High-consequence risks have a distinctive quality. The more calamitous the hazards they involve, the less we have any real experience of what we risk: for if things 'go wrong', it is already too late. Certain disasters give a taste of what could happen – such as the nuclear accident at Chernobyl. As with many such issues, experts are not fully in agreement about what the long-term effects of the escaped radiation from that accident might be on the populations of the countries it affected. It is generally thought to have increased the risks of certain types of disease in the future, and of course has had devastating consequences for the people most immediately affected in the Soviet Union. But it is inevitably counterfactual guesswork to estimate what the outcome of a larger nuclear disaster might be – let alone a nuclear conflict, even a relatively small-scale one.

Risk assessment endeavours in the case of high-consequence risks have to be correspondingly different from those concerned with risks where outcomes can be regularly observed and monitored – although these interpretations have to be constantly revised and updated in the light of new theories and information. The thesis that risk assessment itself is inherently risky is nowhere better borne out than in the area of high-consequence risks. A common method used in the attempted calculation of risks of nuclear reactor accidents is the design of a fault tree. A fault tree is drawn up by listing all known pathways to possible reactor failure, then specifying the possible pathways to those pathways, and so on. The end result, supposedly, is a fairly precise designation of risk. The method has been used in studies of reactor safety in the United States and several European countries. Yet it leaves various imponderables.[16] It is impossible to make a confident calculation of the risk of human error or sabotage. The Chernobyl disaster was the result of human error, as was, at an earlier period, the fire at one of the world's largest nuclear stations at Brown's Ferry in the United States. The fire first started because a technician used a candle to check for an air leak, in direct contravention of established procedures. Some pathways to potential disaster might not be noticed at all. They have been missed on many occasions in more minor risk settings, and for high-consequence risks dangers have sometimes been spotted only by retroactive revisions of data and assumptions. This happened in a hypothetical setting when a study by the American National Academy of Sciences was convened to determine the risks to the food supply given an exchange of nuclear warfare of a certain intensity. The panel carrying out the study concluded that the resulting reduction in the earth's ozone layer would not threaten the survivors' food resources, as many crops that would survive in the atmosphere of increased ultraviolet radiation would continue to be cultivated. No one among the panel noticed, however, that the raised radiation level would make it virtually impossible to work in the fields to grow these crops.[17]

High-consequence risks form one particular segment of the generalised 'climate of risk' characteristic of late modernity – one characterised by regular shifts in knowledge-claims as mediated by expert systems. As Rabinowitch observes: 'One day we hear about the danger of mercury, and run to throw out cans of tuna fish from our shelves; the next day the food to shun may be butter, which our grandparents considered the acme of wholesomeness; then we have to scrub the lead paint from the walls. Today, the danger lurks in the phosphates in our favourite detergent; tomorrow the finger points to insecticides, which were hailed a few years ago as saviours of millions from hunger and disease. The threats of death, insanity and – somehow even more fearsome – cancer lurk in all we eat or touch.'[18] That was written some twenty years ago: since then, further contaminated traces have been found in tuna fish, some types of detergent believed safe in the early 1970s have been banned, while some doctors now say that it is more healthy to eat butter than the low-fat margarines which were previously widely recommended as preferable.

The point, to repeat, is not that day-to-day life is inherently more risky than was the case in prior eras. It is rather that, in conditions of modernity, for lay actors as well as for experts in specific fields, thinking in terms of risk and risk assessment is a more or less ever-present exercise, of a partly imponderable character. It should be remembered that we are all laypeople in respect of the vast majority of the expert systems which intrude on our daily activities. The proliferation of specialisms goes together with the advance of modern institutions, and the further narrowing of specialist areas seems an inevitable upshot of technical development. The more specialisms become concentrated, the smaller the field in which any given individual can claim expertise; in other areas of life she or he will be in the same situation as everyone else. Even in fields in which experts are in a consensus, because of the shifting and developing nature of modern knowledge, the 'filter-back' effects on lay thought and practice will be ambiguous and complicated. The risk climate of modernity is thus unsettling for everyone; no one escapes.

The active courting of risks

Of course, there are differences between risks voluntarily run and those built into the constraints of social life or into a lifestyle pattern to which one is committed. Institutionalised risk environments provide some settings within which individuals can choose to risk scarce resources, including their lives – as in hazardous sports or other comparable activities. Yet the differentiation between risks that are voluntarily undertaken and risks which affect the individual in a less sought-after way is often blurred, and plainly does not always correspond to the division between extrinsic and institutionalised risk environments. The risk factors built into a modern economy, as mentioned before, affect almost everyone, regardless of whether a given individual is directly active within the economic order. Driving a car and smoking provide other examples. Driving is in many situations a voluntary activity; yet there are some contexts where lifestyle commitments or other constraints will make using a car close to a necessity. Smoking may be voluntarily entered into, but once it is an addition it has a compulsive character, as does alcohol consumption.[19]

The active embrace of certain types of risk is an important part of the risk climate. Some aspects or types of risk may be valued for their own sake – the elation that may come from driving fast and dangerously resembles the thrill offered by certain institutionalised risk endeavours. Taking up smoking in the face of its known risks to health may demonstrate a certain bravado that an individual finds psychologically rewarding. To the degree to which this is so, such activities can be understood in terms of dimensions of 'cultivated risk' that will be discussed further below. But for the most part, the passive acceptance of the hazards of such practices as driving and cigarette smoking by large sectors of the population has to be interpreted in different terms. Two types of interpretation have commonly been put forward. One is that the large corporations, and other powerful agencies, conspire to mislead the public about the true levels of risk, or use advertising and other conditioning methods to ensure that a substantial proportion of the population engages in these risk-taking habits nevertheless. The other suggests that most laypeople are not sensitive to individually distributed or to deferred risk – even though they often overreact to collective disasters or to risks that are more 'visible'. Both explanations tend to lay considerable emphasis on apparently irrational components of action. Neither explanation seems particularly convincing, although no doubt each points to factors of some importance. The main influences involved probably derive from certain characteristic features of life-planning and lifestyle habits. Since specific practices are ordinarily geared into an integrated cluster of lifestyle habits, individuals do not always, or perhaps even usually, assess risks as separate items, each in its own domain. Life planning takes account of a 'package' of risks rather than calculating the implications of distinct segments of risky behaviour. Taking certain risks in pursuit of a given lifestyle, in other words, is accepted to be within 'tolerable limits' as part of that overall package.

Individuals seek to colonise the future for themselves as an intrinsic part of their life-planning. As in the case of collective futures, the degree to which the future realm can be successfully invaded is partial, and subject to the various vagaries of risk assessment. All individuals establish a portfolio of risk assessment, which may be more or less clearly articulated, well informed and 'open'; or alternatively may be largely inertial. Thinking in terms of risk becomes more or less inevitable and most people will be conscious also of the risks of *refusing* to think in this way, even if they may choose to ignore those risks. In the charged reflexive settings of high modernity, living on 'automatic pilot' becomes more and more difficult to do, and it becomes less and less possible to protect any lifestyle, no matter how firmly pre-established, from the generalised risk climate.

The argument at this point should not be misunderstood. Much risk assessment proceeds on the level of practical consciousness and, as will be indicated below, the protective cocoon of basic trust blocks off most otherwise potentially disturbing happenings which impinge on the individual's life circumstances. Being 'at ease' in the world is certainly problematic in the era of high modernity, in which a framework of 'care' and the development of 'shared histories' with others are largely reflexive achievements. But such histories often provide settings in which ontological security is sustained in the relatively unproblematic way, at least for specific phases of an individual's life.

Risk, trust and the protective cocoon

The world of 'normal appearances', I stressed earlier, is more than just a mutually sustained show of interaction which individuals put on for one another. The routines individuals follow, as their time-space paths criss-cross in the contexts of daily life, constitute that life as 'normal' and 'predictable'. Normality is managed in fine detail within the textures of social activity: this applies equally to the body and to the articulation of the individual's involvements and projects. The individual must be there in the flesh to be there at all,[20] and the flesh that is the corporeal self has to be chronically guarded and succoured – in the immediacy of every day-to-day situation as well as in life-planning extending over time and space. The body is in some sense perennially at risk. The possibility of bodily injury is ever-present, even in the most familiar of surroundings. The home, for example, is a dangerous place: a high proportion of serious injuries are brought about by accidents in the domestic milieu. 'A body', as Goffman tersely puts it, 'is a piece of consequential equipment, and its owner is always putting it on the line.'[21]

I suggested in chapter 2 that basic trust is fundamental to the connections between daily routines and normal appearances. Within the settings of daily life, basic trust is expressed as a bracketing-out of possible events or issues which could, in certain circumstances, be cause for alarm. What other people appear to do, and who they appear to be, is usually accepted as the same as what they are actually doing and who they actually are. Consider, however, the world of the spy who, in the interests of self-preservation, cannot accept the range of normal appearances in the way that other people usually do. The spy suspends part of the generalised trust which is ordinarily vested in 'things as they are', and suffers tortuous anxieties about what would otherwise be mundane events. To the ordinary person a wrong number may be a minor irritation, but to the undercover agent it may be a disturbing sign that causes alarm.

A feeling of bodily and psychic ease in the routine circumstances of everyday life, as was stressed earlier, is only acquired with great effort. If we mostly seem less fragile than we really are in the contexts of our actions, it is because of long-term learning processes whereby potential threats are avoided or immobilised. The simplest action, such as walking without falling over, avoiding collisions with objects, crossing the road or using a knife and fork, had to be learned in circumstances which originally had connotations of fatefulness. The 'uneventful' character of much of day-to-day life is the result of a skilled watchfulness that only long schooling produces, and is crucial to the protective cocoon which all regularised action presumes.

These phenomena can be usefully analysed using Goffman's notion of the *Umwelt*, a core of (accomplished) normalcy with which individuals and groups surround themselves.[22] The notion comes from the study of animal behaviour. Animals maintain a sensitivity to a surrounding physical area in terms of threats which may emanate from it. The area of sensitivity varies between different species. Some types of animal are able to sense sounds, scents and movements from many miles away; for other animals, the extent of the *Umwelt* is more limited.

In the case of human beings, the *Umwelt* includes more than the immediate physical surroundings. It extends over indefinite spans of time and space, and corresponds to the system of relevances, to use Schutz's term, which enframes the individual's life. Individuals are more or less constantly alert to signals that relate here-and-now activities to spatially distant persons or events of concern to them, and to projects of life-planning of varying temporal span. The *Umwelt* is a 'moving' world of normalcy which the individual takes around from situation to situation, although this feat depends also on others who confirm, or take part in, reproducing that world. The individual creates, as it were, a 'moving wave-front of relevance' which orders contingent events in relation to risk and potential alarms. Time-space movement – the physical mobility of the body from setting to setting – centres the individual's concerns in the physical properties of context, but contextual dangers are monitored in relation to other, more diffuse sources of threat. In the globalised circumstances of today, the *Umwelt* includes awareness of high-consequence risks, which represent dangers from which no one can get completely out of range.

In the settings of modernity, from which *fortuna* has largely retreated, the individual ordinarily separates the *Umwelt* into designed and adventitious happenings. The adventitious forms a continuing backdrop to the foreground relevances from which the individual creates a textured flow of action. The differentiation also allows the person to bracket out a whole host of actual and potential happenings, consigning them to a realm which still has to be watched over, but with minimal carefulness. This has the corollary that each person in an interaction situation presumes that much of what she does is a matter of indifference to others – although indifference still has to be managed in co-present public situations, in the shape of codes of civil inattention.

In contrast to the paranoiac, the ordinary individual is thus able to believe that moments which are fateful for his own life are not the result of fate. Luck is what one needs when one contemplates a risky action, but it has a broader connotation, too, as a means of relating chance to fatefulness (as good or as bad luck). Since the distinction between what is adventitious and what is not is in practice sometimes difficult to draw, however, serious tensions can arise when events or activities are 'misinterpreted' – as where an event affecting another is held to be contrived where it is not, or vice versa. The discovery of contrivance may easily be cause for alarm – a husband is led to suspect infidelity when he finds that an apparently chance meeting between his wife and an ex-lover was actually less than a chance encounter after all. The presumption of generalised trust that the recognition of adventitious happenings involves concerns future anticipations as well as current interpretative understandings. In most circumstances of interaction, an individual assumes that others co-present will not use their current dealings with him as a basis for acts of malevolence at some future time. The future exploitation of current situations, however, is always an area of potential vulnerability.

The protective cocoon is the *mantle of trust that makes possible the sustaining of a viable Umwelt.* That substratum of trust is the condition and the outcome of the routinised nature of an 'uneventful' world – a universe of actual and possible events surrounding the individual's current activities and projects for the future, in which the bulk of what goes on is 'non-consequential' so far as that person is concerned. Trust here incorporates actual and potential events in the physical world as well as encounters and activities in the sphere of social life. Living in the circumstances of modern social institutions, in which risk is recognised as risk, creates certain specific difficulties for the generalised vesting of trust in 'discounted possibilities' – possibilities that are bracketed out as irrelevant to the individual's self-identity and pursuits. The psychological security that conceptions of fate can offer is largely foreclosed, as is the personalising of natural events in the shape of spirits, demons or other beings. The chronic constitutive intrusion of abstract systems into day-to-day life creates further problems influencing the relation between generalised trust and the *Umwelt.*

In modern social conditions, the more the individual seeks reflexively to forge a self-identity, the more he or she will be aware that current practices shape future outcomes. In so far as conceptions of *fortuna* are completely abandoned, assessment of risk – or the balance of risk and opportunity – becomes the core element of the personal colonising of future domains. Yet a psychologically crucial part of the protective cocoon is the deflection of the hazardous consequences that thinking in terms of risk presumes. Since risk profiling is such a central part of modernity, awareness of probability ratios for different types of endeavour or event form one means whereby this can be achieved. What could 'go wrong' can be pushed to one side on the grounds that it is so unlikely that it can be put out of mind. Air travel is usually calculated to be the safest form of transport in terms of various criteria. The risk of being killed in a plane crash, for the regular commercial airlines, is about one in 850,000 per trip – a figure derived by dividing the total number of passenger trips over a given period of time by the number of air-crash victims during that period.[23] It has sometimes been asserted that sitting in a seat in an airliner five miles above the ground is the safest place in the world, given the number of accidents which occur at home, work or in other milieux. Yet many people remain terrified of flying, and a certain minority who have the opportunity or resources to travel by air refuse to do so. They cannot put out of their minds what it would be like if things *did* go wrong.

Interestingly, some such people are willing to travel on the roads without too much worry, even though they are almost certainly aware that the risks of serious injury or death are higher. The weight of the counterfactual seems to matter a lot in this – horrific though road accidents might be, they perhaps do not evoke quite the same degree of dread as the scenario of an air crash.

Deferment in time and remoteness in space are other factors that can reduce the disquiet that awareness of risk as risk might otherwise produce. A young person in good health might be conscious enough of the risks of smoking, but consign the potential dangers to a time that seems impossibly distant in the future – such as when he or she reaches forty – and thus effectively blot out those dangers. Risks remote from an individual's daily contexts of life – such as high-consequence risks – might also be bracketed out of the *Umwelt*. The dangers they present, in other words, are thought of as too far removed from a person's own practical involvements for that individual seriously to contemplate them as possibilities.

Yet notions of fate refuse to disappear altogether, and are found in uneasy combination with an outlook of the secular risk type and with attitudes of fatalism. A belief in the providential nature of things is one sense in which a conception of *fortuna* crops up – an important phenomenon, and one connected with some basic characteristics of modernity itself. Providential interpretations of history were major elements of Enlightenment culture, and it is not surprising that their residues are still to be found in modes of thinking in day-to-day life. Attitudes to high-

consequence risks probably often retain strong traces of a providential outlook. We may live in an apocalyptic world, facing an
array of global dangers; yet an individual might feel that governments, scientists or other technical specialists can be trusted to
take the appropriate steps to counter them. Or else he feels that
'everything is bound to come out all right in the end.'

Alternatively, such attitudes may relapse into fatalism. A fatalistic ethos is one possible generalised response to a secular risk
culture. There are risks which we all confront but which, as
individuals – and perhaps even collectively – none of us can do
much about. The things that happen in life, the proponent of such
an orientation might declare, are in the end a matter of chance.
Therefore we might as well decide that 'whatever will be will be',
and leave matters there. This having been said, it would be
difficult to be fatalistic in all areas of life, given the pressures
today which propel us towards taking an active, innovative attitude towards our personal and collective circumstances. Fatalism
in specific risk contexts tends to devolve into the more encompassing attitudes of what I have elsewhere called 'pragmatic acceptance' or 'cynical pessimism'. The former is an attitude of generalised coping – taking each day as it comes – while the latter repels
anxieties through world-weary humour.[24]

There are many unsought-after events which may puncture the
protective mantle of ontological security and cause alarm. Alarms
come in all shapes and sizes, from the four-minute warning of
Armageddon to a slip on the proverbial banana skin. Some are
bodily symptoms or failings, others are anxieties sparked by an
anticipated or actual failure of cherished projects, or by unexpected events that intrude into the *Umwelt*. The most challenging
situations for the individual to master, however, are those where
alarms coincide with consequential changes – fateful moments.
At fateful moments, the individual is likely to recognise that she
is faced with an altered set of risks and possibilities. In such
circumstances, she is called on to question routinised habits of
relevant kinds, even sometimes those most closely integrated
with self-identity. Various strategies may be adopted. A person
may, for whatever reason, simply carry on with established
modes of behaviour, perhaps choosing to disregard whether or
not these conform well with new situational demands. In some
circumstances, though, this is impossible: for example, someone

who has separated from his spouse can no longer carry on in the same way as he did while married. Many fateful moments by their very nature oblige the individual to change habits and readjust projects.

Fateful moments do not only 'befall' individuals – they are sometimes cultivated or deliberately sought after. Institutionalised risk environments, and other more individualised risk activities, provide a major category of settings in which fatefulness is actively created.[25] Such situations make possible the display of daring, resourcefulness, skill and sustained endeavour, where people are only too aware of the risks involved in what they are doing, but use them to create an edge which routine circumstances lack. Most institutionalised risk environments, including those in the economic sector, are contests: spaces in which risk-taking pits individuals against one another, or against obstacles in the physical world. Contests call for committed, opportunistic action in a way that situations of 'pure chance', like lotteries, do not. The thrills that can be achieved in cultivated risk-taking depend on deliberate exposure to uncertainty, thus allowing the activity in question to stand out in relief against the routines of ordinary life. Thrills can be sought through risk-taking of high order, vicariously in spectator sports, or in activities where the actual level of risk to life and limb is small, but where dangerous situations are simulated (such as a roller-coaster ride). The thrill of risk-taking activities, as Balint says, involves several discernible attitudes: awareness of exposure to danger, a voluntary exposure to such danger, and the more or less confident expectation of overcoming it.[26] Funfairs mimic most of the situations in which thrills are sought elsewhere, but in a controlled way that takes away two key elements: the individual's active mastery; and the circumstances of uncertainty which both call for that mastery and allow it to be demonstrated.

Goffman points out that someone who is strongly inclined towards cultivated risk-taking – like the inveterate gambler – is able to discern opportunities for the play of chance in many circumstances which others would treat as routine and uneventful. Spotting such angles, one might add, is a way of turning up possibilities for developing new modes of activity within familiar contexts. For where contingency is discovered, or manufactured, situations which seem closed and pre-defined can again look open. Cultivated risk here converges with some of the most basic orientations of modernity. The capability to disturb the fixity of things, open up new pathways, and thereby colonise a segment of a novel future, is integral to modernity's unsettling character.

We could say, I think, that cultivated risk-taking represents an 'experiment with trust' (in the sense of basic trust) which consequently has implications for an individual's self-identity. We could redefine Balint's 'confident expectation' as trust – trust that the dangers which are deliberately courted will be conquered. Mastery of such dangers is an act of self-vindication and a demonstration, to the self and others, that under difficult circumstances one can come through. Fear produces the thrill, but it is fear that is redirected in the form of mastery. The thrill of cultivated risk-taking feeds on that 'courage to be' which is generic to early socialisation. Courage is demonstrated in cultivated risk-taking precisely as a quality which is placed on trial: the individual submits to a test of integrity by showing the capacity to envisage the 'down-side' of the risks being run, and press ahead regardless, even though there is no constraint to do so. The search for thrills, or more soberly for the sense of mastery that comes with the deliberate confrontation of dangers, no doubt derives in some part from its contrast with routine. Yet it also takes on psychological fuel from a contrast with the more deferred and ambiguous gratifications that emerge from other types of encounters with risk. In cultivated risk-taking, the encounter with danger and its resolution are bound up in the same activity, whereas in other consequential settings the payoff of chosen strategies may not be seen for years afterwards.

Risk, trust and abstract systems

The abstract systems of modernity create large areas of relative security for the continuance of day-to-day life. Thinking in terms of risk certainly has its unsettling aspects, as was suggested earlier in the chapter, but it is also a means of seeking to stabilise outcomes, a mode of colonising the future. The more or less constant, profound and rapid momentum of change characteristic of modern institutions, coupled with structured reflexivity, mean that on the level of everyday practice as well as philosophical interpretation, nothing can be taken for granted. What is acceptable/appropriate/recommended behaviour today may be seen differently tomorrow in the light of altered circumstances or incoming knowledge-claims. Yet at the same time, so far as many daily transactions are concerned, activities are successfully routinised through their recombination across time-space.

Consider some examples. Modern money is an abstract system of formidable complexity, a prime illustration of a symbolic system that connects truly global processes to the mundane trivialities of daily life. A money economy helps regularise the provision of many day-to-day needs, even for the poorer strata in the developed societies (and even though many transactions, including some of a purely economic nature, are handled in non-monetary terms). Money meshes with many other abstract systems in global arenas and in local economies. The existence of organised monetary exchange makes possible the regularised contacts and exchanges 'at distance' (in time and in space) on which such an interlacing of global and local influences depends. In conjunction with a division of labour of parallel complexity, the monetary system routinises the provision of the goods and services necessary to everyday life. Not only is a much greater variety of goods and foodstuffs available to the average individual than in pre-modern economies, but their availability is no longer governed so directly by the idiosyncrasies of time and place. Seasonal foodstuffs, for example, can often now be bought at any time of the year, and food items that cannot be grown at all in a particular country or region may be regularly obtained there.

This is a colonising of time as well as an ordering of space, since provisioning for the future, for the individual consumer, is rendered unnecessary. In fact, it is of little use to hoard stocks of food – although some might choose to do so in the light of high-consequence risks – for the ordinary business of life in a modern economy that is functioning vigourously. Such a practice would increase costs, since it would commit income that could otherwise be used for different purposes. Hoarding could in any case be no more than a short-term strategy, unless the individual has developed the capacity to furnish his or her own food. So long as the person vests trust in the monetary system and the division of labour, these allow for greater security and predictability than could be achieved by any other means.

As another illustration, consider the provision of water, power for heating and lighting, and sanitised sewage disposal. Such systems, and the expertise on which they draw, act to stabilise many of the settings of day-to-day life – at the same time as, like money, they radically transform them as compared to pre-modern ways of life. In the developed countries, for most of the population, water is available at the turn of a tap, domestic heating and illumination are equally to hand, and personal sewage is quickly flushed away. The organised piping of water has substantially reduced one of the great uncertainties which afflicted life in many pre-modern societies, the inconstant character of water supply.[27] Readily available domestic water has made possible standards of personal cleanliness and hygiene that have made a major contribution to improved health. Constant running water is also necessary for modern sewage systems, and thus for the contribution to health which they have facilitated. Electricity, gas and continually available solid fuels similarly help regulate standards of bodily comfort, and provide power for cooking and the operation of many domestic devices. All these have regularised settings of activity inside and outside the home. Electric lighting has made possible the colonisation of the night.[28] In the domestic milieu, routines are governed by the need for regular daily sleep rather than by the alternating of day and night, which can be cross-cut without any difficulty. Outside the home, an increasing range of organisations operate on a twenty-four hour basis.

Technological intervention into nature is the condition of the development of abstract systems such as these, but of course affects many other aspects of modern social life as well. The 'socialisation of nature' has helped stabilise a variety of previously irregular or unpredictable influences on human behaviour. Control of nature was an important endeavour in pre-modern times, especially in the larger agrarian states, in which irrigation schemes, the clearing of forests and other modes of managing nature for human purposes were commonplace. As Dubos has emphasised, by the modern period Europe was already very largely a socialised environment, shaped by many generations of peasants from the original forests and marshes.[29] Yet over the past two or three centuries the process of human intervention into nature has been massively extended; moreover, it is no longer confined to certain areas or regions, but like other aspects of modernity has become globalised. Many aspects of social activity have become more secure as a result of these developments. Travel, for example, has become regularised, and made safer, by the construction of modern roads, trains, ships and planes. As with all abstract systems, enormous changes in the nature and scope of travel have been associated with these innovations. But it is now easy for anyone with the necessary financial resources casually to undertake journeys that two centuries ago would have been only for the most intrepid, and would have taken much longer to accomplish.

There is greater security in many aspects of day-to-day life – yet there is also a serious price to pay for these advances. Abstract systems depend on trust, yet they provide none of the moral rewards which can be obtained from personalised trust, or were often available in traditional settings from the moral frameworks within which everyday life was undertaken. Moreover, the wholesale penetration of abstract systems into daily life creates risks which the individual is not well placed to confront; high-consequence risks fall into this category. Greater interdependence, up to and including gobally independent systems, means greater vulnerability when untoward events occur that affect those systems as a whole. Such is the case with each of the examples mentioned above. The money a person possesses, however little it may be, is subject to vagaries of the global economy which even the most powerful of nations may be able to do very little about. A local monetary system may collapse completely, as happened in Germany in the 1920s: in some circumstances, which at the moment we might not envisage at all, this might perhaps happen to the global monetary order, with disastrous consequences for billions of people. A prolonged drought, or other problems with centralised water systems, can sometimes have more disturbing results than periodic water shortages might have had in pre-modern times; while any prolonged shortage of power dislocates the ordinary activities of vast numbers of people.

Socialised nature provides a telling – and substantively a massively important – illustration of these characteristics. McKibben argues, with great plausibility, that human intervention in the natural world has been so profound, and so encompassing, that today we can speak of the 'end of nature'. Socialised nature is quite different from the old natural environment, which existed separately from human endeavours and formed a relatively unchanging backdrop to them. 'It is like the old nature in that it makes its points through what we think of as natural processes (rain, wind, heat), but it offers none of the consolations – the retreat from the human world, a sense of permanence, or even of eternity.'[30]

Nature in the old sense, McKibben points out, was quite unpredictable: storms could come without warning, bad summers destroy the crops, devastating floods occur as the result of unexpected rain. Modern technology and expertise have made better monitoring of weather conditions possible, and improved management of the natural environment has allowed many pre-existing hazards to be overcome, or their impact minimalised. Yet socialised nature is in some fundamental respects more unreliable than 'old nature', because we cannot be sure how the new natural order will behave. Take the hypothesis of global warming, a phenomenon which, if it is really occurring, will wreak havoc around the world. McKibben concludes that the available evidence supports the view that the 'greenhouse effect' is real, and in fact argues that the processes involved are already too far under way for them to be effectively countered in the short or medium term. He may be right about this. The point is that, at the time of writing at any rate, no one can say with assurance that it is *not* happening. The dangers posed by global warming are high-consequence risks which collectively we face, but about which precise risk assessment is virtually impossible.

Security, deskilling and abstract systems

Abstract systems deskill – not only in the workplace, but in all the sectors of social life that they touch. The deskilling of day-to-day life is an alienating and fragmenting phenomenon so far as the self is concerned. Alienating, because the intrusion of abstract systems, especially expert systems, into all aspects of day-to-day life undermines pre-existing forms of local control. In the much more strongly localised life of most pre-modern societies, all individuals developed many skills and types of 'local knowledge', in Geertz's sense, relevant to their day-to-day lives. Everyday survival depended on integrating such skills into practical modes of organising activities within the contexts of the local community and the physical environment. With the expansion of abstract systems, however, the conditions of daily life become transformed and recombined across much larger time-space tracts; such disembedding processes are processes of loss. It would be wrong, however, to see such loss as power passing from some individuals or groups to others. Transfers of power do occur in such a way, but they are not exhaustive. For instance, the development of professional medicine has led to the 'sieving off' of knowledge and curative skills once held by many laypeople. Doctors and many other types of professional expert derive power from the knowledge-claims which their codes of practice incorporate. Yet because the specialisation inherent in expertise means that all experts are themselves laypeople most of the time, the advent of abstract systems sets up modes of social influence which no one directly controls. It is just this phenomenon that underlies the emergence of high-consequence risks.

Braverman was mistaken to suppose that, in the sphere of work, a one-way process of deskilling occurs. In the workplace, new skills are continually created, and in some part developed by those whose activities are deskilled. Something similar is true in many other sectors of social activity where the influence of abstract systems has made itself felt. The reappropriation of knowledge and control on the part of lay actors is a basic aspect of what I have sometimes termed the 'dialectic of control'. Whatever skills and forms of knowledge laypeople may lose, they remain skilful and knowledgeable in the contexts of action in which their activities take place and which, in some part, those activities continually reconstitute. Everyday skill and knowledgeability thus stands in dialectical connection to the expropriating effects of abstract systems, continually influencing and reshaping the very impact of such systems on day-to-day existence.

What is involved is not just reappropriation but, in some circumstances and contexts, *empowerment.* Coupled to disembedding, the expansion of abstract systems creates increasing quanta of power – the power of human beings to alter the material world and transform the conditions of their own actions.

The reappropriation of such power provides generic opportunities not available in prior historical eras. Such empowerment is both individual and collective, although the relations between these two levels is often tangled and difficult to unravel, both for the analyst and for the layperson on the level of everyday life.

The profusion of abstract systems is directly bound up with the panoramas of choice which confront the individual in day-to-day activity. On the one hand, there is often a selection to be made between local or lay ways of doing things and procedures on offer from the domain of abstract systems. This is not simply a confrontation of the 'traditional' and the modern, although such a situation is common enough. As a result of processes of reappropriation, an indefinite number of spaces between lay belief and practice and the sphere of abstract systems are opened up. In any given situation, provided that the resources of time and other requisites are available, the individual has the possibility of a partial or more full-blown reskilling in respect of specific decisions or contemplated courses of action.

Empowerment and dilemmas of expertise

Consider, for example, a person with a back problem. What should she do to seek treatment? If she were in Britain, she might go to see a general practitioner under the auspices of the National Health Service. The general practitioner might refer her to a specialist, who may perhaps offer recommendations or provide services which satisfy her. But it could easily happen that she finds that nothing the specialist is able to do offers much help in alleviating the condition. The diagnosis of problems to do with the back is notoriously problematic, and most of the forms of treatment available are controversial both within the medical profession and outside. Some medical specialists, for example, recommend operating on disc ruptures. Yet there are studies indicating that patients with the disc problem concerned are almost as likely to recover without surgery as they are with it. There are large differences between different countries in respect of this issue. Thus the number of patients per thousand for whom operations are recommended for disc troubles in the United States is ten times as high as in Britain, this difference representing, among other things, a variation in generic philosophies of how best to treat back problems between the two countries. If she chooses to inquire further, our patient will discover that within orthodox medical circles there are major differences of opinion about operating techniques, even when an invasive treatment has been agreed on as the best strategy. For instance, some surgeons favour microsurgery over more established spinal surgical procedures.

Investigating a little more deeply, the patient would discover that a variety of other modes of back therapy, held by their proponents to cover ruptured discs as well as many other transitory and more chronic back conditions, are available. These therapies differ not only in the forms of treatment they offer, but in respect of the interpretations they provide of the causal origins of back pains and pathologies. Osteopathy is based on rather different principles from those followed by chiropractors. Each of these orientations also contains competing schools. Other available forms of back treatment include physiotherapy, massage, acupuncture, exercise therapy, reflexology, systems of postural adjustment like the Alexander Method, drug therapies, diet therapies, hands-on healing – and no doubt other therapeutic methods also. One school of thought holds that the vast majority of back problems, including many of a quite serious nature, have their origins in psychosomatic stress, and should therefore be treated by remedying the sources of stress, rather than concentrating directly on the back itself. According to such schools of thought, psychotherapy, meditation, yoga, bio-feedback techniques and other modes of relaxation, or a combination of these, provide the best means of treatment.

At this point the patient might quite reasonably decide that enough is enough and resolve to inform herself about the nature of her complaint and the vying remedies for it. Many non-technical books about the back are available on the popular market. Most give an interpretation of the general state of medical knowledge about the spine and try to provide an informed guide to the competing therapies available. There is, of course, considerable agreement among otherwise differing authorities about the structural anatomy of the body. It would not take long for the sufferer to master a basic understanding of the structural problems which may affect the back. Reskilling/

appropriation would be possible fairly readily in that she could learn about at least the outlines of the different treatments available and how they compare with those suggested by the original specialist. Deciding which to opt for, if any, would be more difficult because she would need to balance off the various claims made by the different approaches. There is no overarching authority to whom she might turn – a characteristic dilemma of many situations in conditions of high modernity.

Yet if such a person takes the trouble to reskill appropriately, a reasonably informed choice can in fact be made. All such choices are not simply behavioural options: they tend to refract back upon, and be mobilised to develop, the narrative of self-identity. A decision to go along with conventional or high-tech medicine, for example, is likely to be only partly a matter of informed choice: ordinarily it also 'says something' about a person's lifestyle. It may mean that an individual is following a fairly pre-established pattern of behaviour, perhaps coupled to certain forms of deference. This might be the case if a person goes to see the general practitioner and then the specialist recommended, and simply follows whatever that specialist suggests, in deference to them both as authoritative members of the medical profession. To opt for a form of alternative medicine, particularly of one of the more esoteric varieties, might signal something about, and actually contribute to, certain lifestyle decisions which a person then enacts.

In most such decisions, conceptions of *fortuna*, fatalism, pragmatism and conscious risk-taking are likely to be mingled together. Since experts so frequently disagree, even professionals at the core of a given field of expertise may very well find themselves in much the same position as a layperson confronting a similar decision. In a system without final authorities, even the most cherished beliefs underlying expert systems are open to revision, and quite commonly they are regularly altered. Empowerment is routinely available to laypeople as part of the reflexivity of modernity, but there are often problems about how such empowerment becomes translated into convictions and into action. A certain element of *fortuna*, or of fatalism, thus allows a person to 'ride along with' a decision which can only be partially warranted in the light of whatever local and expert information is to hand.

Summary: authority, expertise and risk

It was emphasised earlier that no one can disengage completely from the abstract systems of modernity: this is one of the consequences of living in a world of high-consequence risks. Yet, of course, lifestyles and lifestyle sectors can be tailored to navigate a course between the different possibilities offered in a world reconstituted through the impact of abstract systems. Trust may be suspended in some or many of the systems which routinely and more sporadically impinge on the individual's life. It would be very difficult indeed, if not impossible, to withdraw completely from the modern monetary system. Yet an individual could choose to keep whatever assets he had in the form of goods or personal property; and he might have as little to do with banks or other financial organisations as he could. Many possible shadings of scepticism or doubt can be reconciled with a pragmatic or fatalistic attitude towards abstract systems affecting one's life chances.

Others may take lifestyle decisions which propel them back in the direction of more traditional authorities. Religious fundamentalism, for example, provides clear-cut answers as to what to do in an era which has abandoned final authorities: those final authorities can be conjured up again by appeal to the age-old formulae of religion. The more 'enclosing' a given religious order is, the more it 'resolves' the problem of how to live in a world of multiple options. More attenuated forms of religious belief, however, may clearly also offer significant support in shaping significant life decisions.

Most of these dilemmas become particularly acute, or are experienced with special force, during the fateful moments of an individual's life. Since fateful moments, by definition, are highly consequential, the individual feels at a crossroads in terms of overall life-planning. Fateful moments are phases when people might choose to have recourse to more traditional authorities. In this sense, they may seek refuge in pre-established beliefs and in familiar modes of activity. On the other hand, fateful moments also often mark periods of reskilling and empowerment. They are points at which, no matter how reflexive an individual may be in the shaping of her self-identity, she has to sit up and take notice of new demands as well as new possibilities. At such moments, when life has to be seen anew, it is not surprising that endeavours at reskilling are likely to be particularly important and intensely pursued. Where consequential decisions are concerned, individuals are often stimulated to devote the time and energy necessary to generate increased mastery of the circumstances they confront. Fateful moments are transition points which have major implications not just for the circumstances of an individual's future conduct, but for self-identity. For consequential decisions, once taken, will reshape the reflexive project of identity through the lifestyle consequences which ensue.

Hence it is not surprising that at fateful moments individuals are today likely to encounter expert systems which precisely focus on the reconstruction of self-identity: counselling or therapy. A decision to enter therapy can generate empowerment. At the same time, it is important to add, such a decision is not different in nature from other lifestyle decisions made in the settings of modernity. What type of therapy should one pursue, and for how long? As the book *Self-Therapy* shows, it is perhaps possible for an individual effectively to reorient his life without the direct consultation of an expert or professional. On the other hand, many therapists hold that without regular contact with a professional counsellor there is no hope of real personal change. A very considerable diversity of therapies, all of which claim to treat an overlapping range of similar problems, now exist. As a measure of the level of disagreement between different schools, we might compare classical psychoanalysis with behavioural therapy based on conditioning. There are many therapists who abide by the basic tenets Freud established for psychoanalysis, and formulate their therapeutic procedures according to them. Yet some proponents of behaviour therapy claim that psychoanalysis is utterly without validity as a mode of therapy. In addition, a variety of subdivisions of psychoanalysis exist, coupled to dozens of other varying schools of thought and technique. The reflexive encounter with expert systems helping to reconstitute the self therefore expresses some of the central dilemmas to which modernity gives rise.

5
The Sequestration of Experience

It is often said that the overriding emphasis of modernity is on control – the subordination of the world to human dominance. The assertion is surely correct, but put thus baldly it needs considerable elaboration. One thing control means is the subordination of nature to human purposes, organised via the colonising of the future. This process looks at first sight like an extension of 'instrumental reason': the application of humanly organised principles of science and technology to the mastery of the natural world. Looked at more closely, however, what we see is the emergence of *an internally referential system of knowledge and power*. It is in these terms that we should understand the phrase 'the end of nature'. There has taken place a marked acceleration and deepening of human control of nature, directly involved with the globalisation of social and economic activity. The 'end of nature' means that the natural world has become in large part a 'created environment', consisting of humanly structured systems whose motive power and dynamics derive from socially organised knowledge-claims rather than from influences exogenous to human activity.

That nature becomes an internally referential system needs stressing, because the natural environment seems so plainly separate from the universe of social activity. It is perhaps easier to see that social life itself becomes internally referential, along with the mobilising of self-identity. Yet the internal referentiality of modern social life has often been confused with a distinction drawn between 'society' and 'nature'; and, correspondingly, such referentiality has often been thought of as intrinsic to all social systems, rather than primarily to the institutions of modernity.

But social systems only become internally referential, on a thoroughgoing basis at any rate, in so far as they become institutionally reflexive and thereby tied to the colonisation of the future. To the degree that social life is organised according to tradition, taken-for-granted habit or pragmatic adjustment to exogenous nature, it lacks that internal referentiality fundamental to modernity's dynamics. Crucial to these processes is the evaporation of morality, particularly in so far as moral outlooks are integrated in a secure way with day-to-day practice. For moral principles run counter to the concept of risk and to the mobilising of dynamics of control. Morality is *extrinsic* so far as the colonising of the future is concerned.

As distinct from mere habit, tradition always has a 'binding', normative character. 'Normative' here in turn implies a moral component: in traditional practices, the bindingness of activities expresses precepts about how things should or should not be done. Traditions of behaviour have their own moral endowment, which specifically resists the technical power to introduce something new. The fixity of tradition does not derive from its accumulation of past wisdom; rather, coordination of the past with the present is achieved through adherence to the normative precepts tradition incorporates. As Shils comments:

> tradition is thus far more than the statistically frequent recurrence over a succession of generations of similar beliefs, practices, institutions, and works. The recurrence is a result of the normative consequences – sometimes the normative intention – of presentation and of the acceptance of the tradition as normative. It is this normative transmission which links the generations of the dead with the generations of the living in the constitution of a society ... the dead ... are objects of attachment, but what is more significant is that their works and the norms contained in their practices influence the actions of subsequent generations to whom they are unknown. The normative core of tradition is the inertial force which holds society in a given form over time.[1]

Internal referentiality and the lifespan

The development of internally referential social systems is at the origin of the reflexive project of the self. The creation of an internally referential lifespan has been decisively influenced by a series of concurrent social changes. Each of these acts to 'pick out' the lifespan as a distinctive and enclosed trajectory from other surrounding events in the following ways:

1   The lifespan emerges as a separate segment of time, distanced from the life cycle of the generations. The idea of the 'life cycle', indeed, makes very little sense once the connections between the individual life and the interchange of the generations have been broken. As Shils's remarks aptly emphasise, tradition and the continuity of the generations are inherently tied to one another. Generational differences are essentially a mode of time-reckoning in premodern societies. A generation is a distinct kinship cohort or order which sets the individual's life within a sequence of collective transitions. In modern times, however, the concept of 'generation' increasingly makes sense only against the backdrop of standardised time. We speak, in other words, of the 'generation of the 1950s', 'the generation of the 1960s' and so forth. Temporal succession in this sense retains little of the resonance of collective processes of transition characteristic of earlier eras. In traditional contexts, the life-cycle carries strong connotations of renewal, since each generation in some substantial part rediscovers and relives modes of life of its forerunners. Renewal loses most of its meaning in the settings of high modernity where practices are repeated only in so far as they are reflexively justifiable.[2]

2   The lifespan becomes separated from the externalities of place, while place itself is undermined by the expansion of disembedding mechanisms. In most traditional cultures, notwithstanding the population migrations which were relatively common, and the long distances sometimes travelled by the few, most social life was localised. The prime factor that has altered this situation does not lie with increased mobility; rather, place becomes thoroughly penetrated by disembedding mechanisms, which recombine the local activities into time-space relations of ever-widening scope. Place becomes phantasmagoric.[3] While the milieux in which people live quite often remain the source of local attachments, place does not form the parameter of experience; and it does not offer the security of the ever-familiar which traditional locales characteristically display. The intensifying of mediated experience also plays a significant

part here. Familiarity (with social events and people as well as with places) no longer depends solely, or perhaps even primarily, upon local milieux.

Place thus becomes much less significant than it used to be as an external referent for the lifespan of the individual. Spatially located activity becomes more and more bound up with the reflexive project of the self. Where a person lives, after young adulthood at least, is a matter of choice organised primarily in terms of the person's life-planning. Of course, as with all such processes, dialectical forms of counter-reaction are possible. Active attempts to re-embed the lifespan within a local milieu may be undertaken in various ways. Some, such as the cultivation of a sense of community pride, are probably too vague to do more than recapture a glimmer of what used to be. Only when it is possible to gear regular practices to specifics of place can re-embedding occur in a significant way: but in conditions of high modernity this is difficult to achieve.

3   The lifespan becomes more and more freed from externalities associated with pre-established ties to other individuals and groups. Kinship ties of various kinds were plainly the prime external anchor-ings of the individual's life experience in most pre-modern contexts. Kinship relations helped determine, and in many cases completely defined, key decisions affecting the course of events for the individual over the whole lifespan. Decisions about when and whom to marry, where to live, how many children to aim for, how to care for one's children, how to spend one's old age were among the more obvious examples. The externalities of place and kinship normally were closely connected. The transmission of property, including especially family heirlooms and familial dwellings, also played an important part. In modern social conditions, successive family groups only rarely continue residence in the same building. In rural areas, or among a few remaining aristocratic groups, there are still houses which have been lived in by members of the same family for long periods, even centuries. But for the mass of the population such a phenomenon becomes virtually unknown and the notion of 'ances-tors', so central to the lives of many in pre-modern settings, becomes diffuse and difficult to recover.

Lacking external referents supplied by others, the lifespan again emerges as a trajectory which relates above all to the individual's projects and plans. Others always figure in such life-planning, of course, from the members of the family of orientation to subsequent familial partners, children, friends, colleagues and acquaintances. New spheres of intimacy with some such others become crucial elements of frameworks of trust developed by the individual. But these have to be mobilised through the reflexive ordering of the lifespan as a discrete and internally referential phenomenon.

4 The lifespan becomes structured around 'open experience thresholds', rather than ritualised passages. Ritual is itself an external referent and much has been made by social observers of the decline of ritual activities in relation to major transitions of life: birth, adolescence, marriage and death. The relative absence of ritual in modern social contexts, it has been suggested, removes an important psychological prop to the individual's capacity to cope with such transitions. Whether or not such is the case – for, after all, Radcliffe-Brown suggested, in his celebrated debate with Malinowski about this issue, that ritual often produces anxiety rather than alleviates it – what is important for the discussion here concerns the consequences for individual decision-making. Each phase of transition tends to become an identity crisis – and is often reflexively known to the individual as such.[4] The lifespan, in fact, is constructed in terms of the anticipated need to confront and resolve such crisis phases, at least where an individual's reflexive awareness is highly developed.

To speak of the lifespan as internally referential is not the same as arguing from the premises of methodological individualism. The idea of the 'self-sufficient individual' certainly emerged in substantial part as a response to the developing institutions of modernity. But such a methodological standpoint is not implied in the analysis elaborated in this book. Nor does it follow from what has been said above that the individual becomes separated from wider contexts of social events. To some degree, the contrary is the case: the self establishes a trajectory which can only become coherent through the reflexive use of the broader social environment. The impetus towards control, geared to reflexivity, thrusts the self into the outer world in ways which have no clear parallel in previous times. The disembedding mechanisms intrude into the heart of self-identity; but they do not 'empty out' the self any more than they simply remove prior supports on which self-identity was based. Rather, they allow the self (in principle) to achieve much greater mastery over the social relations and social contexts reflexively incorporated into the forging of self-identity than was previously possible.

Institutional influences

The orientation of modernity towards control, in relation to social reproduction and to self-identity, has certain characteristic consequences on the level of moral experience. I shall refer to these consequences generically as the *sequestration of experience.* The phenomenon is directly bound up with the internally referential character of social life and the self. With the maturation of modernity, abstract systems play an increasingly pervasive role in coordinating the various contexts of day-to-day life. External 'disturbances' to such reflexively organised systems become minimised.

We can trace out the origin of these developments by reference to several sets of influences, established during the take-off phase of the modern period, but becoming more and more accentuated with the radicalising and globalising of modern institutions. First, and in some ways most important, is the extension of administrative power brought about by accelerating processes of surveillance.[5] The expansion of surveillance capabilities is the main medium of the control of social activity by social means. Surveillance gives rise to particular asymmetries of power, and in varying degrees consolidates the rule of some groups or classes over others. But it is a mistake to focus too much on this aspect. Much more fundamental is the intensifying of administrative control more generally, a phenomenon not wholly directed by anyone precisely because it affects everyone's activities. Surveillance always operates in conjunction with institutional reflexivity, even in pre-modern systems. It is the condition of institutional reflexivity and at the same time also in some part its product, and thus expresses in a specific institutional form that recursiveness characteristic of all social reproduction. However, in systems in which surveillance is highly developed, conditions of social reproduction become increasingly self-mobilising.

Particularly in the shape of the coding of information or knowledge involved in system reproduction, surveillance mechanisms sever social systems from their external referents at the same time as they permit their extension over wider and wider tracts of time-space. Surveillance plus reflexivity means a 'smoothing of the rough edges' such that behaviour which is not integrated into a system – that is, not knowledgeably built into the mechanisms of system reproduction – becomes alien and discrete. To the degree to which such externalities become reduced to point zero, the system becomes wholly an internally referential one. This statement does not imply that internally referential systems are consensual or free from conflict; on the contrary, they may be internally contradictory and riven with chronic confrontations. However, such conflicts are organised in terms of *system principles*, for their various transformative potentials, rather than in relation to extrinsic criteria or demands.

In practice there are many conflicts brought about by tensions between reflexive system reproduction and the inertia of habit or the externalities of tradition. The case of tradition is complicated, nevertheless, because appeals to traditional symbols or practices can themselves be reflexively organised and are then part of the internally referential set of social relations rather than standing opposed to it. The question of whether tradition can be 'reinvented' in settings which have become thoroughly post-traditional has to be understood in these terms. This observation applies not only to the human connections involved in social relations, but to material artifacts too. Thus in contemporary debates in architecture about postmodernism and the revival of romanticism, the key issue is whether reactions against 'modernism' sustain elements of extrinsic traditional modes, or whether alternatively they have become thoroughly embroiled in an internally referential system. To the degree to which the second of these is the case, attempts at revival of traditional styles are likely rapidly to degenerate into kitsch.

A second important institutional transformation affecting internal referentiality is the reordering of private and public domains. This phenomenon can be understood partly in terms of the creation of spheres of civil society which did not exist in pre-modern systems. The establishing of civil society connects directly with the emergence of the modern form of the state, thus being referentially tied to it. In traditional states, most of day-to-day life, in the rural areas at least, lay outside the scope of the state's administrative power. The local community was for the most part autonomous in terms of its traditions and modes of life, and most forms of personal activity were left more or less completely untouched by the administrative apparatus. However, this external arena was not civil society. Rather, it represented the persistence of modes of life extrinsic to the reflexive order of the political centre.

In the modern social forms, state and civil society develop together as linked processes of transformation. The condition for this process, paradoxically, is the capacity of the state to influence many aspects of day-to-day behaviour. Civil society is structured as the 'other side' of the penetration of the state into day-to-day life. Both state and society, to put things bluntly, are internally referential within the reflexive systems established by modernity. What applies to the state/civil society distinction also applies to that of the public/private. The sphere of the private stands opposed to the public in two senses, both strongly influenced, if not wholly brought about, by the changes associated with the development of modernity. The differentiation of state and civil society marks one of these oppositions. The public domain is that of the state, while the private is that which resists the encroachment of the state's surveillance activities. Since the state is the guarantor of law, the private in this sense is partly a matter of legal definition. It is not just what remains unincorporated into the purview of the state, since the state also helps define private rights and prerogatives in a positive fashion.

The private/public opposition in a second sense concerns what is kept concealed from, and what is more openly revealed to, others. Again, it would be wrong to interpret the growth of privacy (and the need for intimacy) in terms of the erosion of a public sphere which used to exist in more traditional communities. Such a suggestion is contained in the early work of Richard Sennett.[6] Sennett points out that the words 'public' and 'private' are both creations of the modern period. 'Public' had its origin in an emerging sense of commonly owned property and goods, whereas 'private' was first used to refer to the privileges of ruling strata. By the eighteenth century, the terms had come to acquire the senses in which they are used today. 'Public' came to be identified with the electorate – in the sense of 'the public' – and with areas of life open to general scrutiny or with the realm of the common good. The sphere of the 'private' became the areas of life specifically differentiated from the public realm.[7] Sennett argues that the early phase of modernity saw the rise of a public order, centred on the cosmopolitan life of cities, which later declined under the impact of subsequent social changes.

But this thesis is not wholly convincing. What Sennett calls public life belonged as much to more traditional urban settings as to those characteristic of modern social life. Pre-modern cities already enjoyed a flourishing of cosmopolitan culture. In such cities, people already encountered strangers on a regular basis. Yet most urban encounters preserved a collegial character and were dominated by interactions with peers, kin or other familiars. The private has here not yet become a fully concealed or separated domain, as Elias's work makes clear.[8] The public only becomes fully distinguished from the private when a society of strangers is established in the full sense, that is, when the notion of 'stranger' loses its meaning. From that time onwards, the civil indifference, which is the gearing mechanism of generalised public trust, becomes more or less wholly distinct from the private domain, and particularly from the sphere of intimate relationships.

Privacy, and the psychological needs associated with it, were almost certainly strongly conditioned by a further separation, that of childhood from adulthood. In pre-modern times, certainly in Europe and no doubt in most other non-modern cultures also, the child, from quite early on in its life, lived in a collective setting in interaction with adults in non-familial as well as in domestic locales. The emergence of a separate province of 'childhood' demarcated the experience of growing up from outside arenas of activity. Childhood became concealed and domesticated, as well as subject to the core influence of formal schooling. As childhood is separated out from the activities of adults, or at least shaped in distinctive ways, it forms an area of concealment within which private experiences are structured. Schooling is in one sense a public activity, since it is carried on outside the home. But the school remains for the pupils a segregated setting distinct from the adult world of work and other involvements. The gradual concealing of various attributes of development, including major aspects of sexuality, is the outcome of these processes of segregation.[9] This is one important factor explaining the close connections between the emergence of therapy and a focus on childhood learning in relation to therapeutic aims. Childhood as a separate sphere becomes an 'infrastructure' of the personality. This is not to accept the equation of modernity with increasing psychological repression, a view which does not conform to the position established in this book. Rather, therapeutic reconstruction on the basis of childhood experience becomes possible because of the emergence of new 'learning fields' brought about by the 'invention' of childhood.

In both senses distinguished above – privacy as the 'other side' of the penetration of the state, and privacy as what may not be revealed – the private is a creation of the public and vice versa; each forms part of newly emergent systems of internal referentiality. These changes form a fundamental part of the general framework of the transformation of intimacy.

Third, a psychological consequence of the two broad processes described is the increasing prominence of shame, in relation to self-identity, as compared to guilt. Guilt essentially depends on mechanisms extrinsic to the internally referential systems of modernity. Guilt carries the connotation of moral transgression: it is anxiety deriving from a failure, or an inability, to satisfy certain forms of moral imperative in the course of a person's conduct. It is a form of anxiety which is most prominent in types of society where social behaviour is governed according to established moral precepts, including those laid down and sanctioned by tradition. Shame is more directly and pervasively related to basic trust than is guilt, because guilt concerns specific forms of behaviour or cognition rather than threatening the integrity of the self as such. Unlike guilt, shame directly corrodes a sense of security in both self and surrounding social milieux. The more self-identity becomes internally referential, the more shame comes to play a fundamental role in the adult personality. The individual no longer lives primarily by extrinsic moral precepts but by means of the reflexive organisation of the self. This is an important point, since it follows that modern civilisation is not founded, as Freud thought, on the renunciation of desire.

In his writings, Freud uses 'civilisation' in a very broad sense: he is not talking simply of modernity.[10] Civilisation is any form of social and cultural organisation which goes beyond the mere 'primitive'. It is a progressive social order implying increasing complexity of social life. The price paid for such complexity, as well as for the 'higher cultural achievements' which a civilised life makes possible, is increasing repression and, therefore, guilt. Civilisation must presume bodily deprivation because urges which would otherwise lead to misplaced erotic investment with strangers, or unacceptable aggressiveness towards them, must be held in check. Civilised life, Freud accepts, is generally more secure than that of 'primitive beings'. Such security, on the other hand, is exchanged for severe restrictions placed on endemic human tendencies. From this angle, therefore, civilisation is a more moral enterprise than the earlier forms of social order which it increasingly supplants. The aggressiveness repressed by civilisation, conjoined with erotic impulses, are channelled back towards the ego in the form of a harsh moral conscience. This over-weaning super ego produces a pervasive sense of guilt. Civilisation and a strong super ego, 'like a garrison in a conquered city', belong together. Guilt, Freud concludes, is 'the most important problem in the development of civilisation'; 'the price we pay for our advance in civilisation is a loss of happiness through the heightening of this sense of guilt.'[11]

If we equate 'civilisation' with modernity, and look at its early period of development, a connection with guilt and conscience seems to make some sense. If Max Weber's interpretation of the association between the Puritanism and the rise of capitalism is correct, we can see a mechanism for conscience formation.[12] The capitalist, after all, according to Weber's portrayal, provides the impetus for the rise of modern institutions by renouncing the gratifications which accumulated wealth can bring. Yet what about the period afterwards, the very time of the maturation of modernity? Followers of Freud have long had difficulty in reconciling their ideas with the seeming moral permissiveness of late modernity. Perhaps civilisation broke apart under weight of its own demands, allowing individuals the chance to give free play to their desires? Perhaps a period of moral restraint, for whatever reason, has been replaced by one of hedonism? These explanations do not sound convincing. Why would a period of the intensifying and globalising of modern institutions produce a relaxation of guilt if heightened guilt is intrinsically associated with greater civilisational complexity? If we discard the theorem that increasing civilisation means increasing guilt, we can see things in a different light. The characteristic movement of modernity, on the level of individual experience, is away from guilt. Moral conscience, perhaps of the kind described by Weber, may have been of key importance in the early modern period, because it was on this basis that extrinsic moral imperatives became converted into intrinsic parameters of socialised action. Puritan beliefs became mobilising elements in the disembedding of the new economic systems from extrinsic anchoring restraints. Puritanism thus may have been one of the main instruments in a phase of 'take-off' stretching beyond the economic sphere itself – a 'take-off' into a more and more inclusive internally referential ordering of society and nature.

However, rather than promoting a search for new self-identities one could argue that Puritanism provided the 'fixity' which allowed the early entrepreneurs to explore new pathways of behaviour without breaking with their pre-established habits and convictions. The 'ghost of Puritanism' that prowled around in the subsequent systems of modernity from this regard remained a source of externalities to the new social order: it was not, as Marcuse and many others have argued, its main organising impetus. The more the hold of tradition was broken, and the reflexive project of the self came to the fore, the more dynamics of shame rather than guilt come to occupy the psychological centre-stage. Naturally, even in the phase of high modernity, guilt mechanisms remain important, just as key moral involvements persist – for, as I shall argue later, the institutional repression produced by the internally referential orders of modernity is much less than complete.

Arenas of sequestration

The orientation of modernity towards control, in the context of internally referential systems, has well-known connotations on the level of culture and philosophy. Positivistic thought, in one guise or another, became a central guiding thread in modernity's reflexivity. Positivism seeks to expunge moral judgements and aesthetic criteria from the transformative processes it helps set into motion and of which it also provides interpretation and analysis. Rather than concentrating on features of discourse, however, I want to direct attention to their *institutional correlate*, which is the accumulation of processes that effectively make extrinsic influences of limited patience. Processes of institutional sequestration appear in various areas. In each case they have the effect of removing basic aspects of life experience, including especially moral crises, from the regularities of day-to-day life established by the abstract systems of modernity. The term 'sequestration of experience' refers here to connected processes of concealment which set apart the routines of ordinary life from the following phenomena: madness; criminality; sickness and death; sexuality; and nature. In some cases such sequestration is directly organisational: this is true of the mental asylum, the prison and the medical hospital. In other instances, sequestration depends more on more general characteristics of the internally referential systems of modernity. Broadly speaking, my argument will be that the ontological security which modernity has purchased, on the level of day-to-day routines, depends on an institutional exclusion of social life from fundamental existential issues which raise central moral dilemmas for human beings. In order to trace out and develop this theme, a certain amount of historical material is necessary. If we look back, briefly, to the origins of the various arenas of sequestration, we can identify some of the processes underlying the replacement of external by internal criteria in the constitution of modernity's social systems.

Rothman's work, rather than that of Foucault, is most relevant for discussion of the asylum.[13] Although Rothman's research concentrates on the emergence of mental hospitals in the United States, the analysis has very general application. Foucault's discussion of the asylum and of imprisonment relates incarceration to the drive to establish the dominance of bourgeois reason.[14] Those who would seek to contest the sovereign claims of reason are henceforth to be excluded from direct participation in the social order. Suggestive and important as it is, this position has major weaknesses. Without going into these in detail, one can say that it was not so much 'reason' which was at issue as the development of reflexive transformation. What would later be regarded as 'insanity', 'crime' and 'poverty' were treated, prior to the modern period, as extrinsic features of human existence. Madness, crime and poverty were not yet thought of as 'social problems'. Even as late as the eighteenth century, the presence of these characteristics in individuals who would subsequently find themselves placed into one or other of these categories was not regarded as an indicator of either personal or communal failure.

Attitudes towards poverty are revealing here. Use of the term 'poor' in the early eighteenth century encompassed a variety of social conditions. Discussions and legislation about the poor included widows, orphans, the sick, the aged, the disabled and the insane without clear differentiations being observed between them. Morally defined need, rather than the special circumstances which produced it, was the identifying characteristic. A Massachusetts law, which became a model for other states in the US, held that poverty occurs 'when and so often as it shall happen that any person be naturally wanting of understanding, so as to be incapable to provide for him or herself'.[15] This attitude was already a change from preceding eras in Europe. For poverty had by this stage come to be thought of as something needing communal attention, rather than being wholly an extrinsic feature of the circumstances of social life.

How closely these attitudes still remained tied to extrinsic considerations, however, is demonstrated by the treatment of criminality – or more accurately, vagabondage – in eighteenth-century America. Vagabondage, like poverty more broadly, was regarded as largely endemic. It was surrounded by, and connected to, an indefinite set of moral transgressions.

> The colonists judged a wide range of behaviour to be deviant, finding the gravest implications in even minor offences. Their extended definition was primarily religious in origin, equating sin with crime. The criminal codes punished religious offences, such as idolatry, blasphemy, and witchcraft, and clergymen declared infractions against persons or property to be offences against God. Freely mixing the two categories, the colonists proscribed an incredibly long list of activities. The identification of disorder with sin made it difficult for legislators and ministers to distinguish carefully between major and minor infractions. Both were testimony to the natural depravity of man and the power of the devil – sure signs that the offender was destined to be a public menace and a damned sinner.[16]

The idea of secular correction emerged only gradually and should be understood as part of broader processes whereby the social and natural worlds came to be seen as transformable rather than merely given. 'Social control', therefore, was not primarily a means of controlling pre-existing forms of 'deviant' behaviour. 'Deviance' was in fact largely created by the imperatives brought about by the transmutation of naturally given conditions into manageable ones. The sequestration of the mad and the criminal accelerated when these categories became separate from poverty in general, and when it came to be believed that all were intrinsically capable of alteration. Constructing a special setting for deviants provided a means of integrating remedial treatment with the maintenance of regularised control over the settings of day-to-day life on the outside.

The idea that human beings can be subject to correction was necessarily bound up with the notion that social life itself is open to radical change. The early prison reformers – like many professional sociologists later – sought to show that the conditions leading to criminal behaviour derived from the dismal lives people in less fortunate communities were forced to lead. Changing these conditions could at the same time help to alter the behaviour of those who challenged the dominant proprieties. 'The vices of social life', as one official observed of a prisoner in Pennsylvania in the 1840s, 'have heralded the ruin of his fortunes and his hopes.'[17] The existence of crime pointed, not to intractable elements of human nature, but to the inability of the community to live up to its task of creating a responsible citizenry. A properly organised society would both shield potential offenders from temptation and at the same time diminish the circumstances leading to criminal activity.

The impetus which led to the establishment of prisons was originally fuelled by moral considerations. The discipline and regimentation of prison life were to be a form of moral education which, by removing the criminal from the depravity of his or her surroundings, would have rehabilitating effects. The penitentiary was to become a laboratory for social improvement. The routines of prison life, however, in exaggerated form mimicked those established in the social environments of modernity as a whole. The prison henceforth became a laboratory in much the same sense as all the other contexts of modernity are: an environment in which social organisation and change are reflexively engineered, both as a backdrop to individual life and as a medium for the reconstitution of individual identity.

The social incorporation of madness

The history of the asylum encapsulates similar trends of development. Like criminality, madness was in prior eras assumed to be an outcome of God's will, the insane being one group among others worthy of receiving a certain level of care from the community. The image of Pinel removing the chains of the insane could be taken to represent the thrust of modernity as a whole. Indeed, the idea of Prometheus unbound, which so inspired Marx, carries a picture of freedom from the shackles of tradition and custom which reappears many times from the Enlightenment onwards. Insanity came to have an 'open' horizon in common with all other aspects of established behaviour and social relation. The medicalising of insanity, as 'mental illness', is only part of this phenomenon. Insanity was a physical disease, but most forms of insanity were believed to be brought on by social circumstances, and certainly the control of behaviour was a major means of producing supposed cures. Many early psychiatrists, in fact, linked the very aetiological origins of mental illness with social factors, including 'civilisation' itself.

Particularly important, however, was the surfacing of the view that mental illness, in common with criminality, and under specific circumstances, could attack anyone in the population. From being a special, although not clearly distinguishable, characteristic of poverty, and therefore clustered among the least privileged groups, mental illness came to be seen as one of the risks modern life brought in its train. 'Insanity is peculiar to no grade in life. There are none so elevated as to be beyond its reach . . . it has dethroned the monarch, and deepened the gloom of the hovel.'[18]

Asylums were first established with their curative properties in mind. Incarceration was intended to restore mental health through the setting itself, rather than only through the medicines or treatments administered there. The mental hospital was supposed to create an environment which would methodically correct for the deficiencies of the wider social community. Again, a moral dimension to the reform of the afflicted personality was clearly apparent. As in the prison, the maximising of surveillance, in conjunction with the establishing of disciplined routines, were the means of attaining these ends. Insanity, like madness, was actively defined in terms of social incapacity: the inability, or unwillingness, to live the required type of life in the outside world.

What is striking about the asylum, in common with the prison, is how much it shares with the wider social environments of modernity. Foucault is wrong to trace this similarity to discipline as such; the forfeiting of various kinds of social and personal rights on the part of those forcibly incarcerated in prisons and asylums is surely central to their character. What they share in common with the broader frameworks of modernity is the attempt to develop reflexive self-control even among minorities who might seem intrinsically recalcitrant. The moral component in both cases soon took second place to other imperatives. What counted as a 'cure' lost most of its extrinsic characteristics, becoming measured as to whether a person was able and willing to function satisfactorily in the wider social environment. In other respects, simple custody became a dominant feature: incarceration serves at least to protect those in the outside world from unalterable irregularities in the behaviour of the minority.

'Deviance' came to be 'invented' as part of the internally referential systems of modernity, and therefore defined in terms of control. The extrinsic issues and questions which criminality and insanity pose to the population at large are thereby thoroughly repressed. But this is an institutional repression rather than a personal one – it does not presume an intensifying of 'conscience'. It is an exclusion from the core arenas of social life of potentially disturbing issues, values and modes of behaviour. The issues thus repressed are plainly of a moral and existential sort. In behaviour now classified as 'mental illness', for example, alternative visions of what passes for everyday reality are pushed far from the preoccupations of daily life. Once the asylum has become established, few people come into contact with the insane in a regular way. Just as invisible are the connections which once linked 'poverty' in the old sense to extrinsic moral precepts and traditions. Prisons and mental hospitals rapidly lost most of that exotic quality which early on made them spectacles for the outside world to look upon. Instead, they became settings of technical correction, geared to the transformative relations of modernity.

The sequestration of sickness and death

What are now called hospitals only gradually became differentiated from the older organisations which sought to cope with the impact of 'poverty'. The 'hospitals' which were the forerunners of prisons and asylums, as well as of modern medical organisations, mixed together just that range of people noted in previous paragraphs. The emergence of a separate sphere of medical treatment, focused on people with distinct 'physical problems', was part of the self-same processes that created the other carceral organisations.

The development of the hospital in its modern sense was closely bound up with the professionalisation of medicine. The hospital is a setting where medical technology can be concentrated and medical expertise fostered. Yet, like prisons and asylums, the hospital is also a place where those who are disqualified from participating in orthodox social activities are sequestered, and it has similar consequences in terms of the concealment from general view of certain crucial life experiences – sickness and death. As was discussed in the previous chapter, in pre-modern societies chronic sickness was part of many people's lives and contact with death was a more or less commonplace feature of everyone's experience. Elias has pointed out that Ariès's work on the subject probably presents a somewhat slanted view of death in the pre-modern world. Ariès tends to argue that, since death had not yet become hidden away, people were able to meet their end in a serene fashion, surrounded by their loved ones. As Elias says, the presence of others at the deathbed was not necessarily always comforting: sometimes in fact the dying were mocked and taunted by the survivors.[19] Whatever the truth of this may be, and though death may still have been surrounded by fundamental fears and anxieties, it was not then a phenomenon to be concealed.

The point is not just that, today, death is routinely hidden from view. In addition, death has become a technical matter, its assessment removed into the hands of the medical profession; what death is becomes a matter of deciding at what point a person should be treated as having died, in respect of the cessation of various types of bodily function. Death remains the great extrinsic factor of human existence; it cannot as such be brought within the internally referential systems of modernity. However, all types of event leading up to and involved with the process of dying can be so incorporated. Death becomes a point zero: it is nothing more or less than the moment at which human control over human existence finds an outer limit.

The history of capital punishment bears witness to the impulsion to convert death into a pure 'event'. As Foucault and others have shown, in pre-modern settings capital punishment, often combined with other modes of inflicting pain on the body, was frequently a collective spectacle. With the coming of the prison, punishment moves 'out of view' and becomes disciplinary in form. What Foucault does not pursue, although this is quite consonant with his analysis, are the changes affecting capital punishment inside the prison. Public forms of execution were often not just painful, but noisy and prolonged. The whole weight of subsequent development was towards reducing execution to as 'silent' a process as possible.[20] In England, for example, great care was taken to ensure that the condemned spent his or her last night in a cell very close to the place of execution, so as to minimise the duration of the final event. A sequence of technical modifications, designed to make the execution apparatus efficient and silent, was introduced. Death, in other words, was to be instantaneous and unobtrusive. Capital punishment has since been abolished in many countries – a reform prompted by humanitarian motives, but one which also recognises that execution finally puts an individual beyond the possibility of social control.

The privatising of passion

The removal of sexuality behind the scenes is a phenomenon of the *privatisation of passion*. Passion was once a term which referred to the ecstasy and devotion of the religious. It concerned precisely those moments at which an individual felt in contact with cosmic forces, with a realm beyond day-to-day experience. The notion of passion later lost these meanings almost completely, becoming secularised and confined mainly to the sexual sphere. This is part of the very transition by means of which 'sexuality' emerged as a distinct phenomenon, separated from the more general and diffuse eroticism once frequently linked to aesthetics and to the experience of unsocialised nature.[21]

There is no known culture in which sexual behaviour has been carried on in a completely open way under the gaze of everyone. Yet there is plenty of evidence to indicate that, in many non-modern cultures as well as in pre-modern Europe, sexual activity was not strictly kept hidden from the eyes of others. In some part such visibility was unavoidable: in lower socioeconomic groups it was normal practice for parents and children to sleep in the same room, often together with other relatives. Sexual activity carried on more or less casually outside of the dwelling-place also seems to have been something of general occurrence.

The privatising of sexuality might again be thought to be linked to the rise of a new moral conscience. According to such a view, sexuality became increasingly subject to prurient attitudes which condemned it as licence. Foucault has helped to show how misleading this interpretation is. As he says, it suggests a story according to which:

Sexuality was carefully confined: it moved into the home. The conjugal family took custody of it and absorbed it into the serious function of reproduction. On the subject of sex, silence became the rule. . . . A single locus of sexuality was acknowledged in social space as well as at the heart of every household, but it was a utilitarian and fertile one: the parents' bedroom. The rest had only to remain vague; proper demeanour avoided contact with other bodies, and verbal decency sanitised one's speech.[22]

In this interpretation, which conforms broadly speaking to that of Freud, the privatising of sexuality is a matter of repression – that repression which is the price we have to pay for the fruits of civilisation. Foucault does not so much oppose what he calls the 'repressive hypothesis' as contrast it to one which stresses the proliferation of discourses bringing sexuality into the newly con-stituted public arena.

But Foucault's thesis that concern with sexuality becomes obsessive and more or less all-pervasive in the modern world does not seem any more convincing than the conception that it is designed in some part to replace. We can formulate an alternative to both views in the following way. 'Sexuality', in the modern sense, was invented when sexual behaviour 'went behind the scenes'. From this point onwards, sexuality became a property of the individual, and more specifically, the body, as eroticism conjoined to guilt was progressively replaced by an association of sexuality with self-identity and the propensity to shame. The hiding away of sexual behaviour was not so much a prurient concealment from view as a reconstitution of sexuality and its refocusing on an emerging sphere of intimacy. Sexual development and sexual satisfaction henceforth became bound to the reflexive project of the self. The various 'discourses on sexuality' of which Foucault speaks form part of the wider spectrum of the development of reflexive, internally referential systems.

Sexuality has then become, as Luhmann might put it, a 'communicative code' rather than a phenomenon integrated with the wider exigencies of human existence.[23] In sexual behaviour, a distinction had always been drawn between pleasure and procreation. When the new connections between sexuality and intimacy were formed, however, sexuality became much more completely separated from procreation than before. Sexuality became doubly constituted as a medium of self-realisation and as a prime means, as well as an expression, of intimacy. Sexuality has here lost its extrinsic connections with wider traditions and ethics, as well as with the succession of the generations. Sexuality remains, or rather becomes, a central focus for 'experience', and the word 'experience' comes to have a particular significance in relation to sexual life. Yet this 'experience' has little to do with the existential domains with which sex in some sense places us in contact.

Sequestration from extrinsic nature

In each of the respects discussed above, therefore, we can trace out an expanding process of moral sequestration. The major domains of life, including those which seem on the face of things to be more 'biological' than social, come to be brought under the sway of the dual impulsion of self-referentiality and reflexivity. Existential questions become institutionally repressed at the same time as new fields of opportunity are created for social activity and for personal development. The sequestration of experience is in some part the contrived outcome of a culture in which moral and aesthetic domains are held to be dissolved by the expansion of technical knowledge. In some considerable degree, however, it is also the unintended outcome of the endemic structuring processes of modernity, whose internally referential systems lose contact with extrinsic criteria.

We have to add to the processes thus far mentioned the development of the created environment. It has become a commonplace to assert that the core outlooks of modernity treat nature as instrumental, the means to realise human purposes. The *locus classicus* of such a view, it is said, is in none other than Marx himself. The supposed radical critic of modern social life turns out to conform to some of its most deeply ingrained characteristics. The indictment is surely valid. Marx was a critic of capitalism, which he saw as essentially an irrational means of organising modern industry; but he saw the expansion of the productive forces as the very key to a rewarding future for humankind. There are some passages, particularly in Marx's early writings, which suggest a rather more subtle view of nature and its relationship to human aspirations. Yet on the whole the thrust of Marx's account is an instrumental one, and in this respect Marx is more in accord with the dominant line of thinking in Western intellectual thought and culture than critical of it.

However, it is not enough to leave matters there. What is at issue is not just that, with the coming of modernity, human beings treat nature as an inert set of forces to be harnessed to human ends, since this still carries the implication that nature is a *separate domain* from that of human society. As was emphasised earlier, the development of the created environment – or, another phrase for the same thing, the socialisation of nature – cuts much more deeply than this. Nature begins 'to come to an end' in the sense that the natural world is increasingly ordered according to the internally reflexive systems of modernity. In conditions of modernity, people live in artificial environments in a double sense. First, because of the spread of the built environment, in which the vast majority of the population dwell, human habitats become separate from nature, now represented only in the form of the 'countryside' or 'wilderness'. Second, in a profound sense, nature literally ceases to exist as naturally occurring events become more and more pulled into systems determined by socialised influences.

So far as the first of these factors is concerned, we can say that human life becomes sequestered from nature in so far as it unfolds in humanly created locales. In the city, 'nature' still survives as carefully conserved areas of greenery, but for the most part these are artificially constructed: in the form of parks, recreational areas and so forth. Gardens are dug, trees are tended and house plants cultivated; but these are all plainly parts of the created environment, and are only 'natural' in so far as they depend on organic processes rather than on human manufacture alone. The modern city is by far the most extensively and intensively artificial series of settings for human activity that has ever existed. A visit to the countryside or a trek to the wilderness may satisfy a desire to be close to 'nature', but 'nature' here is also socially coordinated and tamed. The notion of a 'wilderness' is a concept which came into prominence during the early period of modern social development. Specifically, it once meant an area of the natural world as yet unexplored by, and unknown to, those from the modern West. Wildernesses now, however, are mostly simply areas where, for one reason or another, cultivation or habitation cannot effectively be maintained, or are simply areas set aside directly for recreational purposes.

In the second sense, nature becomes sequestered from human involvement in an even more fundamental way. Nature is increasingly subject to human intervention, and thereby loses its very character as an extrinsic source of reference. Sequestration from nature in this guise is more subtle, yet more pervasive than in the first sense mentioned. For nature – the alternation of the days and seasons, the impact of climatic conditions – still seems to be 'there': the necessary external environment of human activities, no matter how instrumentally orientated they might be. Yet this feeling is specious. Becoming socialised, nature is drawn into the colonisation of the future and into the partly unpredictable arenas of risk created by modern institutions in all areas subject to their sway.

What is the impact of the sequestration of experience? This is a problem I shall expand upon in subsequent chapters, and only a few general remarks are needed at this point. Such sequestration is the condition of the establishing of large tracts of relative security in day-to-day life in conditions of modernity. Its effect, which as we have seen should be regarded largely as an unintended consequence of the development of modern institutions, is to *repress a cluster of basic moral and existential components of human life* that are, as it were, squeezed to the sidelines.

The institutional repression which moral sequestration signals is not, however, a psychological repression: it does not depend on the internalisation of ever more strict forms of conscience, in the manner suggested by Freud. On the contrary, to repeat, mechanisms of shame, linked to the 'open' nature of self-identity, come in some substantial part to replace those of guilt.

The development of relatively secure environments of day-to-day life is of central importance to the maintenance of feelings of ontological security. Ontological security, in other words, is sustained primarily through routine itself. Although daily existence is in many ways more controlled and predictable in modern social conditions by comparison with the generality of pre-modern cultures, the framework of ontological security becomes fragile. The protective cocoon depends more and more on the coherence of routines themselves, as they are ordered within the reflexive project of the self. Wide areas of day-to-day life, ordered via abstract systems, are secure in Max Weber's sense of providing 'calculable' environment of action. Yet the very routines that provide such security mostly lack moral meaning and can either come to be experienced as 'empty' practices, or alternatively can seem to be overwhelming. When routines, for whatever reason, become radically disrupted, or where someone specifically sets out to achieve a greater reflexive control over her or his self-identity, existential crises are likely to occur. An individual might feel particularly bereft at fateful moments, because at such moments moral and existential dilemmas present themselves in pressing form. The individual, faces a return of the repressed, as it were, but is likely to lack the psychic and social resources to cope with the issues thus posed.

As with other processes of modern social development, it would be wrong to understand the sequestration of experience as all-enveloping and homogeneous, which it is not. It is internally complicated, throws up contradictions, and also generates possibilities of reappropriation. Sequestration, we must stress, is not a

Day-to-day social life becomes sequestered from:

Madness: the expression of traits of personality and behaviour which touch on experiences 'bracketed out' by ordinary attitudes of ontological security.

Criminality: the expression of traits of personality and behaviour which may represent 'alternatives' to routine concerns and involvements (obviously not all concrete forms of criminal activity fall into this category).

Sickness and death: connecting points between social life and external criteria concerning mortality and finitude.

Sexuality: eroticism as a form of connection between individuals and the continuities of the generations.

Nature: the natural environment as constituted independently of human social activity.

Figure 3   *The sequestration of experience*

once-and-for-all phenomenon, and it does not represent a set of frictionless boundaries. The site of oppression, its exclusionary characteristics normally carry connotations of hierarchical differentiation and inequality. The frontiers of sequestered experience are faultlines, full of tensions and poorly mastered forces; or, to shift the metaphor, they are battlegrounds, sometimes of a directly social character, but often within the psychological field of the self.

We also have to consider the impact of mediated experience. Contact with death and serious illness may be rare, except on the part of specialised professionals, but in respect of mediated experience it is very common. Fictional literature and documentary presentations are full of materials portraying violence, sexuality and death. Familiarity with settings of such activities, as a result of the wide-ranging influence of media of various kinds, may in fact often be greater than in pre-modern social conditions. Many popular art forms are essentially morality tales, in which narratives are spun and a moral order assembled. Plainly these fictional worlds in some part supplant those of day-to-day life.

Yet, through mediated language and imagery, individuals also have access to experiences ranging in diversity and distance far beyond anything they could achieve in the absence of such mediations. Existential sensibilities therefore do not simply become attenuated and lost; to some extent they may even be enriched as new fields of experience are opened up.

On the whole it is surely the case that mediated experience furthers sequestration rather than helps to overcome it. A fascination with 'fictional realism', such as soap operas for instance, expresses a concern with the lapsed moralities of everyday life. But such preoccupations tend to confirm the separation of day-to-day activity from the externalities in which they were once embedded. Where individuals are brought face to face with existential demands – as at fateful moments – they are likely to experience both shock and reality inversion. Reality inversion, indeed, may often be a functional psychological reaction which alleviates the anxieties that surge through at such junctures – an unconscious neutralising device.

Narcissism and the self

Sennett: narcissism and character disorders

The foregoing sections imply that self-development in late modernity occurs under conditions of substantial moral deprivation. Sequestered from key types of experience which relate the tasks of day-to-day life, and even longer-term life-planning, to existential issues, the reflexive project of the self is energised against a backdrop of moral impoverishment. Small wonder that in such circumstances the newly constituted sphere of pure relationships may come to bear a heavy burden as an area of experience generating a morally rewarding milieu for individual life development. Does this phenomenon represent a defensive shrinkage of self-identity in the face of a recalcitrant outside world? Some writers have certainly suggested as much and, given their influential nature, their views demand detailed consideration.

The self in modern society is frail, brittle, fractured, fragmented – such a conception is probably the pre-eminent outlook in current discussions of the self and modernity. Some such analyses are linked theoretically to poststructuralism: just as the social world becomes contextualised and dispersed, so also does the self.[24] In fact, for authors writing in a poststructuralist vein, the self effectively ceases to exist: the only subject is a decentred subject, which finds its identity in the fragments of language or discourse. An equally influential view focuses on narcissism. Thus Sennett discusses the rise of 'narcissist character disorders' in relation to his thesis about the demise of public life. As the spheres of public activity shrink, and cities become composed of thoroughfares rather than open meeting places, the self is called on to assume tasks with which it cannot successfully cope.[25]

Narcissism, Sennett says, should not be confused with the lay idea of self-admiration. As a character disorder, narcissism is a preoccupation with the self which prevents the individual from establishing valid boundaries between self and external worlds. Narcissism relates outside events to the needs and desires of the self, asking only 'what this means to me'. Narcissism presumes a constant search for self-identity, but this is a search which remains frustrated, because the restless pursuit of 'who I am' is an expression of narcissistic absorption rather than a realisable quest. Narcissism stands in opposition to the commitment required to sustain intimate relationships; commitment places restrictions on the opportunities the individual has to sample the many experiences demanded in the search for self-fulfilment. Narcissism treats the body as an instrument of sensual gratification, rather than relating sensuality to communication with others. Under the impact of narcissism, intimate relations as well as broader connections with the social world tend to have inherently destructive aspects. The horizons of the person's activity seem bleak and unappealing in spite of, or rather because of, the chronic search for gratification. At the same time, any sense of personal dignity or civic duty tends to evaporate. Authenticity substitutes for dignity: what makes an action good is that it is authentic to the individual's desires, and can be displayed to others as such.

The fact that public space has become 'dead', according to Sennett, is one reason for the pervasiveness of narcissism. People seek in personal life what is denied to them in public arenas. The institutional origins of this situation lie in the decline of traditional authority and the formation of a secular, capitalistic urban culture. Capitalism creates consumers, who have differentiated (and cultivated) needs; secularisation has the effect of narrowing down moral meaning to the immediacy of sensation and perception. 'Personality' replaces the earlier Enlightenment belief in natural 'character'. Personality differentiates between people, and suggests that their behaviour is the clue to their inner selves; in personality development, feelings rather than rational control of action are what matters in the formation of self-identity. The entry of the idea of personality into social life helped prepare the ground for the dominance of the intimate order. Social bonds and engagements increasingly thereafter recede in favour of an endless and obsessive preoccupation with social identity.

> Today, impersonal experience seems meaningless and social complexity an unmanageable threat. By contrast, experience which seems to tell about the self, to help define it, develop it or change it, has become an overwhelming concern. In an intimate society, all social phenomena, no matter how impersonal in structure, are converted into matters of personality in order to have a meaning.[26]

Lasch: the culture of narcissism

The theme of narcissism in relation to the modern self has been more thoroughly explored by Christopher Lasch.[27] Lasch specifically relates the phenomenon to the apocalyptic nature of modern social life. Global risks have become such an acknowledged aspect of modern institutions that, on the level of day-to-day behaviour, no one any longer gives much thought to how potential global disasters can be avoided. Most people shut them out of their lives and concentrate their activities on privatised 'survival strategies', blotting out the larger risk scenarios. Giving up hope that the wider social environment can be controlled, people retreat to purely personal preoccupations: to psychic and bodily self-improvement. Lasch relates this situation to an evaporation of history, a loss of historical continuity in the sense of a feeling of belonging to a succession of generations going back into the past and stretching forwards into the future. Against this backdrop, people hunger for psychic security and a – disturbingly elusive – sense of well-being.

Lasch agrees with Sennett that narcissism is as much about self-hatred as about self-admiration. Narcissism is a defence against infantile rage, an attempt to compensate with omnipotent fantasies of the privileged self. The narcissistic personality has only a shadowy understanding of the needs of others, and feelings of grandiosity jostle with sentiments of emptiness and inauthenticity. Lacking full engagement with others, the narcissist depends on continual infusion of admiration and approval to bolster an uncertain sense of self-worth. The narcissist, according to Lasch, is

> chronically bored, restlessly in search of instantaneous intimacy – of emotional titillation without involvement and dependence – the narcissist is promiscuous and often pan-sexual as well, since the fusion of pregenital and oedipal impulses in the service of aggression encourages polymorphous perversity. The bad images he has internalised also make him chronically uneasy about his health, and hypochondria in turn gives him a special affinity for therapy and for therapeutic groups and movements.[28]

Far from alleviating these symptoms, the therapeutic encounter often merely helps to prolong them because in therapy the individual is encouraged to become the centre-point of reflection and concern.

Consumer capitalism, with its efforts to standardise consumption and to shapes tastes through advertising, plays a basic role in furthering narcissism. The idea of generating an educated and discerning public has long since succumbed to the pervasiveness of consumerism, which is a 'society dominated by appearances'. Consumption addresses the alienated qualities of modern social life and claims to be their solution: it promises the very things the narcissist desires – attractiveness, beauty and personal popularity – through the consumption of the 'right' kinds of goods and services. Hence all of us, in modern social conditions, live as though surrounded by mirrors; in these we search for the appearance of an unblemished, socially valued self.

On the level of personal relations, Lasch agrees, there is a new search for intimacy. However, intimacy becomes unobtainable as a consequence of the very circumstances which lead individuals to be concerned to achieve it. The inability to take a serious interest in anything other than shoring up the self makes the pursuit of intimacy a futile endeavour. Individuals demand from intimate connections with others much greater emotional satisfaction and security than they ever did before; on the other hand, they cultivate a detachment necessary to the maintenance of narcissistic ego defences. The narcissist is led to make inordinate demands on lovers and friends; at the same time, he or she rejects the 'giving to others' that this implies.

The decline of the patriarchal family, and indeed the family in general, according to Lasch, is closely connected to the rise of narcissism. In place of the old 'family authority', and also the authority of traditional leaders and sages, there has arisen a cult of expertise. The new experts are an intrinsic part of the therapeutic culture of narcissism. A 'new paternalism' has arisen in which experts of all types minister to the needs of the lay population. Many modern forms of expertise do not derive from the fulfilment of genuinely felt needs; in some large part the new experts have invented the very needs they claim to satisfy. Dependence on expertise becomes a way of life. Here we reconnect closely with narcissism, because the narcissistic personality originates as a defence against infantile dependency. Since in modern societies dependence extends into most areas of adult life, narcissism becomes intensified as a reaction to the feelings of powerlessness thus engendered.

In subsequent writings Lasch has elaborated, and somewhat modified, his original position. The theme of survival, in an encroaching and disturbing external world, is accentuated. Survival, Lasch emphasises, is the common preoccupation of individuals in day-to-day life as well as of social networks such as peace or ecological movements. In the contemporary era, survival has become a matter of overriding importance; yet the very publicising of the issue, which itself becomes almost an item of routine, produces a lethargic response on the individual level. The dramatising of the risks humanity now faces is a necessary enterprise, and some of the social pressures and movements it has helped to stimulate represent our best hope for the future; yet continual talk of apocalypse creates a siege mentality which is numbing rather than energising. What Lasch previously called the 'culture of narcissism' he has subsequently come to term the 'culture of survivalism'. Modern life increasingly comes to be patterned after the strategies of individuals forced to confront situations of great adversity, in which only a 'minimal self', defensively separated from the outer world, exists. Apathy towards the past, renunciation of the future, and a determination to live one day at a time – such an outlook has become characteristic of ordinary life in circumstances dominated by influences over which individuals feel they have little or no control.

Critical observations

The views of Sennett and Lasch have been applauded by some, criticised by others (Lasch is also critical of Sennett). I do not intend to trace out these debates here, but will concentrate only on certain aspects of them relating directly to the themes developed thus far in this study. I have already expressed disagreement with the idea that a public sphere, distinguishable in the early phases of modernity, subsequently became eradicated, leaving the individual exposed to a complex and overwhelming social world. On the whole one can say that, although fraught with difficulties and reversals, the expansion of the public realm, together with the possibilities which individuals have for effectively participating in it, have advanced with the maturation of modern institutions. This is not a unilinear process of development. Privatism is undoubtedly characteristic of large areas of modern urban life, consequent on the dissolution of place and increased mobility. On the other hand, modern urban areas permit the development of a public, cosmopolitan life in ways that were not available in more traditional communities.[29] For modern urban settings provide a diversity of opportunities for individuals to search out others of like interests and form associations with them, as well as offering more chance for the cultivation of a diversity of interests or pursuits in general.

So far as 'public' life in a broader sense is concerned, we should remember that the mass of the population in the early modern period had few participatory rights in either the political or economic spheres. In the classical capitalistic labour contract, the worker sacrificed all control over his labour power on entering the factory gates; the right to unionise, and the substantial range of capacities made possible by the labour movement, only developed over a very extended period of time. Similarly, rights of effective political participation in local and central government took many years of struggle to achieve. Collective mobilisation in other spheres – in respect, for example, of the multifarious self-help organisations which now exist in most modern societies – were also formed over a lengthy time-period, by means of active struggle. Of course, there is another side to all this, which is the one Sennett and Lasch concentrate on: the growth of large bureaucratic organisations that develop arbitrary powers, and the influence of commodity production, which drains away individual control over daily life. Yet these trends do not go unresisted, and 'bureaucratic capitalism' is internally more fluid and contradictory than these authors assume.

In the work of Lasch, and many others who have produced rather similar cultural diagnoses, one can discern an inadequate account of the human agent. The individual appears essentially passive in relation to overwhelming external social forces, and a misleading or false view is adopted of the connections between micro-settings of action and more encompassing social influences. An adequate account of action in relation to modernity must accomplish three tasks. It must recognise that (1) on a very general level, human agents never passively accept external conditions of action, but more or less continuously reflect upon them and reconstitute them in the light of their particular circumstances; (2) on a collective as well as an individual plane, above all in conditions of modernity, there are massive areas of collective appropriation consequent on the increased reflexivity of social life; (3) it is not valid to argue that, while the micro-settings of action are malleable, larger social systems form an uncontrolled background environment. Let us look at these points in a little more detail.

If we do not see that all human agents stand in a position of appropriation in relation to the social world, which they constitute and reconstitute in their actions, we fail on an empirical level to grasp the nature of human empowerment. Modern social life impoverishes individual action, yet furthers the appropriation of new possibilities; it is alienating, yet at the same time, characteristically, human beings react against social circumstances which they find oppressive. Late modern institutions create a world of mixed opportunity and high-consequence risk. But this world does not form an impermeable environment which resists intervention. While abstract systems penetrate deeply into day-to-day life, responses to such systems connect the activities of the individual to social relations of indefinite extension.

Various forms of dependency – or, to put the matter less provocatively, trust – are fostered by the reconstruction of day-to-day life via abstract systems. Some such systems, in their global extensions, have created social influences which no one wholly controls and whose outcomes are in some part specifically unpredictable. Yet in many respects the expansion of expert systems provides possibilities of reappropriation well beyond those available in traditional cultures.

As an illustration, take the changes now occurring in modes of family life, associated with the emergence of pure relationships. Judith Stacey's work provides a source of evidence here.[30] As she demonstrates, in experiencing the unravelling of traditional family patterns, with all the threats and risks which these changes entail, individuals are actively pioneering new social territory and constructing innovative forms of familial relation. Stacey's research was set against the background of a disturbing and rapidly changing social setting: Silicon Valley in California. Her study itself is highly reflexive: the individuals concerned entered into a continuing dialogue with the author, and their views on their own interview material, and on the text itself, form a key part of the research report.

Stacey's work concerns two extended kinship networks of working-class people who, as she puts it, 'live, love, work and worry' in the Valley. Modern marriage, she points out, unlike its traditional predecessor, depends on enduring voluntary commitment. There are fewer children to be cared for than once was the case, and the division of labour between men and women inside and outside the home has become less clear-cut. The social environment in which marital relationships are formed and sustained has become disturbing and unsettling. The result is certainly that many individuals feel beleaguered and embattled. A concern with day-to-day 'survival', such as that described by Lasch, emerges clearly enough from the lives of the individuals described in Stacey's work. Yet, at the same time, it is strikingly evident that such an outlook does not necessarily, or perhaps even characteristically, promote a withdrawal into a bounded world of the self.

On the contrary, Stacey shows how individuals are actively restructuring new forms of gender and kinship relation out of the detritus of pre-established forms of family life. Such restructurings are not merely local and they are certainly not trivial: what is involved is essentially a massive process of institutional reconstitution, led by those concerned. 'Recombinant families', no longer organised in terms of pre-established gender divisions, are being created; rather than forming a chasm between a previous and a future mode of existence, divorce is being mobilised as a resource to create networks drawing together new partners and former ones, biological children and stepchildren, friends and other relatives. Narcissism is not a trait which emerges with any clarity from studies such as Stacey's where individuals appear not as withdrawing from the outer social world but engaging boldly with it.

Let us look a little more closely at Lasch's characterisation of the 'narcissistic personality of our times'. The features of 'pathological narcissism', he says, in its acute guise appear 'in profusion in the everyday life of our age'.[31] Narcissism is 'the incorporation of grandiose object images as a defence against anxiety and guilt'.[32] It is a reaction formation developed as a means of defending against fears of abandonment. The narcissist is not dominated by a rigid, internalised conscience, or by guilt; she or he is more of a 'chaotic and impulse-ridden character' who needs the admiration of others yet resists intimacy. The narcissist suffers from 'pervasive feelings of emptiness and a deep disturbance of self-esteem'. Narcissism is a defensive strategy which, in Lasch's view, is adaptive in respect of the threatening nature of the modern world. A narcissist forecloses a relation to both past and future, 'destroying' them psychically as a response to dangers the world now presents and to the fear that 'everything may come to an end'.

Surprisingly, Lasch has little to say about one of the main elements of narcissism as ordinarily understood: the relation between self and body. The story of Narcissus concerns his worship of his own appearance, and in most discussions of narcissism as a feature or type of personality the individual's relation to bodily appearance has properly been regarded as fundamental. The cultivation of the body, through consideration of diet, dress, facial appearance and other factors, is a common quality of lifestyle activities in contemporary social life. How far do these concerns represent a form of narcissism? The analysis set out in this and preceding chapters provides the basis of an answer. The body cannot be any longer merely 'accepted', fed and adorned according to traditional ritual; it becomes a core part of the reflexive project of self-identity. A continuing concern with bodily development in relation to a risk culture is thus an intrinsic part of modern social behaviour. As was stressed earlier, although modes of deployment of the body have to be developed from a diversity of lifestyle options, deciding between alternatives is not itself an option but an inherent element of the construction of self-identity. Life-planning in respect of the body is hence not necessarily narcissistic, but a normal part of post-traditional social environments. Like other aspects of the reflexivity of self-identity, body-planning is more often an engagement with the outside world than a defensive withdrawal from it.

Narcissism, in clinical terms, should be regarded as one among several other pathologies of the body which modern social life tends in some part to promote. As a personality deformation, narcissism has its origins in a failure to achieve basic trust. This is particularly true where the child fails satisfactorily to acknowledge the autonomy of the prime caretaker; and is unable clearly to separate out its own psychic boundaries. In these circumstances, omnipotent feelings of self-worth are likely to alternate with their opposite, a sense of emptiness and despair. Carried over into adulthood, these traits create a type of individual who is prone to be neurotically dependent on others, especially for the maintenance of self-esteem, yet possesses insufficient autonomy to be able to communicate effectively with them. Such a person is unlikely to be able to come to terms with the contemplation of risk which modern life circumstances entail. Thus she or he is likely to depend on the cultivation of bodily attractiveness, and perhaps personal charm, as a means of seeking to control life's hazards. The central dynamic of narcissism, to pursue the discussion initiated above, can be seen as shame rather than guilt. The alternating feelings of grandiosity and worthlessness with which the narcissist has to cope are essentially responses to a fragile self-identity liable to be overwhelmed by shame.

In assessing the prevalence of narcissism in late modernity, we have to be careful to separate the world of commodified images, to which Lasch frequently refers, from the actual responses of individuals. In Lasch's account, as we have observed, people appear as largely passive in their reactions – in this case to a world of glossy advertising imagery. Passivity and dependency in the face of the institutions of consumer capitalism, indeed, are among Lasch's main emphases. Yet powerful though commodifying influences no doubt are, they are scarcely received in an uncritical way by the populations they affect.

The uses of therapy

In conclusion, let us return briefly to the question of therapy, seen by Lasch, despite his use of psychoanalytic theory, primarily in negative vein as a form of dependence on experts. Rather than considering Lasch's views directly on this issue, we might turn to the somewhat comparable viewpoint established in the well-known writings of Philip Rieff.[33] Rieff relates the rise of therapy to secularisation and to what he sees as a moral dearth which the weakening of traditional religion has created. What he calls 'therapeutic control' operates to preserve a certain level of 'adequate social functioning' in settings where religion no longer supplies binding guidelines. Formerly if people were miserable, they sought the solace of the church; now they turn to the nearest available therapist. By means of therapy, a person aims to become 'the sane self in a mad world, the integrated personality in the age of nuclear fission, the quiet answer to loud explosions'.[34] Therapy seeks to create a confident and prosperous individual without a sense of higher moralities; it dispenses with the great riddles of life in exchange for a modest and durable sense of well-being. 'The important thing', as Rieff puts it, 'is to keep going.'[35]

There is a certain amount of validity in such a view, but it has to be recast substantially. We should first of all note that therapy does not replicate the 'authority' of previous times, most notably religious authority. There is no authoritative version of therapy. Anyone who seeks therapy, as was pointed out, is confronted with an almost inexhaustible variety of different schools, practices and philosophies, many of which are radically at odds with others. If classical psychoanalysis seems to have a pre-eminent place in intellectual debates about modes of therapy, this is more a tribute to Freud's genius than to any overall acceptance in practice that this particular version of therapy is more legitimate or efficacious than others. Therapy, therefore, is more a specific expression of dilemmas and practices relevant to high modernity than it is a phenomenon substituting for more traditional social or moral forms.

Is therapy only a means of adjusting dissatisfied individuals to a flawed social environment? Is it simply a narrow substitute, in secular vein, for a deeper range of involvements available in pre-modern settings? There is no denying that therapy can be an indulgence, and can perhaps promote narcissistic withdrawal. Most forms of therapy take time and money; therapy is in some degree a cultivated diversion of the privileged.

Yet it is also much more than this.[36] Therapy is an expert system deeply implicated in the reflexive project of the self: it is a phenomenon of modernity's reflexivity. In the shape of psychoanalysis, therapy developed as a means of combating pathologies of the personality. It was formed around a rhetoric of 'illnesses' and 'cures', and the curative properties of diverse forms of therapy – including classical psychoanalysis – continues to be the subject of acrimonious debate. But the prime importance of therapy in circumstances of late modernity does not lie in this direction. Therapy should be understood and evaluated essentially as a methodology of life-planning. The 'capable individual' today not only has a developed self-understanding, but is able to harmonise present concerns and future projects with a psychological inheritance from the past. Therapy is not just an adjustment device. As an expression of generalised reflexivity it exhibits in full the dislocations and uncertainties to which modernity gives rise. At the same time, it participates in that mixture of opportunity and risk characteristic of the late modern order. It can promote dependence and passivity; yet it can also permit engagement and reappropriation.

Therapeutic endeavours, nonetheless, take place against the background of the sequestration of experience and the internally referential systems of modernity. It is not surprising that many – not all – therapies are oriented primarily towards control. They interpret the reflexive project of the self in terms of self-determination alone, thus confirming, and even accentuating, the separation of the lifespan from extrinsic moral considerations.

6
Tribulations of the Self

The self in high modernity is not a minimal self, but the experience of large arenas of security intersects, sometimes in subtle, sometimes in nakedly disturbing, ways with generalised sources of unease. Feelings of restlessness, foreboding and desperation may mingle in individual experience with faith in the reliability of certain forms of social and technical framework. In the light of the analysis developed thus far, let us consider the origins of such sentiments.

The influence of risk and doubt

Radical doubt filters into most aspects of day-to-day life, at least as a background phenomenon. So far as lay actors are concerned, its most important consequence is the requirement to steer between the conflicting claims of rival types of abstract system. Yet it also probably generates more diffuse worries. Adherence to a clear-cut faith – especially one which offers a comprehensive lifestyle – may diminish such anxieties. But it is probably rare for even the most fundamentalist of fundamentalist believers to escape radical doubt entirely. No one today can but be conscious that living according to the precepts of a determined faith is one choice among other possibilities. The very moral outrage which the 'true believer' feels towards outsiders surely often expresses underlying anxiety rather than a feeling of safe adherence to the 'cause'.

Living in a secular risk culture is inherently unsettling, and feelings of anxiety may become particularly pronounced during episodes which have a fateful quality. As mentioned previously, the difficulties of living in a risk culture do not mean that there is greater insecurity on the level of day-to-day life than was true of previous eras – even in institutionalised risk settings. They concern anxieties generated by risk calculations themselves, plus the problem of screening out 'unlikely' contingencies, thus reducing life-planning to manageable proportions. 'Filtering out' is the task of the protective cocoon, but there is no easy boundary to be drawn between a 'well-founded' confidence in present and future events and one that is less secure; this fact is intrinsic to the nature of trust, as a phenomenon which 'brackets ignorance'. The deliberate, and frequently creative, manipulation of this boundary is one of the main inspirations of forms of cultivated risk-taking. Where it cannot be exploited to bring thrills and excitements, however, the borderline remains a focus for anxieties.

Risk assessment is crucial to the colonisation of the future; at the same time, it necessarily opens the self out to the unknown. There are some risk environments where the element of risk, so far as the situated individual is concerned, can be calculated quite precisely. Even here, and even supposing that the element of risk associated with a particular activity or strategy is small, by acknowledging risk the individual is forced to accept that any given situation could be one of those cases where 'things go wrong'. This will not be troubling as a rule if the person concerned has well-established feelings of basic trust. If his sense of basic trust is fragile, however, even contemplating a small risk, particularly in relation to a highly cherished aim, may prove intolerable.

There are many instances, moreover, where riskiness cannot be fully assessed, and others where relevant experts disagree, perhaps in a radical way, about the risks of particular courses of action. The difficulties of living in a secular risk culture are compounded by the importance of lifestyle choices. A person may take refuge in a traditional or pre-established style of life as a means of cutting back on the anxieties that might otherwise beset her. But, for reasons already given, the security such a strategy offers is likely to be limited, because the individual cannot but be conscious that any such option is only one among plural possibilities.

Awareness of high-consequence risks is probably for most people a source of unspecific anxieties. Basic trust is again a determining element in whether or not an individual is actively and recurrently plagued with such anxieties. No one can show that it is not 'rational' to worry constantly over the possibility of ecological catastrophe, nuclear war or the ravaging of humanity by as yet unanticipated scourges. Yet people who do spend every day worrying about such possibilities are not regarded as 'normal'. If most successfully bracket out such possibilities and get on with their day-to-day activities, this is no doubt partly because they assess the actual element of risk involved as very small. But it is also because the risks in question are given over to fate – one aspect of the return of *fortuna* in late modernity. A person may put such contingencies out of mind and assume that things will turn out well, or at least that, should global catastrophes of one kind or another occur, others will bear the brunt of them; alternatively, she might trust to governments and other organizations to cope effectively with the threats that present themselves.

Apocalypse has become banal, a set of statistical risk parameters to everyone's existence. In some sense, everyone has to live along with such risks, even if they make active efforts to help combat the dangers involved – such as by joining pressure groups or social movements. But no amount of bracketing out is likely altogether to overcome the background anxieties produced by a world which could literally destroy itself. The motif of 'survival' which Lasch describes connects such overall anxieties with the life-planning individuals carry out in the more restricted contexts of their action. The satisfaction an individual takes in being a 'survivor' relates primarily to the negotiation of troubles of the reflexively organised life career; but it is surely also infused with a more general sense of anxiety about collective survival in a world of high-consequence risks. There is a good deal of evidence to indicate that unconscious fears of an 'ending to everything' are prevalent among many sectors of the population, and appear with particular clarity in the fantasies and dreams of children.[1]

Ontological security, anxiety, and the sequestration of experience

Processes of change engendered by modernity are intrinsically connected to globalising influences, and the sheer sense of being caught up in massive waves of global transformation is perturbing.[2] More important is the fact that such change is also intensive: increasingly, it reaches through to the very grounds of individual activity and the constitution of the self. Contrary to the thrust of Lasch's analysis, however, no one can easily defend a secure 'local life' set off from larger social systems and organisations. Achieving control over change, in respect of lifestyle, demands an engagement with the outer social world rather than a retreat from it.

Understanding the juggernaut-like nature of modernity goes a long way towards explaining why, in conditions of high modernity, crisis becomes normalised. Much has been written on this subject and there is little need to recapitulate it here. A 'crisis' sounds like a major upheaval, or threatened upheaval, in an existing state of affairs – the original meaning of the word, which comes from a medical context, referred to a life-threatening phase in an illness.[3] In modern social conditions, however, crises become more or less endemic, both on an individual and a collective level. To some extent this effect is rhetorical: in a system open to continual and profound change many circumstances arise which loosely can be thought of as 'crises'. But it is not *just* rhetoric. Modernity is inherently prone to crisis, on many levels. A 'crisis' exists whenever activities concerned with important goals in the life of an individual or a collectivity suddenly appear inadequate. Crises in this sense become a 'normal' part of life, but by definition they cannot be routinised.

On some levels, a certain resigned world-weariness might be enough to cope psychologically with the ubiquity of crises – an attitude which again is only possible under the aegis of a conception of fate. But many crisis situations, even those operating at great distance from the individual, cannot easily be approached in this way, because they have implications for the individual's life circumstances. A person may read of recurrent political crises, for example, and perhaps be scornful about the ability of political leaders to contain them. But many such crises directly affect that person's own activities and capabilities, as when they lead to economic troubles, high unemployment or difficulties in housing markets. The crisis-prone nature of late modernity thus has unsettling consequences in two respects: it fuels a general climate of uncertainty which an individual finds disturbing no matter how far he seeks to put it to the back of his mind; and it inevitably exposes everyone to a diversity of crisis situations of greater or lesser importance, crisis situations which may sometimes threaten the very core of self-identity.

The sequestration of experience serves to contain many forms of anxiety which might otherwise threaten ontological security – but at considerable cost. Existential questions and doubts raise some of the most basic anxieties human beings can face. By and large, under conditions of modernity, such questions do not have to be confronted directly; they are institutionally 'put aside' rather than handled within the personality of the individual. So far as the control of anxiety is concerned, this situation has paradoxical implications. On the one hand, in ordinary circumstances, the individual is relatively protected from issues which might otherwise pose themselves as disturbing questions. On the other hand, whenever fateful moments intervene or other kinds of personal crises occur, the sense of ontological security is likely to come under immediate strain.

On a psychological level, there are close connections between the sequestration of experience, trust and the search for intimacy. Abstract systems help foster day-to-day security, but trust vested in such systems, as I have stressed previously, carries little psychological reward for the individual; trust brackets out ignorance, but does not provide the moral satisfactions that trust in persons can offer.

The sequestration of experience generates a specious control over life circumstances and is likely to be associated with enduring forms of psychological tension. For existential problems concern fundamental aspects of the lives of everyone; institutional repression cannot be by any means complete. We can see here a powerful basis for emotional disquiet, particularly when considered in combination with the backdrop of high-consequence risks. The loss of anchoring reference points deriving from the development of internally referential systems creates moral disquiet that individuals can never fully overcome.

The pure relationship: stresses and strains

In the reflexive project of the self, the narrative of self-identity is inherently fragile. The task of forging a distinct identity may be able to deliver distinct psychological gains, but it is clearly also a burden. A self-identity has to be created and more or less continually reordered against the backdrop of shifting experiences of day-to-day life and the fragmenting tendencies of modern institutions. Moreover the sustaining of such a narrative directly affects, and in some degree helps construct, the body as well as the self.

These stresses have a direct impact on the sphere of personal life. Pure relationships, like many other aspects of high modernity, are double-edged. They offer the opportunity for the development of trust based on voluntary commitments and an intensified intimacy. Where achieved and relatively secure, such trust is psychologically stabilising, because of the strong connections between basic trust and the reliability of caretaking figures. Given that these connections embrace feelings of security in the object-world, as well as in the sphere of personal relations as such, their importance is very considerable. The pure relationship is a key environment for building the reflexive project of the self, since it both allows for and demands organised and continuous self-understanding – the means of securing a durable tie to the other. Of course, many actual relationships exist and endure where little symmetry is found, and where each person is held in thrall by traits in the other which on the surface repel them (co-dependency). But the tendencies towards symmetry in the pure relationship are more than just an ideal: they are in large degree inherent in its nature.

The rise of therapy is closely tied to the emergence of the pure relationship, but not only, or even primarily, because therapeutic work can help heal the psychological damage which such relationships can bring about. The centrality of therapy expresses the fact that the more that pure relationships become dominant, the more crucial becomes an in-depth understanding which allows one to feel 'all right' with oneself. For self-mastery is the condition of that opening-out process through which hope (commitment) and trust are generated in the pure relationship.

Yet pure relationships, and the nexus of intimacy in which they are involved, create enormous burdens for the integrity of the self. In so far as a relationship lacks external referents, it is morally mobilised only through 'authenticity': the authentic person is one who knows herself and is able to reveal that knowledge to the other, discursively and in the behavioural sphere. To be in an authentic relation with another can be a major source of moral support, again largely because of its potential integration with basic trust. But shorn of external moral criteria, the pure relationship is vulnerable as a source of security at fateful moments and at other major life transitions.

Moreover, the pure relationship contains internal tensions and even contradictions. By definition, it is a social relation which can be terminated at will, and is only sustained in so far as it generates sufficient psychic returns for each individual. On the one hand it demands commitment, not only to the other individual, but to the social relation itself: this is again intrinsic to the pure relationship. On the other hand, the relationship can be voluntarily broken, and is acknowledged by both parties to be only 'good until further notice'. The possibility of dissolution, perhaps willingly brought about by the individual in question, forms part of the very horizon of commitment. It is not surprising that rage, anger and depressive feelings swirl through the contexts of pure relationships and, in concrete circumstances, intimacy may be psychically more troubling than it is rewarding.

'Living in the world': dilemmas of the self

In conditions of late modernity, we live 'in the world' in a different sense from previous eras of history. Everyone still continues to live a local life, and the constraints of the body ensure that all individuals, at every moment, are contextually situated in time and space. Yet the transformations of place, and the intrusion of distance into local activities, combined with the centrality of mediated experience, radically change what 'the world' actually is. This is so both on the level of the 'phenomenal world' of the individual and the general universe of social activity within which collective social life is enacted. Although everyone lives a local life, phenomenal worlds for the most part are truly global.

Characterising individuals' phenomenal worlds is difficult, certainly in the abstract. Every person reacts selectively to the diverse sources of direct and mediated experience which compose the *Umwelt*. One thing we can say with some certainty is that in

very few instances does the phenomenal world any longer correspond to the habitual settings through which an individual physically moves. Localities are thoroughly penetrated by distanciated
influences, whether this be regarded as a cause for concern or
simply accepted as a routine part of social life. All individuals
actively, although by no means always in a conscious way, selectively incorporate many elements of mediated experience into
their day-to-day conduct. This is never a random or a passive
process, contrary to what the image of the *collage* effect might
suggest. A newspaper, for example, presents a collage of information, as does, on a wider scale, the whole bevy of newspapers
which may be on sale in a particular area or country. Yet each
reader imposes his own order on this diversity, by selecting which
newspaper to read – if any – and by making an active selection of
its contents.

In some part the appropriation of mediated information follows pre-established habits and obeys the principle of the avoidance of cognitive dissonance. That is to say, the plethora of
available information is reduced via routinised attitudes which
exclude, or reinterpret, potentially disturbing knowledge. From a
negative point of view, such closure might be regarded as prejudice, the refusal seriously to entertain views and ideas divergent
from those an individual already holds; yet, from another angle,
avoidance of dissonance forms part of the protective cocoon
which helps maintain ontological security. For even the most
prejudiced or narrow-minded person, the regularised contact
with mediated information inherent in day-to-day life today is a
positive appropriation: a mode of interpreting information within
the routines of daily life. Obviously there are wide variations in
terms of how open a given individual is to new forms of knowledge, and how far that person is able to tolerate certain levels of
dissonance. But all phenomenal worlds are active accomplishments, and all follow the same basic psychodynamics, from the
most local of ways of life to the most cosmopolitan.

'Living in the world', where the world is that of late modernity,
involves various distinctive tensions and difficulties on the level of
the self. We can analyse these most easily by understanding them
as dilemmas which, on one level or another, have to be resolved
in order to preserve a coherent narrative of self-identity.

Unification versus fragmentation

The first dilemma is that of *unification* versus *fragmentation*. Modernity fragments; it also unites. On the level of the individual right up to that of planetary systems as a whole, tendencies towards dispersal vie with those promoting integration. So far as the self is concerned, the problem of unification concerns protecting and reconstructing the narrative of self-identity in the face of the massive intensional and extensional changes which modernity sets into being. In most pre-modern contexts, the fragmentation of experience was not a prime source of anxiety. Trust relations were localised and focused through personal ties, even if intimacy in the modern sense was generally lacking. In a post-traditional order, however, an indefinite range of possibilities present themselves, not just in respect of options for behaviour, but in respect also of the 'openness of the world' to the individual. 'The world', as indicated above, is not a seamless order of time and space stretching away from the individual; it intrudes into presence via an array of varying channels and sources.

Yet it is wrong to see the world 'out there' as intrinsically alienating and oppressive to the degree to which social systems are either large in scale or spatially distant from the individual. Such phenomena may often be drawn on to supply unifying influences; they are not just fragmenting in their impact on the self. Distant events may become as familiar, or more so, than proximate influences, and integrated into the frameworks of personal experience. Situations 'at hand' may in fact be more opaque than large-scale happenings affecting many millions of people. Consider some examples. A person may be on the telephone to someone twelve thousand miles away and for the duration of the conversation be more closely bound up with the responses of that distant individual than with others sitting in the same room. The appearance, personality and policies of a world political leader may be better known to a given individual than those of his next-door neighbour. A person may be more familiar with the debate over global warming than with why the tap in the kitchen leaks. Nor are remote or large-scale phenomena necessarily factors only vaguely 'in the background' of an individual's psychological make-up and identity. A concern with global warming, for example, might form part of a distinctive lifestyle adopted by a person, even if she is not an ecological activist. Thus she might keep in close contact with scientific debates and adjust various aspects of her lifestyle in relation to the practical measures they suggest.

Fragmentation clearly tends to be promoted by the influences emphasised by Berger and others: the diversifying of contexts of interaction. In many modern settings, individuals are caught up in a variety of differing encounters and milieux, each of which may call for different forms of 'appropriate' behaviour. Goffman is normally taken to be the theorist *par excellence* of this phenomenon. As the individual leaves one encounter and enters another, he sensitively adjusts the 'presentation of self' in relation to whatever is demanded of a particular situation. Such a view is often thought to imply that an individual has as many selves as there are divergent contexts of interaction, an idea which somewhat resembles poststructuralist interpretations of the self, albeit from a differing theoretical perspective. Yet again it would not be correct to see contextual diversity as simply and inevitably promoting the fragmentation of the self, let alone its disintegration into multiple 'selves'. It can just as well, at least in many circumstances, promote an integration of self. The situation is rather like the contrast between rural and urban life discussed previously. A person may make use of diversity in order to create a distinctive self-identity which positively incorporates elements from different settings into an integrated narrative. Thus a cosmopolitan person is one precisely who draws strength from being at home in a variety of contexts.[4]

The dilemma of unification versus fragmentation, like the others to be mentioned below, has its pathologies. On the one hand we find the type of person who constructs his identity around a set of fixed commitments, which act as a filter through which numerous different social environments are reacted to or interpreted. Such a person is a rigid traditionalist, in a compulsive sense, and refuses any relativism of context. On the other hand, in the case of a self which evaporates into the variegated contexts of action, we find the adaptive response which Erich Fromm has characterised as 'authoritarian conformity'. Fromm expresses this in the following way:

The individual ceases to be himself; he adopts entirely the kind of personality offered to him by cultural patterns; and he therefore becomes exactly as all others are and as they expect him to be . . . this mechanism can be compared with the protective colouring some animals assume. They look so similar to their surroundings that they are hardly distinguishable from them.[5]

In such circumstances, we might argue, the false self overrides and blankets out the original acts of thinking, feeling and willing which represent the true motivations of the individual. What remains of the true self is experienced as empty and inauthentic; yet this vacuum cannot be filled by the 'pseudo-selves' brought into play by the individual in different contexts, because these are as much stimulated by the responses of others as drawn from the person's inner convictions. Ontological security in this situation is as weakly founded as in the case of the rigid traditionalist. The individual only feels psychologically secure in his self-identity in so far as others recognise his behaviour as appropriate or reasonable.

Powerlessness versus appropriation

A second dilemma is that of *powerlessness* versus *appropriation*. If there is one theme which unites nearly all authors who have written on the self in modern society, it is the assertion that the individual experiences feelings of powerlessness in relation to a diverse and large-scale social universe. In contrast to the traditional world, it is supposed, where the individual was substantially in control of many of the influences shaping his life, in modern societies that control has passed to external agencies. As specified by Marx, the concept of alienation has served as the centre-point for analyses of this issue. As the forces of production develop, particularly under the aegis of capitalistic production, the individual cedes control of his life circumstances to the dominating influences of machines and markets. What is originally human becomes alien; human powers are experienced as forces emanating from an objectified social environment. Not only the followers of Marx have expressed such a view; it is also found, in somewhat different guise, in the works of the theorists of 'mass society'. The more extensive modern social systems become, according to this position, the more each particular individual feels shorn of all autonomy. Each, as it were, is merely an atom in a vast agglomeration of other individuals.

The ideas I have sought to develop in this book are distinctively different from such a standpoint. In many pre-modern contexts, individuals (and humanity as a whole) were more powerless than they are in modern settings. People typically lived in smaller groups and communities; but smallness is not the same as power. In many small-group settings individuals were relatively power-less to alter or escape from their surrounding social circum-stances. The hold of tradition, for example, was often more or less unchallengeable. There are many other illustrations. Pre-modern kinship systems, for example, were often quite rigid, and offered the individual little scope for independent action. We would be hard pressed to substantiate an overall generalisation that, with the coming of modern institutions, most individuals either are (or feel) more powerless than in preceding times.

Modernity expropriates – that is undeniable. Time-space dis-tanciation and the deskilling effects of abstract systems are the two most important influences. Even if distance and powerless-ness do not inevitably go together, the emergence of globalised connections, together with high consequence risks, represent parameters of social life over which the situated individual has relatively little control. Similarly, expropriation processes are part and parcel of the maturation of modern institutions and reach not only spheres of day-to-day life but the heart of the self.

If we understand such processes in dialectical fashion, however, and if we see that globalisation produces not just extensional but intensional change, a complex picture emerges. We cannot say that all forms of expropriation necessarily provide the possibility of reappropriation, certainly on the level of indi-vidual conduct. Many of the processes transformed by disembed-ding, or reorganised in the light of the intrusion of abstract systems, move beyond the purview of the situated actor. On the other hand, others make possible forms of mastery over life circumstances unavailable in pre-modern situations.

Powerlessness and reappropriation intertwine variously in dif-ferent contexts and at varying times: given the dynamism of modernity, there is little stability in the relations between them. An individual who vests trust in others, or in a given abstract system, normally thereby recognises that she lacks the power to influence them significantly. Yet the vesting of trust can also generate new capacities. Consider the example of money. In order to utilise money, an individual must participate in systems of economic exchange, banking and investment and so forth, over which she has little direct control. On the other hand, this process allows the individual – given sufficient resources – a diversity of opportunities which would otherwise be absent.

The experience of powerlessness, considered as a psychic phenomenon, naturally always relates to aims, projects or aspirations held by the individual, as well as to the composition of the phenomenal world. Powerlessness experienced in a personal relationship may be psychologically more damaging and consequential than powerlessness felt in relation to more encompassing social systems. Of course, these may feed into one another in various ways. Diffuse anxieties about high-consequence risks, for instance, might contribute in a general fashion to feelings of powerlessness experienced by an individual in more local contexts. Conversely, feelings of personal impotence may become diffused 'upwards' towards more global concerns. It seems reasonable to posit that connections of this kind are likely to underlie a 'survival' mentality. A 'survivor' is someone who feels deprived of adequate social mastery in a threatening series of personal and social environments. Yet a survivalist outlook carries connotations of appropriation as well as of powerlessness. Someone who concentrates on surviving in personal relations, as in other spheres of life, cannot be said to have abandoned all autonomy over his or her life's circumstances. Even if only in a somewhat negative sense, the individual clearly seeks active mastery: to survive is to be able in a determined way to ride out the trials life presents and overcome them.

Once again, the dilemma of powerlessness versus appropriation has its pathologies. Where an individual feels overwhelmed by a sense of powerlessness in the major domains of his phenomenal world, we may speak of a process of *engulfment*. The individual feels dominated by encroaching forces from the outside, which he is unable to resist or transcend. He feels either haunted by implacable forces robbing him of all autonomy of action, or caught up in a maelstrom of events in which he swirls around in a helpless fashion. At the other pole of the powerlessness/ appropriation divide is *omnipotence*. Like all personality patholo- gies, it is a fantasy state. The individual's sense of ontological security is achieved through a fantasy of dominance: the pheno- menal world feels as if it is orchestrated by that person as a puppeteer. Since omnipotence is a defence it is brittle, and often links psychologically to the other pole of the powerlessness/ appropriation composition: in other words, under pressure it can dissolve into its contrary, engulfment.

Authority versus uncertainty

A *third* dilemma is that of *authority* versus *uncertainty*. In condi- tions of high modernity, in many areas of social life – including the domain of the self – there are no determinant authorities. There exist plenty of claimants to authority – far more than was true of pre-modern cultures. Tradition was itself a prime source of authority, not located within any particular institution, but pervading many aspects of social life. Diffuse though it may have been, tradition was in an important sense a single authority. Although in the larger pre-modern cultures there may quite often have been clashes between rival traditions, for the most part traditional outlooks and ways of doing things precluded other alternatives. Even where there were vying traditions, involve- ment in a traditional framework was normally quite exclusive: the others were thereby rejected.

When we speak of specific institutions of authority, religion obviously has a leading place. In virtually all smaller pre-modern cultures there was only one main religious order – although such cultures have had their share of sceptics, and magicians and sorcerers were available to those diverging from religious ortho- doxy. Yet these alternatives were scarcely substitutes for the overarching authoritative reach of the dominant religious system. In larger traditional societies, where religious orders sometimes were more diversified, there was little pluralism in the modern sense: orthodoxy confronted various heresies. The local com- munity and the kinship system were two further sources of stabilising authority, directly relevant to the sustaining of trust relations in traditional contexts. Both were the source of 'binding doctrines' as well as of forms of behaviour endowed with strong normative compulsion.

Submission to traditional authorities, no matter how deep, did not remove uncertainty from day-to-day life in traditional cultures. The strength of pre-modern forms of authority could almost be understood as a response to the very unpredictability of daily life and to the number of influences felt to be outside human control. Religious authorities in particular quite often cultivated the feeling that individuals were surrounded by threats and dangers – since only the religious official was in a position to be able either to understand or to seek successfully to control these. Religious authority created mysteries while simultaneously claiming to have privileged access to them.[6]

In modern times some forms of traditional authority continue to exist, including, of course, religion. Indeed, for reasons that are to do precisely with the connections between modernity and doubt, religion not only refuses to disappear but undergoes a resurgence. Yet there is now a basic contrast with the past. Forms of traditional authority become only 'authorities' among others, part of an indefinite pluralism of expertise. The expert, or the specialist, is quite different from the 'authority', where this term is understood in the traditional sense. Except where authority is sanctioned by the use of force (the 'authorities' of the state and legal authority), it becomes essentially equivalent to specialist advice. There are no authorities which span the diverse fields within which expertise is claimed – another way of repeating the point that everyone in modern systems is a lay person in virtually all aspects of social activity. Authority in this situation is no longer an alternative to doubt. On the contrary, modes of expertise are fuelled by the very principle of doubt; in assessing the claims of rival authorities, the lay individual tends to utilise that principle in the sceptical outlook which pluralistic circumstances almost inevitably presuppose.

Of course, day-to-day life is not ordinarily experienced as perennially 'in doubt'. The reorganisation of daily life through abstract systems creates many routine forms of activity having a higher level of predictability than most contexts in pre-modern cultures. Through the protective cocoon, most people are buffered most of the time from the experience of radical doubt as a serious challenge either to the routines of daily activity or to more far-reaching ambitions. The dilemma of authority versus doubt is ordinarily resolved through a mixture of routine and commitment to a certain form of lifestyle, plus the vesting of trust in a given series of abstract systems. Yet this 'compromise package', under pressure, can begin to disintegrate.

Some individuals find it psychologically difficult or impossible to accept the existence of diverse, mutually conflicting authorities. They find that the freedom to choose is a burden and they seek solace in more overarching systems of authority. A predilection for *dogmatic authoritarianism* is the pathological tendency at this pole. A person in this situation is not necessarily a traditionalist, but essentially gives up faculties of critical judgement in exchange for the convictions supplied by an authority whose rules and provisions cover most aspects of his life. We should distinguish this attitude from faith, even faith in fundamentalist religious codes. For faith almost by definition rests on trust. Taking refuge in a dominant authority, however, is essentially an act of submission. The individual, as it were, no longer needs to engage in the problematic gamble which all trust relations presume. Instead, he or she identifies with a dominant authority on the basis of projection. The psychology of leadership plays an important role here. Submission to authority normally takes the form of a slavish adherence to an authority figure, taken to be all-knowing.

At the other pole, we find pathological states in which individuals are virtually immobilised through a tendency towards universal doubt. In its most marked versions, this outlook takes the form of paranoia or a paralysis of the will so complete that the individual effectively withdraws altogether from ordinary social intercourse.

Personalised versus commodified experience

A fourth dilemma is that between *personalised* versus *commodified* experience. Modernity opens up the project of the self, but under conditions strongly influenced by standardising effects of commodity capitalism. In this book I have not sought to trace out in a detailed fashion the impact of capitalistic production on modern social life. Suffice to affirm that capitalism is one of the main institutional dimensions of modernity, and that the capitalist accumulation process represents one of the prime driving forces behind modern institutions as a whole. Capitalism commodifies in various senses. The creation of the abstract commodity, as Marx pointed out, is perhaps the most basic element in the expansion of capitalism as an overall production system. Exchange-value is only created when use-values become irrelevant to the mechanisms whereby the production, sale and distribution of goods and services are carried on. Exchange-value thus allows for the disembedding of economic relations across indeterminate spans of time-space.

Commodification further, crucially, affects labour power: in fact labour power as such only comes into existence when separated as a commodity from 'labour' as a whole. Finally, commodification directly affects consumption processes, particularly with the maturation of the capitalistic order. The establishing of standardised consumption patterns, promoted through advertising and other methods, becomes central to economic growth. In all of these senses, commodification influences the project of the self and the establishing of lifestyles.

We can detail the impact of commodification in the following ways. The capitalistic market, with its 'imperatives' of continuous expansion, attacks tradition. The spread of capitalism places large sectors (although by no means all) of social reproduction in the hands of markets for products and labour. Markets operate without regard to pre-established forms of behaviour, which for the most part represent obstacles to the creation of unfettered exchange. In the period of high modernity, capitalistic enterprise increasingly seeks to shape consumption as well as monopolise the conditions of production. From the beginning, markets promote individualism in the sense that they stress individual rights and responsibilities, but at first this phenomenon mainly concerns the freedom of contract and mobility intrinsic to capitalistic employment. Later, however, individualism becomes extended to the sphere of consumption, the designation of individual wants becoming basic to the continuity of the system. Market-governed freedom of individual choice becomes an enveloping framework of individual self-expression.

The very corruption of the notion of 'lifestyle', reflexively drawn into the sphere of advertising, epitomises these processes. Advertisers orient themselves to sociological classifications of consumer categories and at the same time foster specific consumption 'packages'. To a greater or lesser degree, the project of the self becomes translated into one of the possession of desired goods and the pursuit of artificially framed styles of life. The consequences of this situation have often been noted. The consumption of ever-novel goods becomes in some part a substitute for the genuine development of self; appearance replaces essence as the visible signs of successful consumption come actually to outweigh the use-values of the goods and services in question themselves. Bauman expresses this well:

> Individual needs of personal autonomy, self-definition, authentic life or personal perfection are all translated into the need to possess, and consume, market-offered goods. This translation, however, pertains to the appearance of use value of such goods, rather than to the use value itself; as such, it is intrinsically inadequate and ultimately self-defeating, leading to momentary assuagement of desires and lasting frustration of needs. . . . The gap between human needs and individual desires is produced by market domination; this gap is, at the same time, a condition of its reproduction. The market feeds on the unhappiness it generates: the fears, anxieties and the sufferings of personal inadequacy it induces release the consumer behaviour indispensable to its continuation.[7]

Commodification is in some ways even more insidious than this characterisation suggests. For the project of the self as such may become heavily commodified. Not just lifestyles, but self-actualisation is packaged and distributed according to market criteria. Self-help books, like *Self Therapy*, stand in a precarious position with regard to the commodified production of self-actualisation. In some ways such works break away from standardised, packaged consumption. Yet in so far as they become marketed as prepackaged theorems about how to 'get on' in life, they become caught up in the very processes they nominally oppose.

The commodifying of consumption, it should be made clear, like other phenomena discussed earlier, is not just a matter of the reordering of existing behaviour patterns or spheres of life. Rather, consumption under the domination of mass markets is essentially a novel phenomenon, which participates directly in processes of the continuous reshaping of the conditions of day-to-day life. Mediated experience is centrally involved here. The mass media routinely present modes of life to which, it is implied, everyone should aspire; the lifestyles of the affluent are, in one form or another, made open to view and portrayed as worthy of emulation. More important, however, and more subtle, is the impact of the narratives the media convey. Here there is not necessarily the suggestion of a lifestyle to be aspired to; instead, stories are developed in such a way as to create narrative coherence with which the reader or viewer can identify.

No doubt soap operas, and other forms of media entertainment too, are escapes – substitutes for real satisfactions unobtainable in normal social conditions. Yet perhaps more important is the very narrative form they offer, suggesting models for the construction of narratives of the self. Soap operas mix predictability and contingency by means of formulae which, because they are well known to the audience, are slightly disturbing but at the same time reassuring. They offer mixtures of contingency, reflexivity and fate. The form is what matters rather than the content; in these stories one gains a sense of reflexive control over life circumstances, a feeling of a coherent narrative which is a reassuring balance to difficulties in sustaining the narrative of the self in actual social situations.

Yet commodification does not carry the day unopposed on either an individual or collective level. Even the most oppressed of individuals – perhaps in some ways particularly the most oppressed – react creatively and interpretatively to processes of commodification which impinge on their lives. This is true both within the realm of mediated experience and of direct consumption. Response to mediated experience cannot be assessed purely in terms of the content of what is disseminated: individuals actively discriminate among types of available information as well as interpreting it in their own terms. Even young children evaluate television programmes in terms of their degree of realism, recognising that some are wholly fictional, and treat programmes as objects of scepticism, derision or humour.[8] The fact that commodification is not all-triumphant at a collective level is also important for realms of individual experience. Space, for example, becomes commodified as a fundamental part of disembedding processes. However, space does not thereby become fully commercialised or subject to the standardising impact of commodity production. Many aspects of the built environment, and other spatial forms too, reassert themselves (through the active engagements of agents) in decommodified modes. Commodification is a driving force towards the emergence of internally referential systems; but, as will be discussed in the following section, external anchorings in aesthetic and moral experience refuse to disappear completely.

It is against this complicated backdrop that we should understand processes of individuation. The reflexive project of the self is in some part necessarily a struggle against commodified influences, although not all aspects of commodification are inimical to it. A market system, almost by definition, generates a variety of available choices in the consumption of goods and services. Plurality of choice is in some substantial part the very outcome of commodified processes. Nor is commodification merely the same as standardisation. Where mass markets are at issue, it is clearly in the interests of producers to ensure the large-scale consumption of relatively standardised products. Yet standardisation can often be turned into a mode of creating individual qualities – as in the previously quoted example of clothing. Mass produced clothing still allows individuals to decide selectively on styles of dress, however much the standardising influence of fashion and other forces affect those individual decisions.

A prime type of behaviour pathology associated with commodifying influences is narcissism – in this respect Lasch's thesis is valid, if over-generalised. Of course, narcissism springs from other sources too, especially as a deepseated phenomenon of personality development. But in so far as commodification, in the context of consumerism, promotes appearance as the prime arbiter of value, and sees self-development above all in terms of display, narcissistic traits are likely to become prominent. Individuation, however, also has its pathological aspects. All self-development depends on the mastering of appropriate responses to others; an individual who has to be 'different' from all others has no chance of reflexively developing a coherent self-identity. Excessive individuation has connections to conceptions of gran-

Unification versus fragmentation: the reflexive project of the self incorporates numerous contextual happenings and forms of mediated experience, through which a course must be charted.

Powerlessness versus appropriation: the lifestyle options made available by modernity offer many opportunities for appropriation, but also generate feelings of powerlessness.

Authority versus uncertainty: in circumstances in which there are no final authorities, the reflexive project of the self must steer a way between commitment and uncertainty.

Personalised versus commodified experience: the narrative of the self must be constructed in circumstances in which personal appropriation is influenced by standardised influences on consumption.

Figure 4 *Dilemmas of the self*

diosity. The individual is unable to discover a self-identity 'sober' enough to conform to the expectations of others in his social milieux.

An underlying dynamic: the threat of meaninglessness

If the analysis developed thus far is correct, encounters with the above dilemmas, in the context of the reflexive project of the self, take place against the background of the prevalence of internally referential systems. In other words, the reflexive project of the self has to be undertaken in circumstances which limit personal engagement with some of the most fundamental issues that human existence poses for all of us. It follows that the project of the self has to be reflexively achieved in a technically competent but morally arid social environment. Underlying the most thoroughgoing processes of life-planning – and each of the various dilemmas mentioned above – is the looming threat of *personal meaninglessness*.

The best starting-point for understanding why this should be so is the pervasiveness of abstract systems. Day-to-day life becomes

more calculable than it was in most pre-modern contexts. Calcu-
lability is expressed not only in the provision of stable social
environments, but in the chronic reflexivity whereby individuals
organise their own relations to the encompassing social world.
The threat of personal meaninglessness is ordinarily held at bay
because routinised activities, in combination with basic trust,
sustain ontological security. Potentially disturbing existential
questions are defused by the controlled nature of day-to-day
activities within internally referential systems.

Mastery, in other words, substitutes for morality; to be able to
control one's life circumstances, colonise the future with some
degree of success and live within the parameters of internally
referential systems can, in many circumstances, allow the social
and natural framework of things to seem a secure grounding for
life activities. Even therapy, as the exemplary form of the reflexive project of the self, can become a phenomenon of control – an
internally referential system in itself. Basic trust is a necessary
element in sustaining a sense of the meaningfulness of personal
and social activities within such frameworks. As a taken-for-
granted attitude towards the world as 'right and proper', basic
trust quiets feelings of dread which might otherwise surface. Yet,
as explained earlier, when controlled only by internally referential systems, this attitude is brittle. In fact, we may say that the
more open and general the reflexive project of the self, as further
fragments of tradition are stripped away, the more there is likely
to be a return of the repressed at the very heart of modern
institutions.

The return of the repressed

What are the main social circumstances, or guises, in which the
return of the repressed occurs? We can specify the following
conditions as of prime importance:

1   At *fateful moments*, individuals may be forced to confront
concerns which the smooth working of reflexively ordered
abstract systems normally keep well away from consciousness.
Fateful moments necessarily disturb routines, often in a radical
way. An individual is thereby forced to rethink fundamental

aspects of her existence and future projects. Fateful moments perhaps quite often can be dealt with within the confines of internally referential systems. But just as frequently they pose difficulties for the individual, and quite often for others closely connected with that individual, which push through to extrinsic considerations. Of course, the notion of fateful moments is a broad category. But many such moments do more than bring the individual up short: they cannot easily be dealt with without reference to moral/existential criteria. At fateful moments it is difficult for the individual to continue to think purely in terms of risk scenarios or to confine assessments of potential courses of action to technical parameters.

Most of the main transition points of life represent moments at which external criteria force themselves back into play. Birth and death are the two main mediating transitions between inorganic and organic life whose wider existential implications are difficult to escape. In both instances, institutionalised systems sequester these experiences and their attendant implications for others. In pre-modern cultures, childbirth and death of course were hardly happenings exposed to the view of the whole community. But they normally took place in group or family contexts and were closely integrated with traditional practices, as well as with cosmic interpretations of the passing of the generations. Today, both sets of events tend to happen in the sequestered milieu of the hospital and are there treated as discrete phenomena, having no distinctive connection with either the cycle of the generations or with broader moral issues concerning the relation between human beings and inorganic nature. Death tends to be the more completely hidden away of the two, perhaps because it is the more dangerous in terms of the return of external criteria. For childbirth is a process of entry into life and can be technically managed as such. The process of dying, on the other hand, cannot be seen as anything other than the incipient loss of control: death is unintelligible exactly because it is the point zero at which control lapses.

It is in these terms that we should understand the resurgence of literature concerned with making the phenomenon of death a subject for wider public debate.[9] There are various institutional manifestations of such a trend: one is the development of hospices as environments in which death can be discussed and confronted, rather than merely shunted away from general view. It has often been pointed out that *rites de passage* are relatively lacking in modern societies in respect of basic transitions, including the beginning and end of life. Most such discussions emphasise that, without ordered ritual and collective involvement, individuals are left without structured ways of coping with the tensions and anxieties involved. Communal rites provide a focus of group solidarity at major transitions as well as allocating definite tasks for those involved – such as specifying fixed periods of mourning and modes of behaviour associated with them.

This thesis may very well be valid. However, something more profound is lost together with traditional forms of ritual. *Rites de passage* place those concerned in touch with wider cosmic forces, relating individual life to more encompassing existential issues. Traditional ritual, as well as religious belief, connected individual action to moral frameworks and to elemental questions about human existence. The loss of ritual is also a loss of involvement with such frameworks, however ambiguously they might have been experienced and however much they were bound up with traditional religious discourse. Outside strictly theological circles, discussion of death for us has become largely a preoccupation with sickness. For example, in the case of Aids, what is disturbing is not that the illness, or rather its associated consequences, kills, but that it does so among the relatively young, and in the context of sexual activity. Death is only a 'problem' when it is premature death – when a person has not lived out whatever, given certain risks, a table of life expectancy might suggest.

2   We may detect a return of the repressed in endeavours to promote decarceration in various spheres. The origins of tendencies towards decarceration are no doubt complex. In some part, for example, attempts to set up open prisons or to rehabilitate prisoners in the community, as well as treating the mentally ill by means of community care, have been prompted by economic motives. But an important factor in these changes has also been the reformist belief that it is morally wrong to separate the 'deviant' from the 'normal' members of society. On the surface, decarceration seems to be merely a 'normalising' of deviance – a means of bringing the offender into closer contact with the ordinary population. Yet it may also be the reverse: a means of

encouraging 'normal' individuals to face the potentially perturbing questions raised by those who fail to adhere to central norms governing social life.

Contact with the mentally ill, as many writers have pointed out, in traditional cultures was often thought to be a mode of access to a spiritual experience and even to divine truth. Such contact is hardly likely to reproduce such sentiments today. On the other hand, mental illness, particularly the various kinds of schizophrenia, reminds us of the fragility of the day-to-day conventions by which our experience both of social reality, and the basic parameters of existence more generally, is ordered. The paranoid schizophrenic, for example, might cause us to reflect on why we do not – as she or he does – see malevolence in a glance from another person or an accidental clash of bodies on the street. The person who 'hears voices' may not be in communication with God, but nonetheless might cause us to think afresh about our own 'normality': for perhaps there are aspects to our taken-for-granted views of existence (founded on basic trust) which we can subject to interrogation.

Foucault argued that madness represents all that is excluded from the triumph of modern reason; but we do not need such an exalted view of insanity to see that mental illness reveals to us repressed aspects of our existence. Goffman, rather than Foucault, may be right about mental illness: it represents an incapacity or an unwillingness to conform to some of the most basic 'situational proprieties' that everyday interaction presumes. Looking at the 'other side' of the mundane discloses its contingent, and even arbitrary, character. The mentally ill, or certain groups among them, actually live out the dread which, as Garfinkel's 'experiments with trust' reveal, the constitutive conventions of day-to-day social interaction suppress.

3   We can trace a return of the repressed at the core of sexual behaviour. Passion has become privatised; yet its implications and resonances are far from private. Sexuality has become one main element of the striving for intimacy, but it addresses problems and stimulates feelings which are not restricted to a personal relation between two human beings. In intimate sexual relationships, people today frequently find their greatest moral satisfactions in life. From one angle, this phenomenon can be seen as a

reduction of moral purpose and existential consciousness to a purely personal sphere: a shrinkage which corresponds to the general process of the sequestration of experience. Yet at the same time sexuality breaks out from these confines, and perhaps is quite often the means whereby some of the deeper connotations of 'passion' are rediscovered. Sexuality has become separated from procreation and therefore from cosmic processes of life and death. But it still retains a moral charge and a generalisable significance which separates it from the egoistical concerns of the partners. It cannot be entirely severed from that sense of moral engagement and potential tragedy with which, prior to the rise of romantic involvements, sexual love was ordinarily associated.[10] The very preoccupation of modern discourse with sexuality, of which Foucault speaks, in some degree represents an acknowledgement of these connections. Sexuality both repudiates, and gives substantive form to the involvement of human life with morally transcendent conditions and experiences.

As Alberoni points out, the experience of falling in love – rather than day-to-day sexual encounters – epitomises this phenomenon. Falling in love, in contrast to most forms of sexuality, is intense, exalting and specifically 'extraordinary'. 'At these times, sexuality becomes the means by which life explores the frontiers of the possible, the horizons of the imaginary and of nature.'[11]

4   We may also trace a return of the repressed in a burgeoning preoccupation with the reconstruction of tradition to cope with the changing demands of modern and social conditions. Of course, in many sectors of modern life traditional elements remain, although they are often fragmented and their hold over behaviour partial. Moreover, some of the 'traditional' features of modern social life are in fact inventions dating only from the earlier period of modernity.[12] They are ways of encapsulating and representing modern trends rather than links with a deeply sedimented historical past.

Today, we see a definite tendency to seek to re-establish vanished traditions or even construct new ones. As was mentioned in a previous chapter, whether tradition can effectively be recreated in conditions of high modernity is seriously open to doubt. Tradition loses its rationale the more thoroughly reflexivity, coupled to expert systems, penetrates to the core of everyday life. The establishment of 'new traditions' is plainly a contradiction in terms. Yet, these things having been said, a return to sources of moral fixity in day-to-day life, in contrast to the 'always revisable' outlook of modern progressivism, is a phenomenon of some importance. Rather than constituting a regression towards a 'Romantic refusal' of modernity, it may mark an incipient move beyond a world dominated by internally referential systems.

5   As a phenomenon partly independent of the previous point we might mention the resurgence of religious belief and conviction. Religious symbols and practices are not only residues from the past; a revival of religious or, more broadly, spiritual concerns seems fairly widespread in modern societies. Why should this be? After all, each of the major founders of modern social theory, Marx, Durkheim, and Max Weber, believed that religion would progressively disappear with the expansion of modern institutions. Durkheim affirmed that there is 'something eternal' in religion, but this 'something' was not religion in the traditional sense: symbols of collective unity persist in more secular vein as the celebration of political ideals.

Not only has religion failed to disappear. We see all around us the creation of new forms of religious sensibility and spiritual endeavour. The reasons for this concern quite fundamental features of late modernity. What was due to become a social and physical universe subject to increasingly certain knowledge and control instead creates a system in which areas of relative security interlace with radical doubt and with disquieting scenarios of risk. Religion in some part generates the conviction which adherence to the tenets of modernity must necessarily suspend: in this regard it is easy to see why religious fundamentalism has a special appeal. But this is not all. New forms of religion and spirituality represent in a most basic sense a return of the repressed, since they directly address issues of the moral meaning of existence which modern institutions so thoroughly tend to dissolve.

6   New forms of social movement mark an attempt at a collective reappropriation of institutionally repressed areas of life. Recent religious movements have to be numbered among these, although of course there is great variability in the sects and cults which have developed. But several other new social movements are particularly important and mark sustained reactions to basic

institutional dimensions of modern social life. Although – and in some part because – it addresses questions which antedate the impact of modernity, the feminist movement is one major example. In its early phase, the movement was pre-eminently concerned with securing equal political and social rights between women and men. In its current stage, however, it addresses elemental features of social existence and creates pressures towards social transformations of a radical nature. The ecological and peace movements are also part of this new sensibility to late modernity, as are some kinds of movements for human rights. Such movements, internally diverse as they are, effectively challenge some of the basic presuppositions and organising principles which fuel modernity's juggernaut.

The return of the repressed will occupy us in a more direct way in the next chapter. For it is arguable that the period of high modernity is one of fundamental transition – not just a continuation of modernity's endless dynamism, but the presaging of structural transformations of a more profound type. The expansion of internally referential systems reaches its outer limits; on a collective level and in day-to-day life moral/existential questions thrust themselves back to centre-stage. Focused around processes of self-actualisation, although also stretching through to globalising developments, such issues call for a restructuring of social institutions, and raise issues not just of a sociological but of a political nature.

7
The Emergence of Life Politics

If the conception of the embattled, minimal self were correct, the self would not only be quite separate from the political sphere, but constituted through a defensive rejection of politics in favour of a tightly confined personal realm. Given such a perspective, it would be odd indeed to conclude this study with an exploration of political concerns. I want to propose, however, that not only do the themes developed in the preceding pages have political implications: much more than this, they are relevant to a reconstructing of political endeavours and problems of fundamental importance in the phase of high modernity.

Theodore Roszak has argued that 'we live in a time when the very private experience of having a personal identity to discover, a personal destiny to fulfil, has become a subversive political force of major proportions.'[1] Critics such as Lasch and others, he goes on to say, mistake the new ethos of self-discovery for the 'old-modern' aggrandising individual; they fail to distinguish between new impulses towards personal growth, on the one hand, and capitalistic pressures towards personal advantage and material accumulation on the other. I think this is true, save that the issue has to be theorised rather differently. It is not the reflexive project of the self as such which is subversive; rather, the ethos of self-growth signals major social transitions in late modernity as a whole. These transitions are the ones accentuated throughout this study: burgeoning institutional reflexivity, the disembedding of social relations by abstract systems, and the consequent interpenetration of the local and global. In terms of a political agenda, we can grasp their implications by distinguishing between *emancipatory politics* and *life politics*. Although I shall first of all concentrate on the former of these, it is the latter which is most directly bound up with the themes of this book. I ask the reader's indulgence if, to begin with, the relevance of the discussion of emancipatory politics to these themes is not clear: it will become so, I hope, towards the end of the chapter.

What is emancipatory politics?

From the relatively early development of the modern era onwards, the dynamism of modern institutions has stimulated, and to some extent has been promoted by, ideas of human *emancipation*. In the first place this was emancipation from the dogmatic imperatives of tradition and religion. Through the application of methods of rational understanding, not just to the areas of science and technology, but to human social life itself, human activity was to become free from pre-existing constraints.

If, with appropriate qualifications to cover over-simplification, we recognise three overall approaches within modern politics – radicalism (including Marxism in this category), liberalism and conservatism – we can say that emancipatory politics has dominated all of them, although in rather differing ways. Liberal political thinkers, like radicals, have sought to free individuals and the conditions of social life more generally from the constraints of pre-existing practices and prejudices. Liberty is to be achieved through the progressive emancipation of the individual, in conjunction with the liberal state, rather than through a projected process of revolutionary upheaval. 'Conservatism', the third category, almost by definition takes a more jaundiced view of the emancipatory possibilities of modernity. But conservative thought only exists as a reaction to emancipation: conservatism has developed as a rejection of radical and liberal thought, and as a critique of the disembedding tendencies of modernity.

I define emancipatory politics as a generic outlook concerned above all with liberating individuals and groups from constraints which adversely affect their life chances. Emancipatory politics involves two main elements: the effort to shed shackles of the past, thereby permitting a transformative attitude towards the future; and the aim of overcoming the illegitimate domination of some individuals or groups by others. The first of these objectives fosters the positive dynamic impetus of modernity. The break-away from fixed practices of the past allows human beings to secure increasing social control over their life circumstances. Of course, major philosophical differences have arisen over how this aim is to be achieved. Some have supposed that the emancipatory drive is governed by causal conditions which, in social life, operate in much the same way as physical causation. For others – and this is surely more valid – the relation is a reflexive one. Human beings are able reflexively to 'use history to make history'.[2]

The liberating of human beings from traditional constraints has little 'content' save for the fact that it reflects the characteristic orientation of modernity – the subjection to human control of features of the social and natural worlds that previously determined human activities. Emancipatory politics only achieves a more substantive content when it is focused on divisions between human beings. It is essentially a politics of 'others'. For Marx, of course, class was the agency of emancipation as well as the driving force of history. The general emancipation of humanity was to be achieved through the emergence of a classless order. For non-Marxist authors, emancipatory politics gives more far-reaching importance to other divisions: divisions of ethnicity and gender, divisions between ruling and subordinate groups, rich and poor nations, current and future generations. But in all cases the objective of emancipatory politics is either to release under-privileged groups from their unhappy condition, or to eliminate the relative differences between them.

Emancipatory politics works with a hierarchical notion of power: power is understood as the capability of an individual or group to exert its will over others. Several key concepts and orienting aims tend to be especially characteristic of this vision of politics. Emancipatory politics is concerned to reduce or eliminate *exploitation, inequality* and *oppression*. Naturally, these are defined variously by different authors, and since the main concern of this chapter is not in fact with the nature of emancipatory politics, I shall not try to chart them in a systematic way. Exploitation in general presumes that one group – say, upper as compared to working classes, whites as compared to blacks, or men as compared to women – illegitimately monopolises resources or desired goods to which the exploited group is denied access. Inequalities can refer to any variations in scarce resources, but differential access to material rewards has often been given prime importance. Unlike inequalities in genetic inheritance, for instance, differential access to material rewards forms part of the generative mechanisms of modernity, and hence can in principle (not, of course, in practice) be transformed to any desired degree. Oppression is directly a matter of differential power, applied by one group to limit the life chances of another. Like other aspects of emancipatory politics, the aim to liberate people from situations of oppression implies the adoption of moral values. 'Justifiable authority' can defend itself against the charge of oppression only where differential power can be shown to be morally illegitimate.

Emancipatory politics makes primary the imperatives of *justice*, *equality* and *participation*. In a general way these correspond to the three types of power division just mentioned. All have many variant formulations and can overlap more or less substantially.

Norms of justice define what counts as exploitation and, conversely, when an exploitative relation becomes one of morally defensible authority. A limiting case here would be anarchism, in so far as this doctrine holds that a social order is feasible in which not just exploitation, but authority as such, no longer exists. The fostering of equality, in some schools of thought, is held to be a prime value in itself, and occasionally is seen the overriding aim of emancipatory politics. Most forms of radical and liberal thought, however, regard certain kinds of inequality as legitimate and even desirable – as where material inequalities are justified because they provide economic incentives which generate efficient production. Participation, the third imperative, stands opposed to oppression since it permits individuals or groups to influence decisions that would otherwise be arbitrarily imposed on them. Again ideals of democratic involvement have to specify levels of participation, as hierarchical power is not inevitably oppressive any more than all authority is inherently exploitative.

Since emancipatory politics is concerned above all with over-coming exploitative, unequal or oppressive social relations, its main orientation tends to be 'away from' rather than 'towards'. In other words, the actual nature of emancipation is given little flesh, save as the capacity of individuals or groups to develop their potentialities within limiting frameworks of communal con-straint. The reluctance of most progressivist thinkers since the Enlightenment to think in utopian terms (although there are many exceptions) is one expression of this orientation. Marx's writings provide a characteristically resolute example. 'Utopian socialism' is to be avoided because it gives concrete form to the sought-after society. We cannot legislate in advance as to how people will live in such a social order: this must be left to them, when it actually comes into being.

If there is a mobilising principle of behaviour behind most versions of emancipatory politics it could be called the principle of autonomy.[3] Emancipation means that collective life is orga-nised in such a way that the individual is capable – in some sense or another – of free and independent action in the environments of her social life. Freedom and responsibility here stand in some kind of balance. The individual is liberated from constraints placed on her behaviour as a result of exploitative, unequal or oppressive conditions; but she is not thereby rendered free in any absolute sense. Freedom presumes acting responsibly in relation to others and recognising that collective obligations are involved. Rawls's theory of justice forms a prominent example of a version of emancipatory politics.[4] The basic conditions governing auton-omy of action are worked out in terms of a thematic of justice; Rawls provides a case for justice as an organising ambition of emancipation. Yet how individuals and groups in a just order will actually behave is left open.

Much the same could be said of Habermas's attempt to develop a framework for emancipatory politics in terms of a theory of communication.[5] The ideal-speech situation, held to be imman-ent in all language use, provides an energising vision of emancipa-tion. The more social circumstances approximate to an ideal-speech situation, the more a social order based on the auton-omous action of free and equal individuals will emerge. Individuals will be free to make informed choices about their activities; so will humanity on a collective level. Yet little or no indication is given about what those choices will actually be.

The nature of life politics

Life politics presumes (a certain level of) emancipation, in both the main senses noted above: emancipation from the fixities of tradition and from conditions of hierarchical domination. It would be too crude to say simply that life politics focuses on what happens once individuals have achieved a certain level of autonomy of action, because other factors are involved; but this provides at least an initial orientation. Life politics does not primarily concern the conditions which liberate us in order to make choices: it is a politics *of* choice. While emancipatory politics is a politics of life chances, life politics is a politics of lifestyle. Life politics is the politics of a reflexively mobilised order – the system of late modernity – which, on an individual and collective level, has radically altered the existential parameters of social activity. It is a politics of self-actualisation in a reflexively ordered environment, where that reflexivity links self and body to systems of global scope. In this arena of activity, power is generative rather than hierarchical. Life politics is lifestyle politics in the serious and rich sense discussed in previous chapters. To give a formal definition: life politics concerns political issues which flow from processes of self-actualisation in post-traditional contexts, where globalising influences intrude deeply into the reflexive project of the self, and conversely where processes of self-realisation influence global strategies.

The concerns of life politics flow directly from the principal themes of this book and I shall attempt to document them in some detail below. Although life-political issues can be traced further back, life politics only emerges as a fully distinctive set of problems and possibilities with the consolidating of high modernity. As mentioned previously, the concerns of life politics presage future changes of a far-reaching sort: essentially, the development of forms of social order 'on the other side' of modernity itself.

Emancipatory politics	*Life politics*
1 The freeing of social life from the fixities of tradition and custom.	1 Political decisions flowing from freedom of choice and generative power (power as transformative capacity).
2 The reduction or elimination of exploitation, inequality or oppression. Concerned with the divisive distribution of power/ resources.	2 The creation of morally justifiable forms of life that will promote self-actualisation in the context of global interdependence.
3 Obeys imperatives suggested by the ethics of justice, equality and participation.	3 Develops ethics concerning the issue 'how should we live?' in a post-traditional order and against the backdrop of existential questions.

Life politics, to repeat, is a politics of life decisions. What are these decisions and how should we seek to conceptualise them? First and foremost, there are those affecting self-identity itself. As this study has sought to show, self-identity today is a reflexive achievement. The narrative of self-identity has to be shaped, altered and reflexively sustained in relation to rapidly changing circumstances of social life, on a local and global scale. The individual must integrate information deriving from a diversity of mediated experiences with local involvements in such a way as to connect future projects with past experiences in a reasonably coherent fashion. Only if the person is able to develop an inner authenticity – a framework of basic trust by means of which the lifespan can be understood as a unity against the backdrop of shifting social events – can this be attained. A reflexively ordered narrative of self-identity provides the means of giving coherence to the finite lifespan, given changing external circumstances. Life politics from this perspective concerns debates and contestations deriving from the reflexive project of the self.

In exploring the idea that the 'personal is political', the student movement, but more particularly the women's movement, pioneered this aspect of life politics. But they did so in an ambiguous manner. Members of the student movement, especially those associated with 'situationalism', tried to use personal gestures and 'lifestyle revolts' as a mode of throwing down a challenge to officialdom. They wanted to show not only that daily life expresses aspects of state power, but that by overturning ordinary daily patterns they could actually threaten the power of the state. Seen in this way, however, the politics of the personal only vaguely foreshadows life politics, and remains closer to the emancipatory form. For the objective is to use lifestyle patterns as a means of combating, or sublating, oppression.

Feminism can more properly be regarded as opening up the sphere of life politics – although, of course, emancipatory concerns remain fundamental to women's movements. Feminism, at least in its contemporary form, has been more or less obliged to give priority to the question of self-identity. 'Women who want more than family life', it has been aptly remarked, 'make the personal political with every step they take away from the home.'[6] In so far as women increasingly 'take the step' outside, they contribute to processes of emancipation. Yet feminists soon came to see that, for the emancipated woman, questions of identity become of pre-eminent importance. For in liberating themselves from the home, and from domesticity, women were faced with a closed-off social environment. Women's identities were defined so closely in terms of the home and the family that they 'stepped outside' into social settings in which the only available identities were those offered by male stereotypes.

When Betty Friedan first spoke of 'the problem that has no name', some quarter of a century ago, she meant that being a wife and mother failed to provide the fulfilling life for which many women, almost without knowing it, yearned.[7] Her analysis of this problem led Friedan directly to a discussion of identity and the self. The real 'question which has no name' turns out to be 'who do I want to be?'[8] Friedan specifically related the issue to her own experiences as a young woman. Having just graduated from college, she felt she had many options open to her, including that of following a professional career as a psychologist. Yet instead of taking up a fellowship she had won for a doctoral programme, she abandoned that possible career without really knowing why. She married, had children and lived as a suburban housewife – all the while suppressing her qualms about her lack of purpose in life. In the end, she broke away by acknowledging and facing up to the question of her self-identity, coming to see that she needed self-fulfilment elsewhere.

Betty Friedan's deep disquiet about personal identity, she made clear, only came about because there were now more options available for women. It is only in the light of these alternatives that women have come to see that modern culture does not 'gratify their basic need to grow and fulfil their potentialities as human beings . . .'[9] Her book concluded with a discussion of life-planning, the means of helping women create new self-identities in the previously unexplored public domain. Her 'new life-plan for women' anticipated many features of self-help manuals that were to come later. The new life-plan involved a commitment to personal growth, a rethinking and reconstruction of the past – by rejecting the 'feminine mystique' – and the recognition of risk.

Life politics, body and self

Today, some quarter of a century after Friedan's pathbreaking book first appeared, it has become obvious that many of the issues which at first seemed to concern only women are actually bound up with the relational phenomenon of gender identity. What gender identity is, and how it should be expressed, has become itself a matter of multiple options – ranging up to and including even the choice of whether a person remains anatomically of the same sex into which she or he was born. The politics of self-identity, of course, is not limited to matters of gender differentiation. The more we reflexively 'make ourselves' as persons, the more the very category of what a 'person' or 'human being' is comes to the fore. Many examples can be found to illustrate how and why this is so. For instance, current debates about abortion might seem limited to the body and the rights the body's 'owner' might or might not have over its products. But discussions of abortion also turn in some part on whether or not a foetus is a person and, if so, at what point in its development it can be counted as one. In this issue, as so often in the areas of life politics, we find conjoined problems of philosophical definition, human rights and morality.

As the case of abortion indicates, it is not always easy to distinguish life-political questions concerning self-identity from those that focus more specifically on the body. Like the self the body can no longer be taken as a fixed – a physiological entity – but has become deeply involved with modernity's reflexivity. The body used to be one aspect of nature, governed in a fundamental way by processes only marginally subject to human intervention. The body was a 'given', the often inconvenient and inadequate seat of the self. With the increasing invasion of the body by abstract systems all this becomes altered. The body, like the self, becomes a site of interaction, appropriation and reappropriation, linking reflexively organised processes and systematically ordered expert knowledge. The body itself has become emancipated – the condition for its reflexive restructuring. Once thought to be the locus of the soul, then the centre of dark, perverse needs, the body has become fully available to be 'worked upon' by the influences of high modernity. As a result of these processes, its boundaries have altered. It has, as it were, a thoroughly permeable 'outer layer' through which the reflexive project of the self and externally formed abstract systems routinely enter. In the conceptual space between these, we find more and more guidebooks and practical manuals to do with health, diet, appearance, exercise, lovemaking and many other things.

Reflexive appropriation of bodily processes and development is a fundamental element of life-political debates and struggles. It is important to emphasise this point in order to see that the body has not become just an inert entity, subject to commodification or 'discipline' in Foucault's sense. If such were the case, the body would be primarily a site of emancipatory politics: the point would then be to free the body from the oppression to which it had fallen prey. In conditions of high modernity, the body is actually far less 'docile' than ever before in relation to the self, since the two become intimately coordinated within the reflexive project of self-identity. The body itself – as mobilised in praxis – becomes more immediately relevant to the identity the individual promotes. As Melucci observes,

> the return to the body initiates a new search for identity. The body appears as a secret domain, to which only the individual holds the key, and to which he or she can return to seek a self-definition unfettered by the rules and expectations of society. Nowadays the social attribution of identity invades all areas traditionally protected by the barrier of 'private space'.[10]

We can recognise the problem of 'ownership' of the body as one distinctive issue posed by its double involvement with abstract systems and the reflexive project of the self. As was mentioned before, 'ownership' here is a complex notion bringing in all the problems of defining a 'person'. In the sphere of life politics, this problem includes how the individual is to make choices concerning strategies of bodily development in life-planning, as well as who is to determine the 'disposal' of bodily products and bodily parts.

Body and self are linked in another fundamental domain that has become thoroughly penetrated by the internally referential systems of modernity: reproduction. The term 'reproduction' can be used to refer both to social continuity and to the biological continuance of the species. The terminological connection is not accidental: 'biological' reproduction is by now wholly social, that is, evacuated by abstract systems and reconstituted through the reflexivity of the self. Reproduction clearly was never solely a matter of external determinism: in all pre-modern cultures various kinds of contraceptive methods, for example, have been used. Nonetheless, for the most part the sphere of reproduction belonged irremediably to the arena of fate. With the advent of more or less fail-safe methods of contraception, reflexive control over sexual practices and the introduction of reproductive technologies of various kinds, reproduction is now a field where plurality of choice prevails.

The 'end of reproduction as fate' is closely tied in to the 'end of nature'. For until now reproduction has always been at one pole of human involvement with separated nature – death being at the other. Genetic engineering, whose potentialities have only just begun to be tapped, represents a further dissolution of reproduction as a natural process. Genetic transmission can be humanly determined by this means, thus breaking the final tie connecting the life of the species to biological evolution. In this process of the disappearance of nature, emergent fields of decision-making affect not just the direct process of reproduction, but the physical constitution of the body and the manifestations of sexuality. Such fields of action thus relate back to questions of gender and gender identity, as well as to other processes of identity formation.

Reproductive technologies alter age-old oppositions between fertility and sterility. Artificial insemination and *in vitro* fertilisation more or less completely separate reproduction from the traditional categories of heterosexual experience. The sterile can be made fertile, but various permutations of surrogate parenthood are also thus made possible. The opportunity offered for gay couples, for instance, to produce and rear children is only one among various lifestyle options flowing from these innovations. The fact that sexuality no longer need have anything to do with reproduction – or vice versa – serves to reorder sexuality in relation to lifestyles (although, as always, in large degree only through the medium of reflexive appropriation).

The variety of options now introduced, or likely to be developed soon, in the area of reproductive technologies provides a signal example of the opportunities and problems of life politics. The birth of Louise Brown, on 25 July, 1978, marked a new transition in human reproduction. The creation of new life – rather than the negative control of life through contraception – for the first time became a matter of deliberate construction. *In vitro* fertilisation (IVF) uses many techniques which have been around for some while, but certain key innovations have allowed these to be used to fertilise a human egg outside the body. A further development is pre-implantation sex screening. By means of IVF methods, it is possible to transfer an already 'sexed' embryo to a woman's womb by DNA amplification techniques. Male and female embryos can be distinguished by such techniques, and an embryo of the desired sex implanted. To these techniques can be added embryo freezing. This process allows embryos to be stored for an indefinite length of time, permitting multiple pregnancies without the need for further ovary stimulation and egg collection. Thus it is possible, for example, for identical twins to be born years apart from one another.

Further developments which look at least feasible in the control of human reproduction include ectogenesis and cloning. Ectogenesis is the creation of human life entirely outside the body: the production of children without pregnancy. Cloning, the creation of a number of genetically identical individuals, although perhaps more bizarre, appears closer at hand, and has already been achieved in animal experiments.[11]

Personal lives, planetary needs

The discussion thus far draws in the world of social relations external to the self mainly in terms of their reflexive impact on self-identity and lifestyle. However, personal decisions also affect global considerations – the link in this case is from 'person' to 'planet'. Socialised reproduction connects individual decisions to the very continuity of the species on the earth. To the extent to which the reproduction of the species and sexuality become uncoupled, future species reproduction is no longer guaranteed. Global population development becomes incorporated within internally referential systems. A host of individual decision-making processes, linked through these systems, are likely to produce unpredictabilities comparable to those generated by other socialised orders. Reproduction becomes a variable individual decision, with an overall impact on species reproduction which might be imponderable.

We can trace out yet further connections between lifestyle options and globalising influences. Consider the related topics of global ecology and attempts to reduce risks of nuclear war. In broaching ecological issues, and their relation to political debates, we have to ask first of all why they should be so much the focus of attention today. The answer is partly to be found in the accumulating evidence that the material environment has been subject to more far-reaching and intensive processes of decay than was previously suspected to be the case. Much more decisive, however, are the alterations in human attitudes relevant to the issue. For the fact that nature has 'come to an end' is not confined to the specialist awareness of professionals; it is known to the public at large. A clear part of increased ecological concern is the recognition that reversing the degradation of the environment depends upon adopting new lifestyle patterns. By far the greatest amount of ecological damage derives from the modes of life followed in the modernised sectors of world society. Ecological problems highlight the new and accelerating interdependence of global systems and bring home to everyone the depth of the connections between personal activity and planetary problems.

Grappling with the threats raised by the damaging of the earth's eco-systems is bound to demand coordinated global responses on levels far removed from individual action. On the other hand, these threats will not be effectively countered unless there is reaction and adaption on the part of every individual. Widespread changes in lifestyle, coupled with a de-emphasis on continual economic accumulation, will almost certainly be necessary if the ecological risks we now face are to be minimised. In a complicated interweaving of reflexivity, widespread reflexive awareness of the reflexive nature of the systems currently transforming ecological patterns is both necessary and likely to emerge.

The issue of nuclear power is at the centre of these concerns, and of course forms a link between ecological issues more generally and the existence of nuclear weapons. Debates about whether or not nuclear power stations should continue to be built and, if so, what their relation should be to existing sources of material power exemplify many of the questions raised in the area of life politics. High-consequence risks are involved, some deriving from long-term, incremental factors, others from more immediate influences. Technical calculations of levels of risk here cannot be completely watertight, because they cannot wholly control for human error and because there may be factors as yet unforeseen. A person who wishes to become informed about debates concerning nuclear power will find that experts are as radically divided in their assessments as in other areas where abstract systems prevail. Unless some other – so far unknown – technological breakthrough is made, the widespread use of nuclear power is likely to be unavoidable if global processes of economic growth carry on at the same rate as today, and even more so if they intensify.

Decreasing dependence on nuclear power, or seeking to eliminate nuclear power sources altogether, either in particular regions and countries or on a wider scale, would involve significant lifestyle changes. As in other areas of the expansion of internally referential systems, no one can be quite sure how much damage to human life and to the physical environment might already have been done by existing nuclear power sources; the evidence is controversial. We come back again to personal questions of socialised biology and reproduction. As one author has put it, 'our sperm, our eggs, our embryos and our children' are 'in the front line' in the struggle on the 'toxic frontier'.[12]

As the proponents of 'deep ecology' assert, a movement away from economic accumulation might involve substituting personal growth – the cultivation of the potentialities for self-expression and creativity – for unfettered economic growth processes. The reflexive project of the self might therefore be the very hinge of a transition to a global order beyond the current one. The threat of nuclear war is also linked to the reflexive project of the self. As Lasch says, both throw the problem of 'survival' into sharp relief. Yet one might equally well say that they both throw into relief the possibility of peace: harmonious human coexistence on the global level and psychologically rewarding self-actualisation on the personal plane. The issue of nuclear weaponry enters life politics as a positive appropriation as well as a negative one. It shows with particular clarity the degree to which the personal and global are interconnected because, as in the case of potential ecological disaster, there is nowhere anyone can go on earth to escape. Military technology has become more and more complex, a series of expert systems about which it is difficult for the layperson to get much specialist knowledge (in some part because of the secrecy with which weapon systems are surrounded). Yet this very process makes the potential outbreak of nuclear war no longer just a specific concern of military tacticians and political leaders, but a matter which impinges on the life of everyone. Operating under a negative sign, the danger of nuclear confrontation coincides with other aspects of the life-political field in stimulating reflexive awareness of the socialisation of nature and its implications for personal life.

Summary: the agenda of life politics

Life-political issues place a question mark against the internally referential systems of modernity. Produced by the emancipatory impact of modern institutions, the life-political agenda exposes the limits of decision-making governed purely by internal criteria. For life politics brings back to prominence precisely those moral and existential questions repressed by the core institutions of modernity. Here we see the limitations of accounts of 'postmodernity' developed under the aegis of poststructuralism. According to such views, moral questions become completely denuded of meaning or relevance in current social circumstances. But while this perspective accurately reflects aspects of the internally referential systems of modernity, it cannot explain why moral issues return to the centre of the agenda of life politics. Life-political issues cannot be debated outside the scope of abstract systems: information drawn from various kinds of expertise is central to their definition. Yet because they centre on questions of how we should live our lives in emancipated social circumstances they cannot but bring to the fore problems and questions of a moral and existential type. Life-political issues supply the central agenda for the return of the institutionally repressed. They call for a remoralising of social life and they demand a renewed sensitivity to questions that the institutions of modernity systematically dissolve.

We are now in a position to sum up and systemise the preceding discussion. The agenda of life politics derives from the extension of the internally referential systems of modernity to cover several distinct areas. The invasion of the natural world by abstract systems brings nature to an end as a domain external to human knowledge and involvements. The tremendous extension of human control over nature (which, as in other areas of control, yields new unpredictabilities) comes up against its limits, however. These consist not so much in the environmental degradation and disruption that is thus brought about, as in the stimulus to reintroduce parameters of debate external to modernity's abstract systems. In other words, repressed existential issues, related not just to nature but to the moral parameters of existence as such, press themselves back on to the agenda. The process is not an automatic one: on the level of everyday life, as well as in collective struggles, moral/existential problems are actively recovered and brought forward into public debate. The specific moral arena of such debates concerns, not just what should be done for human beings to survive in nature, but how existence itself should be grasped and 'lived': this is Heidegger's 'question of Being'. The 'end of nature' opens up many new issues for consideration because the field of intrinsic organisation has become so extensive. As with other substantive moral questions, these all in some way involve lifestyle options. All pose difficult analytical problems as well as moral dilemmas.

A second area is biological reproduction. From the point of view of the dominant outlook of modernity, reproduction is a mechanical phenomenon – a matter of genetic processes. But looked at morally, reproduction raises the question of existential contradiction. The main moral arena here concerns transcendence: how human beings should approach the question of their own finitude. As in each of the other domains, how more substantial moral issues bearing on lifestyle options are approached is likely to depend on how the wider questions of existential contradiction and finitude are handled. The problem of what rights a foetus has, for example, is strongly influenced by what one takes 'life' to represent, as a moral as well as an analytic issue.

Globalisation represents a third focus for the expansion of modernity's internally referential systems. The emergence of globalised orders, as has been stressed in this study, means that the world we live 'in' today is different from that of previous ages. Globalisation unifies the overall human community – in some part because of the creation of high-consequence risks which no one living on the earth can escape. New forms of cooperation are called for; although generally acknowledged, in a world of distinct nation-states they are as yet only weakly developed. Given the high-consequence risk factors, the substantive moral questions which arise are partly of a 'containing' kind. Should we declare exceptions to the principle of radical doubt? Should there be limits to the unfettered pursuit of scientific enquiry? Should the possession of nuclear weapons be condemned as morally indefensible? Such questions affect our 'existence' in the concrete sense that they bear on the survival of humanity as a whole. Yet they also connect with more elementary existential issues of intersubjectivity.

Finally, we return to self-identity, focused through the internally referential systems of self and body. Thoroughly penetrated by modernity's abstract systems, self and body become the sites of a variety of new lifestyle options. In so far as it is dominated by the core perspectives of modernity, the project of the self remains one of control, guided only by a morality of 'authenticity'. However, concerning as it does the most intimate human sensibilities, this project becomes a fundamental impetus towards a remoralising of daily life. Substantive questions on the agenda of life politics centre upon rights of personhood and individuality, which connect back to the existential dimensions of self-identity as such.

Connections and implications

What is the sense of 'politics' in 'life politics'? It is conventional in political theory to recognise a narrow and a broad conception of politics. The first refers to processes of decision-making within the governmental sphere of the state; the second sees as political any modes of decision-making which are concerned with settling debates or conflicts where opposing interests or values clash. Life politics is politics in both of these senses.

The narrow sense of politics survives because of the central position which the nation-state and its governmental apparatus continue to hold. A nation-state cannot effectively legislate about issues of life politics so as to produce decisions binding on broader social communities. Thus, for example, a decision to control research into genetic engineering in one state would make little impact on scientific developments in this area globally. A government might decide to ban nuclear power within its own territories, but this act would hardly protect its population in an acceptable way if other countries nearby maintained their nuclear power sources. Yet all issues of life politics involve questions of rights and obligations, and the state thus far continues to be the main administrative locus within which these are settled in law. Life-political issues are likely to assume greater and greater importance in the public and juridical arenas of states. Demands for emancipatory rights, as stressed earlier, do not thereby become any less important. Attempts to extend and sustain citizenship rights, for example, remain fundamental; such rights provide the arenas within which life-political issues can be openly debated.

In the broader sense of politics, life-political issues permeate many areas of social life in later modernity. For numerous spheres of choice on the individual level and collectively are opened up by the extension of abstract systems and the socialisa-

Existential Questions and Life Politics

Domain	Moral arena	Internally referential systems	Substantive moral issues
Existence	Survival and Being	Nature	1 What responsibilities do human beings have towards nature? 2 What are the principles of environmental ethics?
Finitude	Transcendence	Reproduction	1 What are the rights of the unborn? 2 What rights has the foetus? 3 What ethical principles should govern genetic engineering?
Individual and communal life	Cooperation	Global systems	1 What limits should be placed on scientific/technological innovation? 2 What limits should be placed on the use of violence in human affairs?
Self-identity	Personhood	Self and body	1 What rights does the individual have over her/his body? 2 What, if any, gender differences should be preserved? 3 What rights do animals have?

tion of natural processes. It is not my aim to trace out in any detail the likely institutional parameters of life politics in this wider sense. Social movements have played a basic role in bringing life-political issues to the fore, and forcing them on public attention. Whether such movements are harbingers of organisational changes in the domains of political activity is a moot question.[13] In late modernity, where reflexive attempts to colonise the future are more or less universal, many types of individual action and organisational involvement might shape life-political issues. Life-political problems do not fit readily within existing frameworks of politics, and may well stimulate the emergence of political forms which differ from those hitherto prominent, both within states and on a global level.

Thus far, emancipatory politics has been described as though it were merely the preparation for the emergence of life politics. The relation between emancipatory and life politics is, of course, more complicated than such a view would suggest. Emancipatory politics will not come to an end as life politics moves to claim more of the overall political agenda; virtually all questions of life politics also raise problems of an emancipatory sort. In late modernity, access to means of self-actualisation becomes itself one of the dominant focuses of class division and the distribution of inequalities more generally. Capitalism, one of the great driving forces in the expansion of modernity, is a class system which tends to generate major material inequalities – on a global scale as well as within the economically developed societies. The emancipatory struggles which have helped moderate the polarising effects of 'unfettered' capitalist markets are hence directly relevant to the pursuit of life-political endeavours.

Emancipatory politics often does more than simply 'prepare the stage' for life-political concerns. We can explore some possible connections by means of examples. Let me concentrate on two: feminism and the divisions between First and Third World nations.

The women's movement has clear emancipatory objectives. Its aims are to free women from traditional forms of constraint and allow them to participate on an equal level with men in areas of social activity formerly dominated by males. In the first years of the movement, as was indicated earlier, emancipatory interests were clearly in the ascendancy. Yet other concerns were also present from early on. When the women's movement gained its initial momentum in the nineteenth century, some individuals were already proposing that more than sheer emancipation was at stake. Making the voices of women heard, they proposed, would both need far-reaching changes in the actual organisation of social life and bring them about. When women eventually entered the male-dominated sectors of society on an equal basis with men, they would bring with them values and attitudes that would profoundly reshape those male domains.

Among other changes, the emancipation of women, it has been suggested, might influence levels of aggressiveness in society, and might help transform pre-existing attitudes towards the natural environment. Thus feminists early and late have drawn attention to the fact that military power and warfare are quintessentially male domains. Traditional warrior values were always male values, standing opposed to the concerns of women with nurturance in the household and in the family. Most armies, until recent times at any rate, have consisted exclusively of men, and combat on the battlefield has also been a resolutely male affair. Perhaps, therefore, military power and the propensity to war, even in a nuclear age, are bound up directly with male aggressiveness? After all, males specialise in violence: rape, like war, is almost exclusively a male activity.[14] As women become more equal with men, and particularly as they become more and more prominent in public spheres, they may alter the value systems which have been created by men and which underlie warfare and male aggression. Women, it has been claimed, will incorporate nurturing values into arenas of life which were previously subjected by men to their own, more violent, ways of doing things.[15]

Promethean attitudes to nature, technology, and even science itself, it has been argued by some feminist authors, also reflect male orientations. Men's attitude towards the world is essentially an instrumental one, based on domination and manipulation. The outlook of women is characteristically different, and women hence relate in a contrasting way to the natural environment.[16] Mothering and the other nurturant tasks in which women are involved link them to natural reproductive processes much more closely than men. The socialisation of biology and reproduction would, from this perspective, be seen as a further intrusion of male control into these essentially feminine concerns.

In emancipating themselves from male domination, by their very presence women would alter human relations to nature.

These theses are controversial, and are rejected by many.[17] The idea that women would, through their emancipation, substantially alter the nature of military power or the socialisation of nature founders if 'essentialist' theories of gender difference are discarded. For, as many feminist writers would now argue, there are no generic differences between 'men' and 'women'; differences within these categories often override what is shared in common by men or women respectively. Whether or not these conceptions are valid, however, is not what really matters in this context. The point is that we can envisage circumstances in which, because of the changes which ensue from achieving it, emancipation directly affects life-political issues.

Consider in this regard the divisions between First and Third World nations. No one can doubt that reducing global inequalities is essential if long-term global security is to be won. An emancipatory process must be set in motion, although at the moment the mechanisms whereby this might be achieved are not very apparent. It seems difficult to suppose that the disparities between rich and poor countries could be reduced through further global industrialisation on a large scale. Not only would such a process produce a still greater deterioration in global ecology, sufficient resources simply do not exist for the world's population to adopt ways of life comparable to those of the First World societies. Thus a process of emancipation on the part of the world's poor could probably only be achieved if radical lifestyle changes were introduced in the developed countries. Emancipation presumes life-political transformation.

Are there any general formulae connecting emancipatory and life politics? Marx provided one, when he worked out his celebrated formulation of 'the Jewish Question'.[18] Those who fought for the emancipation of the Jews from religious oppression and persecution were not, Marx asserted, struggling for purely sectional interests. For in freeing the Jews from such oppression, they were liberating human beings as a whole. In Marx's argument, this was a generalised freedom from the constraints of religion. But one might generalise the principle yet further: struggles to emancipate oppressed groups can help liberate others by promoting attitudes of mutual tolerance which in the end could benefit everyone.

The emergence of life politics, I have argued, results from the centrality of the reflexive project of the self in late modernity, coupled to the contradictory nature of the extension of modernity's internally referential systems. The capability of adopting freely chosen lifestyles, a fundamental benefit generated by a post-traditional order, stands in tension, not only with barriers to emancipation, but with a variety of moral dilemmas. No one should underestimate how difficult it will be to deal with these, or even how hard it is to formulate them in ways likely to command widespread consensus.[19] How can we remoralise social life without falling prey to prejudice? The more we return to existential issues, the more we find moral disagreements; how can these be reconciled? If there are no transhistorical ethical principles, how can humanity cope with clashes of 'true believers' without violence? Responding to such problems will surely require a major reconstruction of emancipatory politics as well as the pursuit of life-political endeavours.

Notes

1 The Contours of High Modernity

1 Judith Wallerstein and Sandra Blakeslee, *Second Chances* (London: Bantam, 1989).
2 Ibid., quotations from pp. 293, 294, 296, 297 and 308.
3 A fuller exposition of the major points of the next few sections can be found in Anthony Giddens, *The Consequences of Modernity* (Cambridge: Polity, 1990).
4 Anthony Giddens, *The Nation-State and Violence* (Cambridge: Polity, 1985).
5 See Giddens, *Consequences of Modernity*.
6 Georg Simmel, *The Philosophy of Money* (London: Routledge, 1978), p. 179.
7 Alan Fox, *Beyond Contract* (London: Faber, 1974). For one of the few generalised discussions of trust in systems, see Susan P. Schapiro, 'The social control of impersonal trust', *American Journal of Sociology*, 93, 1987.
8 Cf. Paul Connerton, *How Societies Remember* (Cambridge: Cambridge University Press, 1989).
9 Giddens, *Central Problems in Social Theory* (London: Macmillan, 1979).
10 Claude Lévi-Strauss, *Structural Anthropology* (London: Allen Lane, 1968).
11 Walter J. Ong, *Interfaces of the Word* (Ithaca: Cornell University Press, 1977).
12 Harold Innis, *Empire and Communications* (Oxford University Press, 1950); Marshall McLuhan, *Understanding Media* (London: Sphere, 1967).
13 Christopher Small, *The Printed Word* (Aberdeen: Aberdeen University Press, 1982).

14 J. M. Strawson: 'Future methods and techniques', in Philip Hills (ed.), *The Future of the Printed Word* (London: Pinter, 1980), p. 15.

15 Susan R. Brooker-Gross, 'The changing concept of place in the news', in Jacquelin Burgess and John R. Gold, *Geography, the Media and Popular Culture* (London: Croom Helm, 1985), p. 63.

16 Cf. E. Relph, *Place and Placelessness* (London: Pion, 1976). Joshua Meyrowitz, *No Sense of Place* (Oxford: Oxford University Press, 1985).

17 Especially Jean Baudrillard. See Mark Poster, *Jean Baudrillard* (Cambridge: Polity, 1989).

18 Yi-Fu Tuan, *Topophilia* (Englewood Cliffs: Prentice-Hall, 1974); Robert David Sack, *Conceptions of Space in Social Thought* (London: Macmillan, 1980).

19 Giddens, *Consequences of Modernity*. For an important analysis which uses a rather different metaphor, see James R. Rosenau, *Turbulence in World Politics* (London: Harvester, 1990).

20 Ulrich Beck: *Risikogesellshaft: Auf dem Weg in eine andere Moderne* (Frankfurt: Suhrkamp, 1986).

21 On this issue, see Zygmunt Bauman, *Modernity and Ambivalence* (Cambridge: Polity, 1990).

2 The Self: Ontological Security and Existential Anxiety

1 Anthony Giddens, *Central Problems in Social Theory* (1979) and *The Constitution of Society* (Cambridge: Polity Press, 1984).

2 Harold Garfinkel, 'A conception of, and experiments with, "trust" as a condition of stable concerted actions', in O. J. Harvey, *Motivation and Social Interaction* (New York: Ronald Press, 1963); see on this issue also John Heritage, *Garfinkel and Ethnomethodology* (Cambridge: Polity Press, 1984).

3 For a fuller exposition, see Anthony Giddens, *The Consequences of Modernity*; and, in the original source, Erik Erikson, *Childhood and Society* (New York: Norton, 1950).

4 D.W. Winnicott, *The Maturational Processes and the Facilitating Environment* (London: Hogarth, 1965), pp. 57, 86.

5 D. W. Winnicott, 'Creativity and its origins', in his *Playing and Reality* (Harmondsworth: Penguin, 1974), p. 83.

6 Sigmund Freud, *Introductory Lectures on Psychoanalysis* (Harmondsworth: Penguin, 1974), p. 395.

7 Sigmund Freud, 'Anxiety', in ibid.

8   Harry Stack Sullivan, *Conceptions of Modern Psychiatry* (New York: Norton, 1953).
9   Ibid., p. 14.
10 Cf. Rollo May, *The Meaning of Anxiety* (New York: Washington Square Press, 1977).
11 Freud, 'Anxiety'.
12 Erving Goffman, *Relations in Public* (London: Allen Lane, 1971).
13 Sören Kierkegaard, *The Concept of Dread* (London: Macmillan, 1944), p. 99.
14 Anthony Giddens, *New Rules of Sociological Method* (London: Macmillan, 1981).
15 Paul Tillich, *The Courage to Be* (London: Collins, 1977).
16 Sören Kierkegaard, *Concluding Unscientific Postscript* (Princeton: Princeton University Press, 1941), p. 147.
17 Quotations from Martin Heidegger, *Being and Time* (Oxford: Blackwell, 1962), pp. 143–5.
18 Sören Kierkegaard, *The Sickness Unto Death* (Harmondsworth: Penguin, 1989).
19 René Descartes, *Meditations on First Philosophy* (Cambridge: Cambridge University Press, 1986), p. 98.
20 Of course, this issue has been much debated by philosophers, particularly following the lead of Hume. A very large literature relevant to the problem has accumulated over the past twenty years.
21 R. D. Laing, *The Divided Self* (Harmondsworth: Penguin, 1965).
22 In ibid., p. 108.
23 Ibid., p. 112.
24 Charles Taylor, *Sources of the Self* (Cambridge: Cambridge University Press, 1989). On narratives of self-identity see also Alasdair MacIntyre, *After Virtue* (London: Duckworth, 1981).
25 Giddens, *Constitution of Society*, ch. 2.
26 Goffman, *Relations in Public*.
27 Ibid., p. 248.
28 Ibid.
29 Michel Foucault, *Discipline and Punish* (London: Allen Lane, 1979).
30 Goffman, *Relations in Public*, p. 250.
31 Kierkegaard, *Sickness Unto Death*.
32 Bruno Bettelheim, *The Informed Heart* (London: Palladin, 1970). For further discussion, see Giddens, *Central Problems*.
33 Sigmund Freud, *Beyond the Pleasure Principle* (London: Hogarth, 1950).
34 Laing, *Divided Self*, p. 144.

35   Harold Garfinkel, *Studies in Ethnomethodology* (Cambridge: Polity Press, 1984).
36   For this analysis, I draw on the work of Thomas J. Scheff and Suzanne Retzinger, *Emotion and Violence* (New York: Lexington Books, 1991), although I do not, as they do, pursue the connections between shame, rage and violence.
37   See Rom Harré, *Personal Being* (Oxford: Blackwell, 1983).
38   Jean-Paul Sartre, *Being and Nothingness* (London: Methuen, 1969).
39   Gabriele Taylor, *Pride, Shame and Guilt* (Oxford: Clevedon Press, 1985).
40   Helen B. Lewis, *Shame and Guilt in Neurosis* (New York, International Universities Press, 1971).
41   Helen M. Lynd, *Shame and the Search for Identity* (London: Routledge, 1958), pp. 46–7.
42   Heinz Kohut, *The Analysis of the Self* (New York: International Universities Press, 1971).
43   G. Piers and M. Singer, *Shame and Guilt* (New York: Norton, 1953).
44   Ibid., p. 142.
45   Kohut, *Analysis of the Self*, p. 108.
46   Heinz Kohut, *The Restoration of Self* (New York: International Universities Press, 1977), pp. 238, 241.
47   Erikson, *Childhood and Society*, p. 242.

3   The Trajectory of the Self

1   Janette Rainwater, *Self-Therapy* (London: Crucible, 1989), p. 9.
2   Ibid.
3   Ibid., p. 11.
4   Ibid., p. 56.
5   Ibid., p. 194.
6   Ibid., p. 209.
7   Roy F. Baumeister, *Identity. Cultural Change and the Struggle for Self* (New York: Oxford University Press, 1986).
8   Emile Durkheim, *The Division of Labour in Society* (London: Macmillan, 1984).
9   Rainwater, *Self-Therapy*, p. 15.
10   John O. Lyons, *The Invention of the Self* (Carbondale: Southern Illinois University Press, 1978).
11   Rainwater, *Self-Therapy*, p. 172.

12 Sharon Wegscheider-Cruse, *Learning to Love Yourself* (Deerfield Beach, Fa: Health Communications, 1987).
13 Ibid., p. 79.
14 Dennis H. Wrong, 'The influence of sociological ideas on American culture', in Herbert J. Gans, *Sociology in America* (Beverly Hills: Sage, 1990).
15 Pierre Bourdieu, *Distinction* (Cambridge, Mass.: Harvard University Press, 1986).
16 Peter Berger et al., *The Homeless Mind* (Harmondsworth: Penguin, 1974).
17 Anthony Giddens, *The Constitution of Society*, ch. 4.
18 Joshua Meyrowitz, *No Sense of Place*.
19 Cf. Berger et al., *Homeless Mind*, pp. 69ff.
20 See Harvey Sacks, 'On members' measurement systems', *Research on Language and Social Interaction*, 22, 1988–9.
21 Rainwater, *Self-Therapy*, pp. 56ff.
22 Anthony Giddens, *The Consequences of Modernity*.
23 Pat Easterling, 'Friendship and the Greeks', in Roy Porter and Sylvana Tomaselli, *The Dialectics of Friendship* (London: Routledge, 1989), p. 11.
24 Shere Hite, *Women and Love* (London: Viking, 1988).
25 Ibid., p. 526.
26 Ibid., p. 655.
27 See, for example, Kenneth Solomon and Norman B. Levy, *Men in Transition* (London: Plenum, 1983).
28 See, for example, Shere Hite, *Sexual Honesty* (New York: Warner, 1974).
29 There is now a very large literature on co-dependency, particularly in the United States, ranging from technical texts to popular explanations and therapeutic programmes. For a representative example, see Melody Beattie, *Co-Dependent No More* (New York: Harper, 1987).
30 See the celebrated analysis by Norbert Elias, *The Civilising Process*, vol. 1 (Oxford: Blackwell, 1978).
31 Goffman has a great deal of interest to say about how privacy is sustained in day-to-day life, and why individuals regard it as so important; on the other hand, he implies that privacy is a universal need, and rarely places his account of it in a historical context.
32 Joseph Bensman and Robert Lilienfeld, *Between Public and Private* (New York: Free Press, 1979).
33 Wegscheider-Cruse, *Learning to Love Yourself*, p. 96 (emphasis added).
34 Ibid., p. 100.

35   Giddens, *Consequences of Modernity*, pp. 114ff.
36   Wegscheider-Cruse, *Learning to Love Yourself*, pp. 101–3.
37   Vernon Coleman, *Bodysense* (London: Sheldon Press, 1990).
38   Ibid., pp. 23–4.
39   Ibid., p. 25.
40   Joan Jacobs Brumberg, *Fasting Girls: The Emergence of Anorexia Nervosa as a Modern Disease* (Cambridge, Mass.: Harvard University Press, 1988).
41   Ibid., p. 100.
42   Cf. in particular Hilde Bruch, *The Golden Cage: The Emergence of Anorexia Nervosa* (London: Routledge, 1978).
43   This description appears as chapter 8 in Marilyn Lawrence, *The Anorexic Experience* (London: Women's Press, 1984).
44   Cf. Marcia Millman, *Such a Pretty Face* (New York: Berkley Books, 1981); Kim Chernin, *The Obsession: Reflections on the Tyranny of Slenderness* (New York: Harper, 1981).
45   Susie Orbach, *Hunger Strike: The Anorexic's Struggle as a Metaphor for Our Age* (London: Faber, 1986).
46   Ibid., pp. 27ff.
47   J. A. Sours, *Starving to Death in a Sea of Objects* (New York: Aronson, 1981).

4   Fate, Risk and Security

1   Liz Greene, *The Astrology of Fate* (London: Allen and Unwin, 1984).
2   Max Weber, *The Sociology of Religion* (Boston: Beacon, 1963).
3   Niccolo Machiavelli, *The Prince*, quoted from *The Portable Machiavelli* (Harmondsworth: Penguin, 1979), pp. 159–60.
4   Cf. Torsten Hägerstrand, 'Time and culture', in G. Kirsch et al., *Time Preferences* (Berlin: Wissenschaftszentrum, 1985); Helga Nowotny, *Eigenzeit: Entstehung und Strukturierung eines Zeitgefühls* (Frankfurt: Suhrkamp, 1989), ch. 2.
5   Erving Goffman, *Interaction Ritual* (London: Allen Lane, 1972).
6   Ibid.
7   Goffman does not include the second of these in his discussion of fatefulness, but from the point of view of an individual contemplating his or her life, and how to act from a given point onwards, the acquisition of fateful information forms a crucial conjuncture.
8   Quoted from John Keats, 'Ode to a Nightingale', in Roy Porter and Dorothy Porter, *In Sickness and in Health* (London: Fourth Estate, 1988).

9   John Urquhart and Klaus Heilmann, *Risk Watch* (New York: Facts on File, 1984).
10   Ibid., p. 12.
11   Raymond Firth, 'Suicide and risk-taking in Tikopia society', *Psychiatry*, 24, 1961.
12   James M. A. Weiss, 'The gamble with death in attempted suicide', *Psychiatry*, 20, 1957.
13   Peter G. Moore, *The Business of Risk* (Cambridge: Cambridge University Press, 1983), pp. 104ff.
14   R. A. Brearley and S. Myers, *Principles of Corporate Finance* (New York: McGraw-Hill, 1981).
15   Urquhart and Heilmann, *Risk Watch*, ch. 4.
16   Paul Slovic and Baruch Fischoff, 'How safe is safe enough?', in Jack Downie and Paul Lefrere, *Risk and Chance* (Milton Keynes: Open University Press, 1980).
17   P. M. Boffey, 'Nuclear war', *Science*, no. 190, 1975.
18   E. Rabinowitch, 'Living dangerously in the age of science', *Bulletin of the Atomic Scientists*, 28, 1972.
19   Urquhart and Heilmann, *Risk Watch*, p. 89.
20   Goffman, *Interaction Ritual*, p. 166.
21   Ibid., p. 167.
22   Erving Goffman, *Relations in Public*, pp. 252ff.
23   Urquhart and Heilmann, *Risk Watch*, p. 45.
24   Anthony Giddens, *The Consequences of Modernity*.
25   Cf. Charles W. Smith, *The Mind of the Market* (Totowa: Rowman and Littlefield, 1981).
26   Michael Balint, *Thrills and Regressions* (London: Hogarth, 1959). This work is drawn on extensively by Goffman in *Interaction Ritual*.
27   Murray Melbin, *Night as Frontier* (New York: Free Press, 1987).
28   René Dubos, *The Wooing of Earth* (London: Athlone, 1980).
29   Ibid.
30   Bill McKibben, *The End of Nature* (New York: Random House, 1989), p. 96.

5   The Sequestration of Experience

1   Edward Shils, *Tradition* (London: Faber, 1981), p. 25.
2   John Kotre, *Outliving the Self* (Baltimore: Johns Hopkins University Press, 1984).
3   Anthony Giddens, *The Consequences of Modernity*.
4   Cf. Erik Erikson, *Identity: Youth and Crisis* (London: Faber, 1968).

5   Cf. Giddens, *A Contemporary Critique of Historical Materialism*, vol. 1.
6   Richard Sennett, *The Fall of Public Man* (Cambridge: Cambridge University Press, 1977).
7   Ibid., ch. 5.
8   Norbert Elias, *The Civilising Process*, vol. 1.
9   Ibid., pp. 175ff.
10 Sigmund Freud, *Civilisation and its Discontents* (London: Hogarth, 1950).
11 Ibid., pp. 61, 71.
12 Max Weber, *The Protestant Ethic and the Spirit of Capitalism* (London: Allen and Unwin, 1976).
13 David J. Rothman, *The Discovery of the Asylum* (Boston: Little, Brown, 1971).
14 Michel Foucault, *Discipline and Punish*.
15 Rothman, *Discovery*, p. 4.
16 Ibid., p. 15.
17 Ibid., pp. 72–3.
18 Ibid., p. 124.
19 Norbert Elias, *The Loneliness of the Dying* (Oxford: Blackwell, 1985).
20 John Lofland, *State Executions* (Montclair: Patterson Smith, 1977).
21 Niklas Luhmann, *Love as Passion* (Cambridge: Polity, 1986).
22 Michel Foucault, *The History of Sexuality* (Harmondsworth: Penguin, 1981), pp. 3–4.
23 Luhmann, *Love as Passion*.
24 See, for example, Michael R. Wood and Louis A. Zurchner, *The Development of a Postmodern Self* (New York: Greenwood, 1988).
25 Sennett, *Fall of Public Man*.
26 Ibid., p. 219.
27 Christopher Lasch, *The Culture of Narcissism* (London: Abacus, 1980) and *The Minimal Self* (London: Picador, 1985).
28 Lasch, *Culture of Narcissism*, pp. 85–6.
29 Cf. Claude Fischer, *To Dwell Among Friends* (Berkeley: University of California Press, 1982).
30 Judith Stacey, *Brave New Families* (New York: Basic, 1990).
31 Lasch, *Culture of Narcissism*, p. 74.
32 Ibid., p. 79.
33 Philip Rieff, *The Triumph of the Therapeutic* (Harmondsworth: Penguin, 1966).
34 Ibid., p. 34.
35 Ibid., p. 35.
36 Two relevant discussions, which set out to contest Lasch's interpre-

tations in relation to the United States are Daniel Yankelovich, *New Rules: Searching for Self-fulfilment in a World Turned Upside Down* (New York: Bantam, 1982); and Peter Clecak, *America's Quest for the Ideal Self* (Oxford: Oxford University Press, 1983). A trenchant critique of Lasch is to be found in Dennis H. Wrong, 'Bourgeois values, no bourgeoisie? The cultural criticism of Christopher Lasch', *Dissent*, Summer 1979.

6 Tribulations of the Self

1 Cf. Dorothy Rowe, *Living with the Bomb* (London: Routledge, 1985); Robert Jay Lifton and Richard Falk, *Indefensible Weapons* (New York: Basic, 1982).
2 Arnold Gehlen, *Man in the Age of Technology* (New York: Columbia University Press, 1980).
3 Cf. Jürgen Habermas, *Legitimation Crisis* (London: Heinemann, 1976).
4 Cf. Claude S. Fischer, *The Urban Experience* (New York: Harcourt Brace Jovanovich, 1984).
5 Eric Fromm, *The Fear of Freedom* (London: Routledge, 1960), p. 160.
6 W. Warren Wagar, *Terminal Visions* (Bloomington: University of Indiana Press, 1982).
7 Zygmunt Bauman, *Legislators and Interpreters* (Cambridge: Polity, 1989), p. 189.
8 Robert Hodge and David Tripp, *Children and Television* (Cambridge: Polity, 1989), p. 189. Cf. also John Fiske, *Understanding Popular Culture* (London: Unwin Hyman, 1989).
9 Cf. in particular Norbert Elias, *The Loneliness of the Dying*.
10 Niklas Luhmann, *Love as Passion*, chs 13, 14.
11 Francesco Alberoni, *Falling in Love* (New York: Random House, 1983), p. 13.
12 Eric Hobsbawm and Terence Ranger, *The Invention of Tradition* (Cambridge: Cambridge University Press, 1983).

7 The Emergence of Life Politics

1 Theodore Roszak, *Person-Planet: The Creative Destruction of Industrial Society* (London: Gollancz, 1979), p. xxviii.
2 Cf. Jürgen Habermas, *Knowledge and Human Interests* (Cambridge: Polity, 1987) – the classic discussion of this issue.

3 See David Held, *Models of Democracy* (Cambridge: Polity, 1987), concluding chapter.
4 John Rawls, *A Theory of Justice* (Oxford: Clarendon, 1972).
5 Jürgen Habermas, *Theory of Communicative Action* (Cambridge: Polity, 1987).
6 Barbara Sichtermann, *Femininity: The Politics of the Personal* (Cambridge: Polity, 1986), p. 2.
7 Betty Frieden, *The Feminine Mystique* (Harmondsworth: Pelican, 1965).
8 Ibid., p. 61.
9 Ibid., p. 68.
10 Alberto Melucci, *Nomads of the Present* (London: Hutchinson Radius, 1989), p. 123.
11 David Suzuki and Peter Knudtson, *Genethics: The Ethics of Engineering Life* (London: Unwin Hyman, 1989).
12 John Elington, *The Poisoned Womb* (Harmondsworth: Penguin, 1986), p. 236.
13 Cf. Melucci, *Nomads*.
14 Susan Brownmiller, *Against Our Will* (London: Secker and Warburg, 1975).
15 Cf. Jean B. Elshtain, *Women and War* (New York: Basic, 1987).
16 For a sophisticated discussion of this question, see Carolyn Merchant, *The Death of Nature* (New York: Harper, 1980).
17 Cf. Teresa Brennan, *Between Feminism and Psychoanalysis* (London: Routledge, 1989).
18 Karl Marx, 'On the Jewish Question', in T. B. Bottomore, ed., *Karl Marx, Early Writings* (New York: McGraw-Hill, 1962).
19 These are issues which I take up in a book in preparation, which forms the third volume of *A Contemporary Critique of Historical Materialism*, but is also a companion work to this one. The book concentrates upon the institutional parameters of modernity rather than upon the domain of self-identity.

Glossary of Concepts

Abstract systems: symbolic tokens and expert systems taken generically.

Basic trust: trust in the continuity of others and in the object-world, derived from early infantile experience.

Bodily demeanour: the stylised conduct of the individual within the contexts of day-to-day life, involving the use of appearance to create specific impressions of self.

Collage effect: the juxtaposition of heterogeneous items of knowledge or information in a text or format of electronic communication.

Colonisation of the future: the creation of territories of future possibilities, reclaimed by counterfactual inference.

Deskilling of day-to-day life: the process whereby local skills are expropriated into abstract systems and reorganised in light of technical knowledge. Deskilling normally goes along with complementary processes of reappropriation.

Dialectic of the local and global: the oppositional interplay between local involvements and globalising tendencies.

Disembedding: the lifting out of social relationships from local contexts and their recombination across indefinite time/space distances.

Emancipatory politics: the politics of freedom from exploitation, inequality or oppression.

Existential contradiction: the contradictory relation of human beings to nature, as finite creatures who are part of the organic world, yet set off against it.

Existential questions: queries about basic dimensions of existence, in respect of human life as well as the material world, which all human beings 'answer' in the contexts of their day-to-day conduct.

Expert systems: systems of expert knowledge, of any type, depending on rules of procedure transferable from individual to individual.

Extrinsic criteria: influences on social relations or social life not governed by the institutional reflexivity of modernity.

Fateful moments: moments at which consequential decisions have to be taken or courses of action initiated.

High-consequence risks: risks which are pervasively consequential in terms of their implications for very large numbers of people.

High (or late) modernity: the current phase of development of modern institutions, marked by the radicalising and globalising of basic traits of modernity.

Historicity: the use of history to make history, a fundamental aspect of the institutional reflexivity of modernity.

Institutional reflexivity: the reflexivity of modernity, involving the routine incorporation of new knowledge or information into environments of action that are thereby reconstituted or reorganised.

Internal referentiality: the circumstance whereby social relations, or aspects of the natural world, become organised reflexively in terms of internal criteria.

Life-planning: the strategic adoption of lifestyle options, organised in terms of the individual's projected lifespan, and normally focused through the notion of risk.

Life politics: the politics of self actualisation, in the context of the dialectic of the local and global and the emergence of the internally referential systems of modernity.

Lifestyle sector: a time/space 'slice' of an individual's overall activities, within which a fairly consistent set of social practices is followed.

Mediated experience: the involvement of temporally/spatially distant influences with human sensory experience.

Narrative of the self: the story or stories by means of which self-identity is reflexively understood, both by the individual concerned and by others.

Ontological security: a sense of continuity and order in events, including those not directly within the perceptual environment of the individual.

Open human control: future-oriented human intervention in the social and natural worlds, in which colonising processes are regulated by risk assessment.

Place as phantasmagoric: the process whereby local characteristics of place are thoroughly invaded by, and reorganised in terms of, distanciated social relations.

Privatising of passion: the contracting of passion to the sexual sphere and the separation of that sphere from the public gaze.

Protective cocoon: the defensive protection which filters out potential dangers impinging from the external world and which is founded psychologically upon basic trust.

Pure relationship: a social relation which is internally referential, that is, depends fundamentally on satisfactions or rewards generic to that relation itself.

Reflexive project of the self: the process whereby self-identity is constituted by the reflexive ordering of self-narratives.

Regimes: regularised modes of behaviour relevant to the continuance or cultivation of bodily traits.

Risk culture: a fundamental cultural aspect of modernity, in which awareness of risk forms a medium of colonising the future.

Risk profiling: the portrayal of clusters of risks, in given environments of action, in the light of current circumstances of technical knowledge.

Self-identity: the self as reflexively understood by the individual in terms of his or her biography.

Separation of time and space: the disentangling of separated dimensions of 'empty' time and 'empty' space, making possible the articulation of disembedded social relations across indefinite spans of time/space.

Sequestration of experience: the separation of day-to-day life from contact with experiences which raise potentially disturbing existential questions – particularly experiences to do with sickness, madness, criminality, sexuality and death.

Symbolic tokens: media of exchange that have standard value and are thus interchangeable across an indefinite variety of contexts.

Trajectory of the self: the formation of a specific lifespan in conditions of modernity, by means of which self-development, as reflexively organised, tends to become internally referential.

Trust: the vesting of confidence in persons or in abstract systems, made on the basis of a 'leap into faith' which brackets ignorance or lack of information.

Umwelt (Goffman): a phenomenal world with which the individual is routinely 'in touch' in respect of potential dangers and alarms.

Index

on madness 205
on sexuality 163–4, 206
on surveillance 15
fragmentation 4–5, 27, 84,
    137, 189–91
Freud, Sigmund 60, 62, 143,
    163, 180
on civilisation 153–4
on fear and anxiety 43–4,
    45, 49
on guilt 8, 64
on repression 167
on shame 66, 67
Friedan, Betty 216–17
friendship, as relationship 87,
    90, 92
Fromm, Erich 190–1
fulfilment 79
fundamentalism, religious 142,
    196, 207
future,
colonisation 114, 125, 129,
    133, and end of nature
    144–5, 166; and
    morality 145, 228; and
    risk assessment 3–4, 29,
    111–12, 117–19, 182
and fate 109–11
fear of 73
organisation 75, 77
and risk 48, 109, 111
and self-therapy 72, 85–7

Garfinkel, Harold 36–7, 39,
    56, 63, 205
Geertz, Clifford 138
gender,
and identity 216–17, 219
as learned 63, 230
generation 146, 203
genetic engineering 8, 219, 226

globalisation,
and 'end of nature' 144
and high-consequence risk
    122, 183–4
and morality 225
of social activity 21
and time and space 21, 32,
    192
Goffman, Erving,
on body and self 56–7, 126
on civil indifference 46–7
on fragmentation of the self
    190
on mental illness 205
on privacy 236 n.31
on time 113
on the *Umwelt* 127–32
greenhouse effect 137
guilt 8, 64–5, 67–8, 153–5, 167

Habermas, Jürgen 213–14
habit, and routine 40, 62
Heidegger, Martin 49–50, 78,
    224
Heilmann, Klaus 115–116
high modernity,
as apocalyptic 4
existential parameters 27–32
and personal problems 10–14
history,
loss of 171
shared 97, 126
Hite, Shere 88, 90–4
hospice movement 203–4
hospitals, and sequestration of
    illness 156, 161–2
hostility, and anxiety 46
Hume, David 234 n.20
humiliation, and shame 65
Husserl, Edmund 50–1
hyperreality 5, 27

Index compiled by Meg Davies (Society of Indexers)